WILD FLOWERS

Golden Chincherinchee
(Ornithogalum miniatum)

Una van der Spuy

WILD FLOWERS
of South Africa
for the Garden

Hugh Keartland Publishers

HUGH KEARTLAND (PUBLISHERS) (PTY) LTD
Nicholson Street, Denver
Johannesburg

First edition 1971
This edition 1976

ISBN 0 949997 01 3

Filmset in 10 on 12 pt Century
Lithographed by Keartland Press (Pty) Ltd, Johannesburg

Contents

PART I
Introduction

I

Photographs
Acknowledgements
Names of plants
Change of names
Getting to know the plants around you
Have your own herbarium
The meanings of some species names

◁ Mauve Senecio, orange Ursinias, yellow Dimorphotheca and blue Heliophila

Introduction

Beautiful wild flowers are to be found in many parts of Southern Africa. They can be seen beside our roads, in fields and meadows, in vleis, in sand along the seashore, on arid plains and on mountain slopes. Nature's munificent gift to mankind! Lovely as they are against their natural background most of them become even lovelier when grown in the garden, where they respond to care and attention by producing a greater abundance of flowers, often larger in size and with longer stems.

Whilst this book has been written as a guide to gardeners in Southern Africa, who have been slow in getting to know and grow their native plants, it will, I hope, also serve to introduce more of these plants to gardeners and horticulturists in other countries. It may also be of value to botanical students and plant collectors who wish to learn about some of the plants of Southern Africa.

Only those plants which I feel can be used to enhance the beauty of the garden and home are described. Some of these may not be as decorative as some of the beautiful plants from other countries, and I do not suggest that gardens in Southern Africa should be planted only with our native flowers. We should learn, however, to combine the best of our indigenous plants with the exotic flora which at present we tend to plant almost exclusively.

Southern Africa has a rich treasure of native plant material, as varied as it is beautiful. We have, moreover, a vast number of plants which will grow under difficult conditions; and, when I hear would-be gardeners lamenting that they have given up gardening because of the harsh climatic conditions in which they live, I wish they could see the glorious natural displays which occur in some parts of Southern Africa where either climate or soil, or both, make the growing of exotics extremely difficult. In late winter and early spring, sparkling fields of flowers appear, as if by magic, north of Cape Town up to the Orange River and in parts of the Karoo. Here, masses of flowers of infinite variety emerge spontaneously from the soil despite the low annual rainfall, the long hot and dry summers, and the low temperatures which occur at night over much of this region in winter. In the sandy soil near Darling, fifty kilometres north of Cape Town, the veld in spring becomes a tapestry embroidered with a myriad lovely little flowers—nemesias, sparaxis, romulea, ixias, babiana, and that most colourful little plant known as the Bok Bay vygie or ice plant. Further to the east and north-east of Cape Town, in the dry Karoo, succulents make

Drosanthemum makes a colourful show in dry areas of the Western Cape and parts of the Karoo.

glowing splashes of colour on the sun-bleached soil. In all parts of South Africa, in Swaziland, Rhodesia, Botswana and Malawi there are numerous veld flowers worthy of a place in our gardens.

One would imagine that, having this splendid array of wild flowers provided for us by nature, gardeners in Southern Africa would long ago have made greater use of them to beautify their gardens, because obviously what grows naturally in the country should, for the most part, be easier to grow than plants from other lands. Unfortunately, however, it is only within the last ten to twenty years that we have begun to grow indigenous plants in our gardens, and it is generally the larger plants such as the proteas which are planted, whilst the smaller ones are still neglected.

This is a pity because these smaller plants are as decorative as the larger ones and, because they are smaller, they are better suited to gardens of small or average size. Moreover, some of them have been grown in other countries for many years and visitors to Southern Africa naturally expect to find them growing in our gardens, too.

In all countries of Europe, hybrids developed from our Barberton or Transvaal daisy are grown by the million in glass-houses, to provide flowers for florists, but in Southern Africa one seldom finds the species or the lovely new hybrids in gardens or florists' shops. Our enchanting little lachenalia was popular as a pot plant in England in Victorian times. Our sparaxis was introduced into Australia years ago and one can now see them growing "wild" along the roadsides in some parts of that country. Our nerina, with its lovely pink and red flowers, has been grown on the Channel Islands so successfully and for so long, to supply flowers for the florists of London and Paris, that it was thought to be a native of the islands! Yet, one seldom sees it in gardens or flower shops in its homeland.

About seventy years ago, Hildagonda Duckitt, better known for her book on cookery, sent some seed of nemesia which she had collected at her home about fifty kilometres north of Cape Town, to a seed firm in England. Today, many English gardens are a riot of colour in early summer with beautiful hybrids developed from plants raised from these seeds, yet one rarely comes across nemesias in our gardens.

Our mesembryanthemums or vygies are being used all over the world to beautify gardens and roadsides, and to prevent the erosion of banks along highways. I have come across them in parts of America, in England, in Spain, Portugal, France, Italy and Israel. These plants, which

9

Blue Flax (Heliophila) and Dimorphotheca in fields near Cape Town

grow like weeds in Southern Africa, have in some cases to be raised in glass-houses overseas before being planted out, but they are so beautiful that gardeners there consider them well worth that effort. In South Africa they are only now becoming popular.

Our pelargoniums, of which we have over 200 species, have been hybridized in different countries, and each year millions of plants are sold in the Northern Hemisphere to provide plants for the garden and for pot culture.

The tall, stately gladioli acclaimed for so long both as a garden flower and for floral work, were developed by the crossing of wild ones from the southern part of Africa with Asiatic species. The newest hybrids now becoming popular both amongst florists and gardeners in Europe, Australia and the United States, are much smaller, and more closely related to some of our small species in size and colouring, even to displaying the fascinating "spade" marking which characterises some of our small wild gladioli.

Our crane flower *(Strelitzia reginae)*, first introduced to England 200 years ago and named after the wife of George III of England, still steals the limelight and draws the crowds when it appears on flower shows in Europe. In the western United States it commanded much admiration, and it grows so well in Southern California that it has been adopted as the civic emblem of Los Angeles.

Our ericas have been grown in New Zealand by gardeners there and also to produce flowers for florists, but in South Africa it is difficult to find more than a few species on display in any garden, public or private, and only recently have some enterprising flower-farmers started growing them commercially. In New Zealand, too, our montbretia can be found making flaming patches of colour along the roadsides where it has become naturalized.

Why have we neglected our admirable floral heritage for so long? No precise answer can be given to this question, but I think that it is partly due to the fact that for many years seedsmen have not carried stocks of our native plants and few nurserymen, even now, have many indigenous plants, bulbs or seeds for sale. One cannot, however, blame the nurserymen for being tardy in stocking these plants for they cannot afford to cultivate plants which are not in general demand. And so the wheel goes full circle. Unfortunately some of the plants described in this book are still not available from nurserymen and seedsmen, but, once the general public begins to ask for plants, our seedsmen and nurserymen will find it worthwhile propagating them. I hope therefore, that this book will encourage gardeners to grow South African plants, and that before long it will

10

be a common thing to see the plants of Southern Africa bringing beauty to gardens far and wide.

A list of the names and addresses of nurseries which stock indigenous plants is obtainable on application to the Department of Agricultural and Technical Services, Pretoria. It is suggested also that those who wish to grow South African plants should join the Botanical Society of South Africa, the address of which is:

Kirstenbosch, Newlands, C.P. South Africa. Members are entitled to receive a certain number of packets of seeds free of charge each year, and they also receive the interesting and informative Journal of the Society. Seeds of many of the plants mentioned in this book are obtainable from this Society.

PHOTOGRAPHS

With the exception of the pictures enumerated below, the photographs in this book are my own. The ideal, in a book of this kind, would be to show a close-up of the flower and a picture of the whole plant to illustrate its manner of growth. This, however, would have made the book too expensive. In many cases, therefore, I thought it best to take close-up pictures against a plain back-ground, so that the details of the flowers would show up clearly enough to help readers to identify the plants.

In some cases the colours are not true to nature. This is due to the fact that some shades do not register correctly on the film available. This applies particularly to some shades of cyclamen and blue, and to certain tones of orange-red.

ACKNOWLEDGEMENTS

I am deeply indebted to the following persons for the assistance given:

Dr. John Rourke, of the Compton Herbarium, who was never too busy to provide information on indigenous plants and who spent many hours identifying specimens for me; Miss W. Barker, curator of the Compton Herbarium, for information on lachenalias; the staff of the Botanical Research Unit at Stellenbosch University and Mr. H. Herre and Mr. E. Meyer, who also assisted with the naming of plants; Mrs. Mauve and the Botanical Research Institute in Pretoria and Mr. O. Kerfoot of the Botanical Department of the Witwatersrand University, for checking the names and advising where changes were neces-

White Arums grow in abundance beside the roads in the South-Western Cape

The deep rich orange colour of Ursinia contrasts well with the yellow of the flowers of Mimosa

sary; Dr. and Mrs. R. White, for reading the manuscript in its early stages; Mrs. G. Lipp for reading at a later stage; Mr. and Mrs. F. C. Batchelor who welcomed me to their beautiful garden of wild flowers at Protea Heights, Stellenbosch, and allowed me to photograph specimens there; Miss Marion Kelder and Miss Louise Hofmeyr for helping with the sorting of some of the photographs; Mr. J. Sinton and Mr. R. Meintjes for helping with the checking of the manuscript; Mr. John Mashati for tending the flowers in my garden; Mr. Andrew Mahoney, who cheerfully acted as bearer for camera equipment on some expeditions up steep slopes; and, last, but by no means least, my husband, who gave helpful criticism of the manuscript, and who accompanied me on many long and sometimes arduous expeditions, to study and photograph plants in their natural surroundings.

As regards photographs—I must express my gratitude first to Miss Alice Mertens, Head of the Department of Photography of the University of Stellenbosch, who taught me what I know about photography, and to the following for the loan of the photographs indicated:

Mrs. C. Giddy for pictures of aloes, *Leonotis leonurus*, *Haemanthus natalensis* and *Boophane disticha*. Mrs. Nancy Gardiner for the pictures of *Brunsvigia radulosa* and *Cyrtanthus tuckii;* Mrs. M. C. Staples for some pictures of lampranthus growing in her garden in New Zealand; Dr. F. Rousseau for a slide of *Brunsvigia orientalis*, and Dr. F. le Roux for a picture of *Vallota speciosa*.

NAMES OF PLANTS

The plants in this book have been arranged under their botanical names with the common names given after the botanical ones. Although some gardeners find it difficult to remember botanical names, it is important that these should be used in order to be sure of obtaining the plant one really wants, as common names can be misleading.

Sometimes a plant has several different common names, used in different parts of the country or the world. For example, a particular species of cyrtanthus may be known in one area as a fire lily and in another as a Kei lily; and, what is known in Southern Africa as the Barberton daisy is known abroad as the Transvaal daisy. Very often, also, a single common name is used to describe many different flowers. For example, the name gousblom is applied to several different

Dorotheanthus-
Beauty from the Sand

plants with daisy-like flowers, the correct names of which may be dimorphotheca, gazania or arctotis.

Botanical names are used internationally and, if one knows them, one can always be certain of procuring the plant or seeds one wants, whereas of one asks for plants by their common names, one may get a different plant from that required.

In order to learn the botanical names more easily, it is advisable to know something about the system used in naming plants. Plants are classified into different categories as follows: family, genus, species, variety and cultivar.

GENUS: (plural *genera*) The genus name of a plant may be compared to the surname of a person. Jones, Smith, Van der Merwe and De Villiers are surnames which help us to identify different people; and, in the same way, names such as agapanthus, gladiolus, gazania and watsonia are names which help us to identify different kinds of plants. All the plants in a genus are closely related, and a family is made up of a few or many genera which also show a certain relationship to one another. The genus name may have been adopted to indicate some special characteristic of the plant or its general impression. For example, lampranthus is derived from the Greek

The silver leaves and golden flowers of Didelta, growing on the seashore, make a colourful foreground to Table Mountain

13

The beautiful Flame Lily *(Gloriosa superba)* can be found in coastal bush and on plains, from the Eastern Cape north into the Transvaal and Rhodesia.

The Sabie Star (Adenium) grows wild in dry areas of the lowveld of the Transvaal and in Rhodesia.

14

lampros (shining) and *anthos* (flower), and is the genus name of a group of plants with eye-catching flowers which shine and sparkle in the sunlight. The genus name may also be derived from a person, e.g. Zaluzianskya—named after a Polish botanist of the sixteenth century—Zaluziansky.

The genus name is always written first, starting with a capital letter, and it is followed by the species name. Should the genus be mentioned again shortly afterwards, it is not necessary to use more than the initial letter only of the genus. For example, when writing about indigenous gladioli one may write about *Gladiolus alatus* followed by another species of gladiolus, such as *G. blandus*. There is no necessity to write out the whole word gladiolus the next time it appears.

SPECIES: The species (or specific) name of a plant corresponds to the Christian or first name of a person. If you want to know to which Smith someone is referring, you ask for his first or Christian name. Similarly if you wish to know to which indigenous gladiolus someone is referring you ask for its species name. This name is written immediately after the genus (surname) but with a small initial letter. e.g. in *Gladiolus alatus*—the word *alatus* is the species name.

Each genus may include one, a few, or a great number of species. Very often the species name is based on some characteristic of the plant. For example, one species of native gladiolus which has flowers rather like an orchid in form and colouring is named *Gladiolus orchidiflorus*, whilst another species with flowers shaped rather like a parrot's beak is known as *G. psittacinus*, the word *psittacinus* being the Latin word describing this. Sometimes the species name is an indication where the plant is abundant or where it was first found, e.g. *Aloe pretoriensis*, a particular aloe common in the district of Pretoria. Often the specific name is that of the person who first discovered or named the plant, and naturally such names would usually be those of plant collectors or botanists. Occasionally however, others are honoured in this way. For example, *Watsonia vanderspuyae* was named after one of our first and most enthusiastic convenors of wild flower shows who used this, until then unknown watsonia from the Piketberg district, in an arrangement of wild flowers she made for a show in Cape Town; and *W. ardernei* was named after Mr. Arderne who collected this lovely species in the Tulbagh district and grew it in his famous garden in Cape Town.

Because it is generally simpler to remember names if one knows their significance, the meanings of some specific names are given at the end of this section.

VARIETY: Having labelled a plant with a genus (surname) and a species (first or Christian) name, botanists sometimes discover that, because of slight differences in a species, it is necessary to add another name. The differences are not sufficient to warrant giving the plant a different specific name, so a variety name is then added.

CULTIVAR: This word has only recently been introduced into botanical nomenclature mainly to differentiate between a variety which occurs in nature, as indicated above, and a distinct sport which occurs naturally or a man-made hybrid, both of which are propagated for horticultural purposes. Named hybrids, which hitherto the gardener would refer to as varieties, should therefore now be referred to as cultivars. The cultivar name is always given in inverted commas and written with initial capital letters, e.g. a named hybrid of nerina is known as *Nerine sarniensis* 'Pink Beauty'.

FAMILY: The word family refers to a large group of plants which include different genera having common characteristics. This term is of interest to keen gardeners and plant collectors who like to know the relationships between plants. The names of families usually end with "*aceae*". The following are examples:

1. *Iridaceae* (iris family) which includes native plants such as aristea, babiana, gladioli, moraea, sparaxis and watsonia.

2. *Liliaceae* (lily family) includes the true lilies and native plants such as agapanthus, aloes, bulbine, dipidax, lachenalia and tulbaghia.

CHANGES OF NAMES

Because botanical names are often long and cumbersome many people find it difficult to remember them, and it is not surprising that some irritation is expressed by nurserymen and gardeners when names, which they have learned with difficulty, are changed to others just as difficult to remember and to spell. The reasons why it is sometimes necessary to change the names are given briefly below.

The system of classification of plants used today whereby all plants have two names, was initiated by Linnaeus, a Swedish botanist, who lived in the eighteenth century. From that time onwards, as plant collectors sent or took plant material, either

Wild flowers
effectively planted in
Kirstenbosch Gardens

On the left: Gazania
with grey leaf
(hybrid); blue
Charieis, orange
Ursinias.
On the right:
white Venidium and
cyclamen Watsonias

The bold beauty of the Tree Aloe (*Aloe arborescens*)
highlights the garden in winter

in dried form or as bulbs or living plants, back to
herbaria in their own countries or to Sweden,
names were given to the plants. As a great deal of
plant material was collected during this period,
and as communications between countries at that
time were not particularly good, it is not surprising that sometimes the same plant was given
different names in different countries, or even in
different herbaria in the same country. It follows
quite naturally that only with the passage of time
would it be discovered that some plants had more
than one botanical name.

When such a discovery is made one name
naturally has to be dropped. The international
rules laid down some fifty years ago state that the
botanical name FIRST given shall be accepted
and any subsequent names must be abandoned,
even if the subsequent name is more descriptive
of the plant.

A more valid reason for the changing of botanical names of plants is due to the fact that some of
the plants of Southern Africa have not yet been
properly classified, and, until this is done, which
will take many years, one must expect name
changes to occur, due to re-classification. It will,
therefore, be some time before the names of our
plants are finalised. In the text of this book, where

The glistening flowers of Lampranthus bring colour to the rock-garden

there has been a recent change of name, the new botanical name is given.

GETTING TO KNOW THE PLANTS AROUND YOU

I am sure that there are many people who, after a walk in the country or an expedition into the mountains, have come back full of admiration for the wild flowers they have seen, and eager to know the names of the plants. The names of plants can be ascertained by sending pressed specimens to one of the following herbaria:

The National Herbarium, Division of Botany, Pretoria

The Compton Herbarium, Kirstenbosch, Newlands, Cape

The Natal Herbarium, Botanic Gardens Road, Durban

The Albany Museum Herbarium, Grahamstown

The Herbarium and Botanic Gardens, Causeway, Salisbury

Before picking any plants, make sure that you are not thereby transgressing the laws of the province in which you live, relating to the picking of wild flowers. For example, no flowers may be picked along a public road, and certain other flowers are protected wherever they may be growing.

Specimens sent for identification should be prepared in the following way. Choose a spray or twig with leaves and flowers and/or fruit. Put it between sheets of newspaper or between the pages of a magazine with absorbent pages, to dry out. It is not necessary to use blotting paper as ordinary newspaper will do. If a large number of specimens is to be collected, have ready a couple of sheets of thick cardboard or thin plywood and tape or straps to go around them, so that the specimens can be pressed inside covers of this kind as they are collected. Change the newspaper covering after a couple of days to prevent mildew.

When sending specimens to an herbarium, give some particulars about the plant to aid in its identification or to add to existing information on the plant. State its approximate height and spread, in what locality you found it, whether it was in damp soil or along a stream, in a dry place, in sand or clay, on a plain or on a mountain, in sun or in shade.

The specimen sent will no doubt already have been named, but there is always the exciting possibility that you may have come across a new species which has not yet been discovered and that it may then be named after you!

HAVE YOUR OWN HERBARIUM

If the idea of collecting plants fascinates you, why not start your own herbarium? Make quite sure that your specimens are dry before mounting them. This may take two or three weeks in some cases, and even longer in others. Keep the sheets of newspaper enclosing the specimens under a weight, in a plant-press or under a carpet, so that the specimens are pressed flat. With plants which take a long time to dry out it may be necessary to change the newspaper several times. Inspection every few days will indicate whether they are dry or not.

Insects, some of which are invisible to the naked eye, or their eggs, may be present in plants, and, if the specimens are to be preserved it is advisable to treat them. If they are to be kept for only a short time dip the specimens in methylated spirits before drying them out. Where they are to be preserved for a long period, as in an herbarium, they should be treated with poison after being pressed. Each specimen should be dipped in a solution of 2 per cent Mercuric Chloride in rectified spirits, or in a solution made by mixing 50 cc of Mystox with white spirit to make up a total quantity of a litre. The specimens should then be dried before mounting them.

When dry, they can be mounted on sheets of stiff paper or thin cardboard of uniform size. The usual herbarium size is 30 × 45 cm. The mounting is done by securing the specimen to the paper or cardboard with strips of Scotch tape. The mounted sheets should then be labelled with the botanical and common names, where collected, the date collected and other pertinent information. They should then be stored in file covers in a dry, cool cupboard.

Charming flower pictures can be made from dried flowers, and those with patience and artistic ability will find the composing of such pictures a rewarding hobby. Be warned, however, that the indiscriminate picking of wild flowers is forbidden by law and, before picking any for this purpose, get into touch with the Department of Nature Conservation of your Province, to ascertain exactly what the laws are regarding the picking of wild flowers in your area.

The Heavenly Blue Daisy *(Charieis heterophylla)* forms a gay border to a bed of orange Urisinias (New name is *Felicia heterophylla)*

Blue Flax and orange Urisinias make a fine show in the Caledon Gardens in spring

An artistic planting of Vygies or Mesems turned a stone quarry into a lovely garden

THE MEANINGS OF SOME SPECIES NAMES

acaulis . . . . . stemless, or apparently stemless.
adenocarpum . . . with glandular fruit
aethiopica . . . . pertaining to Southern Africa
alata . . . . . winged
alba . . . . . . white
albomaculata . . . spotted white
alooides . . . . like an aloe
amelloides . . . . like amellus (small type of daisy)
angustiloba . . . with narrow lobes
arenarius . . . . growing in sand
argentea . . . . silver
argyrophyllum . . with silvery leaves
aristata . . . . with a stiff bristle-like awn tapering to an apex
anthemoides . . . like anthemis (chamomile)
aurea . . . . . golden
baccifera . . . . bearing berries
barbata . . . . . bearded
bella . . . . . beautiful
belladonna . . . . beautiful lady
bellidiformis . . . in the shape of bellis— i.e. a small daisy
bergiana . . . . after Bergius—a Swedish botanist
blandus . . . . . flattering
bulbifera . . . . having a bulb
bullatus . . . . . blistered or puckered
caerulea . . . . sky-blue
cakilefolia . . . . with very divided leaves
calenduliflora . . having flowers like a calendula
calocephalum . . with a beautiful head
campanulatus . . bell-shaped
capensis . . . . of the Cape
capitatum . . . . with a knob-like head
cardinalis . . . . cardinal red
carinatus . . . . keeled
carmineus . . . . carmine
carneum . . . . flesh-coloured
caudata . . . . . having a tail
caulescens . . . . with a stem above or on the ground
ciliata or ciliaris . with a fringe of fine hairs
circinata . . . . curled inward from the tip
citrina . . . . . lemon-yellow

clavata . . . . . club-shaped
coccinea . . . . scarlet
coma-aurea . . . with a yellow crest
comosum . . . . tufted
cordata . . . . . heart-shaped
corifolia . . . . leathery leaves.
cornuta . . . . . horn-like
corymbosa . . . . having flowers arranged in corymbs
crocata . . . . . tinted yellow
cruentus . . . . bloody
cucullatus . . . . hooded
cuneata . . . . . wedge-shaped or triangular
debilis . . . . . weak
decipiens . . . . deceiving
discolor . . . . varying in colour
disticha . . . . leaves or flowers in two ranks on opposite sides of stem and in same plane
elatus . . . . . tall
elegans . . . . . elegant
erosa . . . . . with irregularly toothed margins
eximia . . . . . excellent
fastuosa . . . . proud
filifolia . . . . . thin, fine leaves
flava . . . . . pale yellow
floribunda . . . . with an abundance of flowers
flos-solis . . . . flowers of the sun
foetidum . . . . smelly
frutescens . . . . growing in a shrubby fashion
fruticosa . . . . shrubby
glaucina . . . . bluish, sea-green
graminicola . . . growing among grasses
grandiflorum . . with large flowers
grandis . . . . . large
guttata . . . . . exuding tears
heterophylla . . . with leaves of different forms
hirsuta . . . . . hairy
hyalina . . . . . colourless or transparent
igneum . . . . . flame-coloured
inapertus . . . . not open
incanum . . . . with silvery-grey flush on leaves

20

THE MEANINGS OF SOME SPECIES NAMES

incrassatum . . .	thickened
integerrima . . .	entire—with leaf margin not serrated
jucundum	pleasing or charming
juncea	like a reed or rush
lacteum	white as milk
lacticolor	the colour of milk
laevis	smooth or polished
lanata	with a woolly covering
lanceolata . . .	lance-shaped
leicarpa	with smooth seeds
leonurus . . .	with a lion's tail
leptalea	slender, thin, narrow
linearifolia . . .	with narrow or linear leaves
lineata	narrow
longifolia . . .	with long leaves
luteus	deep, golden-yellow
macrantha . . .	large-flowered
macrocarpa . . .	with large fruit
maculatus . . .	spotted or blotched
maritima . . .	of the seaside
miniata	the colour of red lead
monadelpha . .	one sheath (stamens united)
multiflorus . . .	with many flowers
nana	dwarf or small
neochilus . . .	new-lipped
paniculata . . .	with flowers arranged in a panicle
palustris	of marshy places
papilionacea . .	like a butterfly
patens	spreading
pavonia	like a peacock
perigrinum . . .	wandering around
pes-caprae . . .	like the foot of a goat
petiolata . . .	with a petiole or stalk
pictus	adorned with colour
platyphyllus . .	flat-leaved
plicata	folded into pleats
pluvialis . . .	relating to rain
polystachya . .	with many spikes
prunifolius . . .	with leaves like a cherry or plum
psittacinus . . .	parrot-like
pulchra	beautiful
pulcherrima . .	very or most beautiful
puniceus . . .	crimson or phoenician purple

ramosissima . . .	very much branching
repens	creeping
rigens	stiff or rigid
rigescens . . .	rather stiff
rigidus	rigid
ringens	gaping
rotundifolius . .	having round leaves
sabulosum . . .	liking the sand
sanguineus . . .	blood-red
sericea	like silk
serrata	with finely-toothed margins to leaves
sesamoides . . .	granular—like the seed of sesame
sessiliflora . . .	bearing flowers close to the stem—without stalks
setaceus . . .	bristle-like
speciosa . . .	handsome, showy, splendid
spectabilis . . .	very showy
spuria	false
stenophylla . .	narrow-leaved
stoechadifolia . .	with leaves like a stoechadium
stricta	straight, upright or narrow
strumosa . . .	with a swelling
tagetes	like a marigold
tenella	delicate
thyrsiflora . . .	flowers arranged in a thyrsis
tomentosa . . .	hairy
tricolor	of three colours
tristis	dull colour
turbinata . . .	cone-shaped
undulata . . .	wavy
uniflora	single-flowered
uvaria	with rounded parts, like a bunch of grapes
vegeta	fresh, vigorous
velutina	velvety or covered with short, soft hairs
venusta	beautiful or graceful
vestita	clothed
villosa	shaggy-haired
virescens . . .	turning green
viridiflorum . .	with green flowers

Osteospermums look
effective cascading
over a wall

**Flowers to
decorate a rock-
garden or a dry
bank or wall**

The flowers of orange
Lampranthus show
up beautifully against
the stone wall

Lampranthus planted
along a bank as a
border to the garden

The Bokbay Vygie or
Iceplant
(*Dorotheanthus
bellidiformis,*) is an
ideal plant for the
rock-garden

Part II
Growing South African Plants

Climate

Water

How much water to give and how often

Frost

Soil

Shade

Measurements

◁ Plant Gazanias to brighten the garden

Growing South African Plants

In Southern Africa we have a wide range of climatic conditions which are encountered also in other countries of the world, and the plants mentioned in this book are eminently suited for cultivation in countries where similar climatic conditions prevail. Many species flourish out-doors in places as widely apart as Australia, California and the southern States of America, the south of France, the south of England and New Zealand. In regions with colder winters a number of them are grown indoors, or raised in glass-houses and planted out for a summer display in the garden.

CLIMATE

Climate undoubtedly plays a most important part in determining what plants may be grown in a particular locality, but fortunately many plants are adaptable and adjust to climatic conditions widely different from those of their natural habitat. To grow plants more easily, however, it is desirable to know something about the con-ditions in which they grow in nature, and for this reason I have stated in what areas of Southern Africa the plants can be found growing naturally.

Southern Africa may be broadly divided into two main climatic zones according to the season when the rains fall. There is the WINTER-RAINFALL region of the Cape Peninsula and the north-western and south-western Cape, and there is the SUMMER-RAINFALL region which covers the rest of South Africa and Rhodesia. In the winter-rainfall region the amount of rain varies from dry areas of the north-western Cape and the southern part of South West Africa where it is less than 250 mm (10 inches) a year, to mountainous areas in the south-western Cape where it may be more than 1250 mm (50 inches) a year. Although sharp frosts are not uncommon in parts of this region really severe cold is seldom experienced except on the mountains where some plants endure snowy conditions on and off during the winter. In the winter-rainfall region the sum-mers are hot and dry, except for a strip of the coastal belt from Knysna to near Port Elizabeth, which has some rain during the summer months.

The summer-rainfall region may be divided into several different areas as follows:

(i) The coastal belt which varies from tem-perate in the south to sub-tropical in Natal and Zululand.

(ii) The Karoo which has a low rainfall, often with warm days during winter followed by frosty nights, and hot summers.

A colourful corner of daisies: Blue Charieis, orange Urisinias, mauve Senecio, and white Dimorphotheca

(iii) The highlands of the north-eastern Cape and eastern Orange Free State and Lesotho, where severe frosts are experienced at night for the whole of winter, and where snowfalls are not infrequent.

(iv) The dry western part of the Orange Free State, the western Transvaal and parts of South West Africa, where frosts are moderate to severe and where the rainfall is low.

(v) The Transvaal highveld and parts of Rhodesia, where frosts are moderate and occasionally severe, and the rainfall is about 750 mm (30 inches) a year

(vi) The northern Transvaal and parts of Rhodesia where the rainfall is meagre and winters are mild.

(vii) The lowveld of the Transvaal and Rhodesia where winters are always mild and the annual rainfall is about 500 mm (20 inches).

(viii) The highlands of Natal and Rhodesia where the rainfall is good, averaging 750 mm (30 inches) or more a year and where the frosts in winter are moderate and occasionally severe.

In growing plants the most limiting factors are the degrees of cold experienced during winter and the moisture available throughout the year. Plants which grow naturally in the warmer parts of the country, such as the eastern Cape coastal strip, the coastal region of Natal, and the lowveld of Rhodesia and the Transvaal, are likely to be damaged by severe frosts when grown in areas which are much colder, but many of the plants native to the south-western and north-western Cape are able to stand severe frosts once they are established, and provided that they are not allowed to become too dry during the winter months. Dryness during winter is more likely to kill plants native to this particular region than cold.

WATER

There is a tendency to assume that since the rainfall over a great part of Southern Africa is low, indigenous plants need very little water. This is true only of succulents which grow naturally in desert-like or dry areas of the country.

The greatest concentration of beautiful plants is to be found in that part of Southern Africa which has its rains in winter, and in the descriptions of plants, where it is stated that a plant is from the Cape Peninsula or from the north-western or south-western Cape, this should serve as an indication that such plants should be watered

27

during autumn to spring. Plants native to areas which have their rains in summer will flourish if left somewhat dry in winter.

HOW MUCH WATER TO GIVE AND HOW OFTEN

This is a question which is often posed and is one which requires careful and scientific analysis. The great mistake made in watering is in giving too little water too often. A sprinkling of the surface of the soil may give one a feeling of satisfaction because wet soil looks better than dry soil, but this kind of watering does more harm than good for the following reasons:

Water moves down through the soil by wetting soil particles progressively, and it is only when the top few centimetres have been wet that it moves down to the particles below. The object of watering is to supply moisture to the ROOTS of the plants and it is therefore imperative that the water should percolate down to the root zone. This happens only when water has been applied for a long enough period to allow it to seep down. A daily sprinkling of the surface of the soil tends to encourage the roots to remain near the surface where they dry out rapidly, whereas deep watering encourages them to go down in their search for water. A soaking of the soil twice a week is therefore more beneficial than a daily sprinkling, and in the end it takes less time.

To be sure of watering properly it is advisable to measure how much water your pipes deliver in a given time. Allow the sprinklers to run for an hour in the morning, and later in the day, dig down to see how far the water has penetrated into the soil. This will give you an idea as to how long the sprinklers should be left in one position in order to get water down to the roots of plants. This, however, gives only a rough idea because the amount of water from a sprinkler varies from near the sprinkler to the outside edge of the spray.

A garden made from a rocky outcrop showing succulents charmingly grouped

A gay arrangement of
yellow Bulbinella and
golden-orange Ixias
and Satyriums

Yellow, blue and
orange flowers form a
pleasing combination

Psilothonna tagetes
(yellow), *Felicia
bergeriana* (blue) and
Ursinia (orange)

29

Arctotis
look charming in a
small, simple
arrangement

Generally it is least near the sprinkler and at the outside edge and most in the middle area.

Two other factors should also be taken into account when calculating how much water to give and how often. Soils differ in their capacity for absorbing and retaining water. Clay absorbs water slowly and loses it slowly, whereas sand takes up water quickly and loses it quickly. As a rough guide it can be assumed that 25 mm (1 inch) of rain will penetrate 30 cm (12 inches) in sandy soil, about 18 cm (7 inches) in loam, and only about 10 cm (4 inches) in clay. It will therefore be necessary to water clay for a longer period at a time, but less frequently than sandy soil.

The other factor of importance to consider when estimating how often one should water is the weather. During periods when hot, dry winds prevail it will be necessary to water more frequently than during periods of still or cool, cloudy weather.

Gardeners in areas where the rainfall is low and where little water is available for irrigation should grow mainly drought-tolerant plants. In such areas mulching the soil with layers of straw, grass or stones is recommended to reduce the rate of evaporation of moisture from the soil and to aid in keeping plants from drying out.

FROST

Whilst moderate to sharp frosts are common in many regions of Southern Africa, really severe frosts occur only in parts of the Orange Free State, mainly near the Maluti mountains, in certain areas near Bethal, in the Transvaal, near Sutherland in the western Cape, and in parts of the north-eastern Cape near Maclear. The frosts which occur elsewhere often damage young plants, but once a plant has become established frost-damage is very much reduced.

An arrangement of
spring-flowering bulbs.
Yellow Ixias and
mauve Tulbaghia at
the back, with
Freesias, Sparaxis and
Babiana in front

There are various ways of protecting plants from frost. Annuals, perennials and bulbs may be protected by mulching the soil with straw, and, where manure is available, a layer of fresh manure near the plants and under the straw will help to generate heat and obviate frost-damage. Fresh manure should not, however, be allowed to touch the plants. Tall plants which are susceptible to frost-damage may be protected by having a cardboard carton put over them at night, or they can be covered with plastic sheets during periods when severe frost threatens.

Very often the damage done to plants during winter occurs in the early morning, when the sun, striking frosted leaves, heats them up too quickly and so causes damage to the tissues. If the leaves warm up slowly this kind of damage is unlikely to occur. One appreciates the significance of this if one recalls how sharply one's hands tingle if put into luke-warm water when they are ice-cold. Plants which are not hardy to frost should therefore be planted in a position where they are shaded from the first rays of the early morning sun in winter, so that the warm air can dissipate the frost before the sun shines onto the leaves or flowers.

Watering plants in winter tends to mitigate damage from frost, for moist soil holds and releases more heat than dry soil. Walls and hedges also help to reduce frost-damage and tender plants should be set out near a north-facing wall in the Southern Hemisphere, and a south-facing one in the Northern. Such walls absorb heat during the day and radiate it at night, thus warming plants near them.

SOIL

Because so many of the plants of Southern Africa are to be found growing in impoverished-looking soil some gardeners assume that they should be planted in the garden without thought being given to soil improvement. It is true that astonishingly beautiful flowers can be found growing in sandy wastes, in gravel on mountain slopes or else in clay so hard that it is almost impossible to get a fork into it. More often than not, however, these plants will do far better when planted in soil to which some humus has been added.

The two extremes of soil are clay and sand. Clay consists of powder-fine particles which pack closely together when wet and which therefore tend to exclude all air from the soil. Sand, on the other hand, consists of large particles which remain loose under all circumstances. The advantage of clay is that it retains water and nutrients and the advantage of sand is that it is easy to work. Both, however, have disadvantages. Clay is difficult to work and tends to pack solid and suffocate plants, and sand loses water and nutrients rapidly and it is therefore necessary to water it very much more frequently than is the case with clay.

Both types of soil can be improved by the addition of compost and leaf mould and by heavy mulching, allowing the mulching material to rot down and become part of the soil. When improving the soil it should be remembered that it is better to add the compost and leaf mould BELOW the surface of the soil. This should be done for two reasons:

(a) to be sure that its benefit in encouraging micro-organisms to flourish occurs in the area where roots develop, and

(b) to prevent it being leached out by strong sunshine, as is likely to happen when it is applied on the surface.

Good soil or loam is neither of the extremes mentioned above. It is composed of medium-sized particles in which there is a high proportion of humus.

An arrangement of
Ixia scillaris

Lampranthus aureus (Orange Lampranthus) makes a good ground cover in hot, dry gardens

SHADE

Where the sun shines brightly for most days of the year, as it does in many parts of Southern Africa, Australia and much of the southern part of the United States, lack of shade is a factor likely to limit the development of some plants which flourish naturally near the coast. Plants which occur naturally in coastal regions are protected from intense sunshine by the humidity which is present in the atmosphere, and when these plants are grown inland at a high elevation they may find the intensity of the sun too much. This also applies to many plants which grow naturally on mountain slopes and which are shaded by the slopes from the afternoon sun, or which are protected to some extent by mist or fog which occurs high up on the slopes. In planning a garden it is therefore advisable to plant trees or tall shrubs to shade some of the smaller plants from the heat of the mid-day or afternoon sun.

MEASUREMENTS

The size to which plants grow, and even the size of the flowers and leaves, depends to some extent on the nature of the soil and climatic conditions, so measurements of plants must be regarded as being approximate. The figures below serve as an aid in the conversion of metric to English measurements.

$$10 \text{ mm} = .39 \text{ in}$$
$$25.40 \text{ mm} = 1 \text{ in}$$
$$254 \text{ mm} = 10 \text{ in}$$
$$2.54 \text{ cm} = 1 \text{ in}$$
$$25.4 \text{ cm} = 10 \text{ in}$$
$$30.48 \text{ cm} = 12 \text{ in}$$
$$1 \text{ m} = 3.28 \text{ ft}$$
$$1 \text{ litre} = 0.22 \text{ gallons}$$
$$1 \text{ km} = 0.62 \text{ miles}$$

33

III

PART III
Plant Selection Guide

Plants for the rock-garden

Plants for coastal gardens

Plants for a difficult climate

Plants for shady places

Plants to cascade over a wall or grow on a bank

Plants which are quick-growing

Plants with pleasing foliage

Plants for containers

Plants which provide material for arrangements

Flower colour through the seasons

◁ Dorotheanthus does well in dry sandy soil

Plant Selection Guide

Those who are new to gardening and even many with a great deal of gardening experience behind them know little of the plants native to Southern Africa, and have difficulty, therefore, in selecting the right plants for the right places.

In order to make it easier to choose plants, whether it be for a rock garden, a coastal garden, for a shady place or to provide material for arrangements, lists have been compiled and are given in the section which follows.

To facilitate the selection of plants to give year-round interest in the garden this section also contains a table of the plants which flower during the different seasons, together with an indication as to their colour.

More detailed information on the plants in these lists is given in the text.

PLANTS FOR THE ROCK-GARDEN

A rock-garden may be lovely or it may be an eyesore. Far too often one sees rock-gardens which are really ugly. They are poorly planned, badly sited and wrongly planted.

A rock-garden should not be a collection of stones set haphazardly in the ground at various angles with odd plants growing between them, nor should it be a mound of soil with stones jutting out from it. A rock-garden must be designed with care in the right setting, to look like a natural rocky outcrop on a hillside, with the rocks emerging from the soil—not projecting in an unnatural fashion. The plants between the rocks should be those which will emphasize the rocks and the skill with which they have been sited; they should not be plants of such exuberant growth as to hide the rocks from view. Obviously the right place for a rock-garden is on a slope, although it is possible, also, to create a rock-garden on a flat site.

Planting a rock-garden calls for a careful selection of plant material because the growth of the plants must be in proportion to the garden and to the size of the rocks, and the roots should not be so invasive as to get under the rocks and eventually prove impossible to keep under control.

Although in South Africa we are fortunate in having many succulents which withstand long periods without water, one should not regard the rock-garden as the kind of garden where only succulents are to be grown. Many of the plants which look decorative in a rock-garden are those which need good soil and care, such as regular watering and occasional feeding. If the soil is not good take the trouble to improve it, after setting the rocks in position.

It is advisable, also, to group plants according to the conditions which suit them best. Succulents which like sandy soil and good drainage should not be interplanted with those plants which need rich soil and plenty of moisture; and, plants which like to be dry at one season should be set apart from those which need an abundance of water at that season.

The plants listed below include some which are suitable for the small rock-garden as well as those suitable for the large one.

Annuals and Perennials

Anemone capensis
Aptosimum indivisum
Arctotis species and hybrids
Castalis spectabilis
Charieis heterophylla
Chironia baccifera
Chrysocoma coma-aurea
Cotula species
Diascia species
Dicoma zeyheri
Dimorphotheca species and hybrids
Felicia species
Gazania species and hybrids
Geranium incanum
Gerbera jamesonii and hybrids
Grielum grandiflorum
Helichrysum species
Heliophila sonchifolia
Heterolepis aliena
Limonium perigrinum

Lobelia species
Monopsis lutea
Monsonia speciosa
Nemesia species and hybrids
Orphium frutescens
Osteospermum species and hybrids
Pelargonium species
Pentzia grandiflora
Phoenocoma prolifera
Psilothonna species
Roella ciliata
Sebaea exacoides
Selago species
Senecio arenarius
Senecio elegans
Sutera species
Ursinia species
Vellozia retinervis
Zaluzianskya villosa

Bulbs

Agapanthus species
Albuca species
Amaryllis belladonna
Ammocharis coranica
Anapalina species
Anomalesia cunonia
Antholyza ringens
Aristea macrocarpa
Babiana species and hybrids
Boophane disticha
Brunsvigia species
Bulbine species
Bulbinella species
Clivia species
Crocosmia species
Cyrtanthus species
Dietes species
Dilatris corymbosa
Engysiphon pictus
Eucomis clavata
Eucomis punctata
Freesia species and hybrids
Geissorrhiza species
Gladiolus species
Gloriosa superba
Haemanthus species
Homoglossum species

Ixia species
Kniphofia species
Lachenalia species
Lanaria lanata
Lapeirousia species
Littonia modesta
Melasphaerula ramosa
Moraea species
Nerine species and hybrids
Ornithogalum species
Oxalis species
Pterygodium species
Romulea
Sandersonia aurantiaca
Satyrium species
Sparaxis species and hybrids
Spiloxene capensis
Strelitzia parvifolia
Strelitzia parvifolia var. juncea
Strelitzia reginae
Synnotia variegata
Tritonia species and hybrids
Tulbaghia species
Veltheimia species
Watsonia species and hybrids
Zantedeschia species

Succulents

Adenium species
Aloe species, particularly the smaller ones
Carpobrotus species
Cephalophyllum species
Conicosia pugioniformis
Cotyledon species
Crassula species
Delosperma species
Didelta carnosa var. tomentosa

Dorotheanthus species
Drosanthemum species
Euphorbia (small species)
Lampranthus species
Rochea coccinea
Rochea subulata
Ruschia species
Semnanthe lacera
Senecio haworthii

PLANTS FOR COASTAL GARDENS

The climate along the coastline of Southern Africa varies considerably from the western to the eastern seaboard. On the west coast the rainfall may be scanty, as it is from a little north of Cape Town to South West Africa, or it may be fairly heavy in the winter, as it is further south near Cape Town and east towards Mossel Bay, with a long, dry period in the summer. The coastal area near George and Knysna has good rains throughout the year with no long dry period. East from Port Elizabeth towards East London the rains fall in summer and the climate is mild throughout the year with a long dry period from autumn to spring. Further east up to the northern border of Natal the climate tends to become sub-tropical, with rain in summer and humid conditions throughout the year. Some of the plants which flourish in the south-western Cape will not do well in sub-tropical gardens.

The force of the wind and the intensity of the sunlight varies, but coastal gardens in most parts experience fairly severe wind at different seasons of the year. For this reason it is important that shelter from wind should be provided for small plants which are most likely to be affected, and that the trees and shrubs planted should be those which can stand windy conditions.

Most coastal gardens can grow a wide variety of plants but those just above high-water mark will be limited because there are few plants which tolerate salt-laden air and spray from the sea.

Where the soil is a porous sand, as it often is in coastal gardens, it should be improved before any planting is done, because, although some plants do not mind sandy soil the majority grow far better if they are planted in soil to which humus has been added. The addition of humus in the form of compost or manure with plenty of litter not only encourages the development of bacteria which promote the growth of plants, but it also makes gardening easier, as plants grown in soil rich in humus require less watering than those growing in sandy soils deficient in humus.

Annuals and Perennials

Anemone capensis
Arctotis species and hybrids
Asparagus species
Castalis spectabilis
Chironia baccifera
Chrysocoma coma-aurea
Coleus neochilus
Cotula species
Diascia species
Dimorphotheca species and hybrids
Felicia species
Gazania species and hybrids
Geranium incanum
Helichrysum species
Heterolepis aliena
Leonotis leonurus
Limonium perigrinum
Lobelia species and hybrids

Monsonia speciosa
Nemesia species
Orphium frutescens
Osteospermum species
Pelargonium species
Pentzia grandiflora
Phoenocoma prolifera
Plectranthus species
Psilothonna species
Salvia africana-coerulea
Scabiosa species
Sebaea exacoides
Selago species
Senecio elegans
Senecio glastifolius
Sutera species
Ursinia species
Zaluzianskya species

Bulbs

Agapanthus species
Albuca species
Amaryllis belladonna
Aristea species
Bulbine species
Bulbinella species
Chasmanthe floribunda
Clivia species
Crinum species

Cyrtanthus species
Dierama species
Dietes species
Dilatris species
Eucomis species
Freesia species and hybrids
Gladiolus species
Gloriosa species
Haemanthus species

Kniphofia species
Lachenalia species
Moraea species
Ornithogalum species
Oxalis species
Pterygodium species
Sandersonia aurantiaca
Satyrium species
Scilla natalensis

Sparaxis species and hybrids
Spiloxene capensis
Strelitzia species
Tritonia species and hybrids
Tulbaghia species
Veltheimia viridifolia
Watsonia species and hybrids
Zantedeschia species (arum, calla)

Succulents

Aloe arborescens
Aloe saponaria
Aloe striata
Aloe tenuior
Aloe thraskii and others
Carpobrotus species
Cephalophyllum species
Conicosia pugioniformis
Cotyledon species
Crassula species

Delosperma species
Didelta carnosa var. tomentosa
Dorotheanthus species
Drosanthemum species
Lampranthus species
Portulacaria afra
Rochea coccinea
Ruschia species
Semnanthe lacera

PLANTS FOR A DIFFICULT CLIMATE

There are regions of Southern Africa where harsh climatic conditions make gardening difficult. Similar conditions exist also in many parts of Australia and in some of the southern states of America. In these regions temperatures in summer may reach 38°C or more, whilst in winter, although the days may be warm, the temperatures drop to below freezing at night. In addition to being subject to a wide range of temperatures these areas have a low rainfall. Fortunately we have many native plants in South Africa which grow naturally in regions where the climatic conditions are as described above.

In places where the rainfall is low the soil tends to be brak or alkaline and this is another factor which inhibits the growth of plants in such areas. As most plants do best in soil which is acid, gardeners in regions of low rainfall are advised to have their soil tested, and if it is excessively alkaline to dig in acid compost and peat, and to use aluminium sulphate and sulphur to make the soil more suitable for those plants which do well only in acid soil.

The list given below includes some plants which are tolerant of alkaline soil and some which are not. It includes also some plants which stand severe frost and some which do not. All of the plants listed are able to tolerate fairly long periods without water. This does not mean, however, that they should not be watered. Many of them will not die if left without water for weeks on end, but they are not likely to progress and may wither if they do not receive some water during their growing season. Those marked with an * are more tolerant of dry conditions than the others.

Annuals and Perennials

*Aptosimum indivisum
*Arctotis species and hybrids
Castalis spectabilis
Charieis heterophylla

Chironia baccifera
*Chrysocoma coma-aurea
Coleus neochilus
Cotula species

*Dimorphotheca species and hybrids
Felicia species
*Gazania species and hybrids
Gerbera jamesonii
Grielum grandiflorum
Helichrysum species
Leonotis leonurus
Limonium perigrinum

*Osteospermum species
Pelargonium species
*Pentzia grandiflora
Psilothonna species
Salvia species
Senecio species
*Ursinia species
Zaluzianskya species

Bulbs

*Agapanthus species
Albuca (some species)
Amaryllis belladonna
*Antholyza ringens
Boophane disticha
*Brunsvigia gregaria
Brunsvigia radulosa
*Bulbine species
*Bulbinella species
Cyrtanthus breviflorus
Cyrtanthus galpinii
Cyrtanthus sanguineus
Dietes species
Freesia species and hybrids
Gladiolus ecklonii
Gladiolus milleri

Gladiolus oppositiflorus
Gladiolus orchidiflorus
Gladiolus psittacinus
Gladiolus salmoneus
Gloriosa superba
Haemanthus species
*Lapeirousia speciosa
Moraea species
Nerine filifolia
Nerine krigei
Nerine masonorum
Ornithogalum species
Sparaxis species and hybrids
Tritonia species
Tulbaghia species
Veltheimia capensis

Succulents

* All the succulents mentioned in the text should be tried in gardens in dry areas.

PLANTS FOR SHADY PLACES

There are shady places in all gardens, for the walls of a house create a certain amount of shade. In a hot country, however, it is important to plant trees and large shrubs to provide additional shade for the house and garden.

In the Southern Hemisphere a limited area along the south wall of the house has shade all day throughout the year, whilst along the other walls there will be shade for only part of the day. Many plants thrive when grown along a wall facing east where they get full morning sun and little or no afternoon sun, but few plants do well when planted along a wall which cuts off the morning sun and subjects them to the full heat of the afternoon sun.

The degree and intensity of shade varies according to its source. That provided by a wall is open shade, whereas a pergola or trees provide overhead shade. A large, spreading tree with dense foliage has heavy shade near its bole and light shade at its perimeter, whilst one which has feathery foliage or which is small, will create only light shade. When choosing plants for shady places it is advisable to plant only shade-loving ones in deep shade or in places which are shaded all day, but in areas where there is shade for only part of the day or where there is filtered sunlight a large number of different plants may be grown.

It is impossible to state categorically just how much shade a plant needs as this differs according to situation. Many plants which grow well in the open near the coast will not thrive in hot areas inland where the sunlight is intense, unless they have shade for part of the day. Other plants grow naturally in forests or under trees near the coast or inland. These are the shade-loving ones and they do best when planted in shade or semi-shade. The shade-loving plants are marked in the list below with an *. The other plants listed do best if shaded for only part of the day, preferably during the hot afternoon, or when grown in filtered shade.

Annuals and Perennials

Anchusa capensis
Anemone capensis
*Asparagus species
Coleus neochilus
Geranium incanum
Hypoestes aristata
Monsonia speciosa

Orphium frutescens
*Plectranthus species
Scabiosa species
Sebaea exacoides
Selago species
*Streptocarpus
Wahlenbergia species

Bulbs

Agapanthus species
*Amaryllis belladonna
Anapalina species
Anomalesia cunonia
Babiana species
Brunsvigia species
Bulbine alooides
Bulbine caulescens
Bulbinella species
*Chasmanthe floribunda
*Chlorophytum species
*Clivia species and hybrids
Crinum species
Cyrtanthus species
Dierama species
Dietes species
Disa species
Eucomis species
Freesia species and hybrids

Gladiolus (spring-flowering species)
Haemanthus species
Homoglossum species
Kniphofia species
Lachenalia species
Lapeirousia laxa
*Littonia modesta
Melasphaerula ramosa
Nerine species and hybrids
*Sandersonia aurantiaca
*Schizostylis coccinea
Scilla natalensis
Sparaxis species and hybrids
Tritonia species and hybrids
*Tulbaghia fragrans
*Vallota speciosa
*Veltheimia viridifolia
*Zantedeschia aethiopica

Succulents

Aloe aristata
Aloe ciliaris
Aloe microstigma
Aloe petricola
Aloe polyphylla
Aloe tenuior
Aloe thompsoniae

Crassula falcata
*Crassula multicava
Crassula perfoliata
Crassula portulacea
Rochea coccinea
Rochea subulata

PLANTS TO CASCADE OVER A WALL
OR GROW ON A BANK

In gardens on steeply sloping sites it is sometimes necessary to build a retaining wall to keep the soil from being washed down the slope. Because sloping terrain tends to dry out more quickly than level ground careful thought should be given when making a selection of plants to clothe such a wall or bank.

The plants listed below can be used to cascade over a wall or be planted on a slope to hold the soil. Some of them have attractive foliage as well as flowers. Some need full sunshine whilst other prefer partial or full shade. Details of their cultural requirements are given in the text.

Name of Plant	Remarks
Aloe ciliaris	Is a scrambling species of aloe producing charming coral flowers in sun or partial shade.
Arctotis stoechadifolia	This plant, from which many beautiful hybrids have evolved, grows quickly, has greyish foliage and beautiful flowers in late winter and early spring.
Asparagus densiflorus	Is an evergreen with pleasing stems of decorative foliage. Likes shade.
Carpobrotus species	These plants spread quickly. Most species are suitable for large gardens rather than small ones. They are useful for checking erosion along road and railway embankments and for holding coastal sand.
Cephalophyllum species	Succulent plants with flowers of brilliant colours in spring. Fine for holding the drift of sand along the coast and for hot dry gardens.
Coleus neochilus	Bears spikes of jacaranda-blue flowers in spring and summer. Is quick-growing. Suitable for sun or partial shade.
Crassula multicava	A quick-growing succulent which roots where it touches the ground and grows in shade or sun. It makes a good ground cover.
Delosperma species and hybrids	Are colourful succulents which do well on dry banks and walls and in sandy soil.
Diascia species	These are charming annuals and perennials with pretty pink flowers.
Didelta carnosa var. tomentosa	This is a splendid ground cover or plant for banks and walls in seaside gardens.
Dimorphotheca pluvialis	Is an easy-to-grow annual with sparkling white flowers in late winter.
Dimorphotheca sinuata and hybrids	Bears charming daisy-like flowers of shades of yellow and orange in late winter and spring.
Dorotheanthus species	Include delightful and most colourful and easy-to-grow spring-flowering annuals.
Drosanthemum species	These succulents tend to root where the stems are in close contact with the soil. They stand drought and a good deal of frost.
Felicia amelloides	This is a delightful shrubby perennial with flowers of sky to azure blue.

43

Name of Plant	Remarks
Gazania rigens var. leucolaena	Has pretty, slender, silvery leaves and canary-yellow flowers on and off through the year.
Gazania rigens var. uniflora	This decorative species bears trailing stems of silvery-grey leaves and bright yellow flowers.
Gazania: other species and hybrids	There are several species and very lovely hybrids to bind the soil and make the dry slope or bank colourful.
Geranium incanum	Is a charming little perennial with pretty foliage and flowers. Likes good soil and some shade.
Grielum grandiflorum	Is a pretty little plant with beautiful shining yellow flowers. It likes sandy soil
Helichrysum argenteum	A sun-loving plant which grows into a mound of silvery-grey leaves.
Helichrysum argyrophyllum	Has silver leaves throughout the year and yellow flowers in late summer and early autumn.
Heterolepis aliena	Is a low-growing perennial with gay yellow flowers in mid-spring.
Lampranthus species	Lampranthus include prostrate and bushy succulents which are ideal for dry banks and walls.
Malephora crocea	Is a pretty succulent to have growing on a bank. Dry conditions suit it.
Osteospermum species and hybrids	Include delightful plants for trailing over a wall or bank. Some species tolerate partial shade.
Pelargonium species	These are quick-growing plants which are ideal for large banks and walls.
Plectranthus ciliatus and Plectranthus verticillatus	Both are sprawling plants which quickly clothe a bank. They need shade, good soil and regular watering.
Ruschia species	Do well in hot dry gardens. They have succulent leaves and pretty little flowers.
Senecio haworthii	Is a bushy little plant with unusual and decorative silver-grey leaves.
Thunbergia alata	A quick-growing climber which makes a pretty show falling over a wall or bank.
Ursinia sericea	A shrubby species with attractive grey foliage—suitable for a large bank.

PLANTS WHICH ARE QUICK-GROWING

Probably the first fact which most gardeners want to know about a plant is how quickly it grows. Fortunately a number of our South African native plants are quick-growing.

The rate of growth of a plant is an inherited characteristic of a genus or species, but climatic conditions undoubtedly play a part, too. A plant which is quick-growing in a subtropical climate may prove slow in a region where winters are cold or where it has insufficient moisture, and those which like a temperate climate may not progress well under hot or dry conditions. The care given a plant will also influence its rate of growth. Generally it can be said that those planted in good soil and watered liberally and regularly will grow more rapidly than those which are neglected.

The plants listed below are quick-growing when given the kind of conditions which suit them. Before making a selection of plants it is advisable therefore to read the details of their cultural requirements, which is given in the text.

Annuals and Perennials

Anchusa capensis
Arctotis species and hybrids
Asparagus species
Castalis spectabilis
Charieis heterophylla
Chironia species
Chrysocoma coma-aurea
Coleus neochilus
Cotula species
Diascia species
Dimorphotheca species and hybrids
Felicia species
Gazania species and hybrids
Geranium incanum
Helichrysum species

Heliophila sonchifolia
Leonotis leonurus
Lobelia species
Nemesia species and hybrids
Orphium frutescens
Osteospermum species and hybrids
Pelargonium species
Pentzia grandiflora
Plectranthus species
Psilothonna species
Salvia species
Selago species
Senecio species and hybrids
Ursinia species

Bulbs

Agapanthus species
Albuca species
Amaryllis belladonna
Anapalina species
Babiana species and hybrids
Bulbine species
Bulbinella species
Chasmanthe floribunda
Chlorophytum
Clivia species and hybrids
Crinum species and hybrids
Crocosmia species and hybrids
Cyrtanthus species
Dierama species
Dietes species and hybrids
Eucomis species.
Freesia species and hybrids
Galtonia candicans
Gladiolus (many species)

Gloriosa species
Homeria species
Homoglossum species and hybrids
Ixia species and hybrids
Kniphofia species and hybrids
Lachenalia species and hybrids
Littonia modesta
Moraea species
Ornithogalum species
Oxalis species
Romulea species
Satyrium species
Sparaxis species and hybrids
Tritonia species and hybrids
Tulbaghia species
Veltheimia viridifolia
Watsonia species and hybrids
Zantedeschia species (arum)

Succulents

Aloe arborescens
Aloe chabaudii
Aloe ciliaris

Aloe comptonii
Aloe ferox
Aloe microstigma

Succulents

Aloe saponaria
Aloe striata
Aloe tenuior
Carpobrotus species
Cephalophyllum species
Conicosia pugioniformis
Cotyledon species
Crassula (most species)
Delosperma species

Dorotheanthus species
Drosanthemum species
Euphorbia species
Lampranthus species
Portulacaria afra
Rochea coccinea
Rochea subulata
Ruschia species
Semnanthe lacera

PLANTS WITH PLEASING FOLIAGE

When selecting plants for the garden do not be guided solely by the flowers they bear but consider the leaves, too. Flowers are ephemeral in nature whereas the leaves may keep the garden looking attractive for a much longer time. Leaves may be decorative because of their form; e.g. they may be lacy or feathery, long and slender, oval, broad or heart-shaped; or they may be attractive because of their texture; e.g. they may be glossy, hairy, silky rough or leathery; or they may beautify the garden because of their colour. There are many different shades of green and grey, and an artistic combination of these different shades can make the garden attractive throughout the year.

Annuals and Perennials

Anemone capensis
Asparagus species
Coleus neochilus
Gazania species and particularly
Gazania rigens var. leucolaena
Gazania rigens var. uniflora
Geranium incanum
Grielum grandiflorum
Helichrysum argenteum

Helichrysum argyrophyllum
Monsonia speciosa
Pelargonium (several species)
Pentzia grandiflora
Plectranthus species
Senecio (many species)
Ursinia species, and particularly
Ursinia sericea

Bulbs

Agapanthus
Bulbine species
Chasmanthe floribunda
Chlorophytum comosum and hybrids
Clivia species and hybrids
Dierama species
Eucomis species
Gloriosa superba

Littonia modesta
Sandersonia aurantiaca
Strelitzia reginae
Strelitzia parvifolia
Strelitzia parvifolia var. juncea
Vallota
Veltheimia viridifolia
Zantedeschia species

46

Succulents

Aloe (see species mentioned on page 240)
Conicosia pugioniformis
Cotyledon (some species)
Crassula (many species)
Delosperma
Didelta carnosa var. tomentosa

Dorotheanthus
Drosanthemum
Lampranthus
Malephora crocea
Portulacaria afra
Senecio haworthii

PLANTS FOR CONTAINERS

Plants growing in containers are now used extensively to decorate the house inside and to bring life to a patio or terrace outside. There are certain advantages in growing plants in containers for indoor and outdoor show. The plants, in their containers, can be kept in an out-of-the-way part of the garden or in a shed, and brought on show only when they are at their best. In this way your indoor pot plants and window-boxes, and pots or tubs on the terrace will always look decorative because the plants are on display only when they have reached their peak. Well-nourished plants in good containers can add great beauty to the home or garden from season to season.

Growing plants in containers is also a way of producing special plants where soil or other conditions make gardening difficult. If the soil in your garden is alkaline and you want to grow plants (such as ericas and proteas) which like acid soil, then grow them in large containers filled with an acid soil mix, and if you live in an area where severe frosts preclude your growing some of your favourite plants, try growing them in containers which can be stored in a sheltered corner during the most severe weeks of winter.

Containers: Containers are of many different kinds and it is advisable to give careful thought to the type of containers needed for different plants. House plants are generally grown in fairly small clay pots, which can be displayed individually, hidden inside more decorative pots, or they may be grouped together in ornamental window-boxes. It is easier to keep a window-box looking attractive if the plants in it are grown in individual pots rather than planted in soil in the window-box itself. This makes it easy to take out any plant which is past its prime and to put in another pot plant to take its place. Plants which are to be grown outdoors should be planted in large containers as, to make a good show, they must be encouraged to grow fairly large. Well-made plant boxes of durable timber, tubs or large pots are the best containers to use. Whatever container is used, it is important to see that there are drainage holes at the bottom. If the water cannot drain through the soil becomes sour and the plant will eventually die.

Soil: The soil in the container should be rich in humus and friable in texture. Clay is not suitable because it packs into a mass as solid as a block of cement. For plants which like acid soil see that the mixture is acid, adding peat when necessary. For succulents use more sand in the mixture.

Water: No specific rules can be laid down as to how often to water plants in containers. This is something one has to learn by experience. How much water to give and how often to water depends on the nature of the plant, that is, whether it likes damp growing conditions or prefers to be somewhat dry (e.g. succulents), and it depends also on the weather. Obviously during periods of dry weather, and particularly when it is windy, plants need to be watered far more frequently than during periods of rain or when the air is still. Test the soil with your fingers and if it is dry beneath the surface, water the plant until the water seeps through the drainage holes. If the water comes out too fast at the bottom it may mean that the plant has dried out to such a degree that the soil has shrunk away from the sides of the container thus allowing the water to run out quickly down the sides. Where this has happened soak the container in a bucket of water or plug the drainage holes and let water seep into the container slowly until the soil is saturated right through.

Food: It is only natural that plants in containers will sooner or later absorb the nutrients originally available in the soil. If they are in small containers and do not mind being moved from one container to another they can be repotted in fresh soil, but generally it is easier to keep plants going by feeding them with additional nutrients in the form of fertilizer. Frequent light applications of fertilizer are better for a plant than a large dose occasionally. The plant itself may indicate when it needs extra nutrients. Should the leaves appear to be turning pale green or yellow instead of remaining their original shade, or, should they seem to be smaller in size than the leaves originally were, it is time to fertilize. If you are new to gardening remember that certain plants, such as some of the succulents, seldom need additional nutrients and that others require regular feeding in order to flourish. Remember also that some plants become dormant every year either after their flowering period or in winter, and that the leaves of such plants will turn yellow or wither, or do both, and that this prelude to dormancy does not indicate that they need any food. Plants need no extra nutrients when they become dormant, but before they start into new growth the following season they should be repotted in fresh soil or given some extra food. Fertilizers are available in tablet or powder form with particulars as to their application given on the container. If in doubt rather under-fertilize than over-fertilize. Some bulbs do not flower if they are moved each year. Such plants should be grown in the same container without repotting for several seasons.

Containers vary in size, and in the list which follows the size of containers is indicated as follows:
Large: diameter at the top more than 35 cm (14 inches).
Medium: diameter at the top of 20-35 cm (8-14 inches).
Small: diameter at the top of 15-20 cm (6-8 inches).

Annuals and Perennials

Name of Plant	Sun or Shade	LARGE	MEDIUM	SMALL	Remarks
Anemone capensis	Part shade			•	Pretty foliage; flowers in spring.
Arctotis species and hybrids	Sun	•	•		Flowers late winter and early spring.
Asparagus asparagoides	Shade			•	Indoor or outdoor plant with good foliage.
Asparagus densiflorus	Shade	•	•		Elegant stems of leaves throughout the year.
Asparagus setaceus	Shade	•	•	•	Outdoor or indoor plant with decorative foliage. Needs support of some kind.
Chironia baccifera	Sun		•	•	Pink flowers in summer followed by red berries.
Coleus neochilus	Sun or Shade	•	•		Pretty but has unpleasant smell when touched.
Diascia integerrima	Sun	•	•		Pink flowers from spring to summer.
Felicia amelloides	Sun	•	•		Blue flowers in spring and summer.

48

Annuals and Perennials

Name of Plant	Sun or Shade	LARGE	MEDIUM	SMALL	Remarks
Gazania rigens var. uniflora	Sun	●	●		Pretty silver leaves and yellow flowers; trailing stems.
Gazania species and hybrids	Sun		●	●	Brilliant colours in late winter and early spring.
Geranium incanum	Sun or Shade		●	●	Decorative foliage and mauve flowers in late winter and spring.
Gerbera jamesonii	Sun		●	●	Colourful flowers in spring.
Helichrysum argenteum	Sun	●	●		Silver leaves. White flowers in spring.
Helichrysum argyrophyllum	Sun	●	●	●	Neat, silver leaves, and small yellow flowers in late summer and autumn.
Heterolepis aliena	Sun		●	●	Scrambling, low-growing plant with bright yellow flowers.
Lobelia species	Sun		●	●	Blue flowers in spring and summer.
Orphium frutescens	Sun or Shade		●	●	Glistening flowers of a charming cyclamen pink in summer.
Osteospermum jucundum	Sun	●	●	●	Mauve flowers on trailing stems; late winter.
Monsonia speciosa	Part shade			●	Pink flowers in late winter.
Nemesia species and hybrids	Sun		●	●	Many colours; flowers in late winter and early spring.
Plectranthus ciliatus	Shade	●	●		Trailing stems with pinky-mauve flowers in autumn.
Roella ciliata	Part shade			●	Blue/mauve flowers in spring.
Streptocarpus species and hybrids	Shade		●	●	Mauve, blue, white. Do best indoors and in sheltered gardens.

Name of Plant	Sun or Shade	LARGE	MEDIUM	SMALL	Remarks
Agapanthus species	Sun or Shade	●	●		Good foliage and fine flowers in summer.
Albuca species	Sun or part shade		●	●	Flowers of unusual form and colouring. Mostly in spring and summer.
Amaryllis belladonna	Part shade		●		Magnificent flowers late summer and early autumn.
Anapalina species	Part shade		●	●	Flowers in spring and summer.
Anomalesia cunonia	Part shade		●	●	Luminous coral-red flowers in late winter, early spring.
Antholyza ringens	Sun		●	●	Most unusual shape; flowers in late winter and early spring.
Brunsvigia species and hybrids	Part shade	●	●		Pink to red flowers; spring to summer.
Chlorophytum	Shade		●	●	For indoor or outdoor show. Green/white foliage.
Clivia miniata	Shade		●	●	For indoor or outdoor show; flowers in spring.
Crocosmia aurea	Sun		●	●	Outstanding plant for summer flowers.
Cyrtanthus species	Sun or part shade		●	●	Pretty little flowers in spring and summer.
Dilatris species	Sun or part shade		●	●	Round heads of lavender-blue flowers in mid-spring.
Disa species	Part shade		●	●	Difficult but beautiful. See text.
Eucomis punctata and E. clavata	Sun	●	●		Handsome and unusual flowers in summer.
Freesia species and hybrids	Sun or part shade		●	●	Species more sweetly scented than hybrids.
Geissorrhiza rochensis	Sun		●	●	Most beautiful flowers in late winter or early spring.
Gladiolus (small species)	Sun or part shade		●	●	Flowers from late winter through spring, and some in summer.

Bulbs

Name of Plant	Sun or Shade	LARGE	MEDIUM	SMALL	Remarks
Gloriosa species	Part shade	●	●		Exceptional flower for indoor or outdoor show in summer. Needs support.
Lachenalia species	Sun or part shade		●	●	Make fine winter-spring pot plants indoors or outside. For colours see text.
Littonia modesta	Part shade	●	●	●	Golden flowers in summer. Needs support.
Moraea villosa and other small species	Part shade		●	●	Enchanting little flowers for a spring display.
Nerine species and hybrids	Part shade		●	●	Flowers of red, rose, cerise, pink, mauve, white in summer.
Ornithogalum miniatum	Sun			●	Bright golden or orange flowers in spring.
Oxalis species	Sun			●	Charming little flowers from late winter to early spring.
Romulea rosea	Sun			●	Most colourful in late winter and early spring.
Sandersonia aurantiaca	Part shade	●	●		Pretty flowers in summer. Plant needs support.
Satyrium carneum and S. coriifolium	Part shade or sun		●	●	Flowers of unusual form in spring.
Schizostylis coccinea	Part shade		●	●	Handsome scarlet flowers in summer.
Sparaxis species and hybrids	Sun or part shade		●	●	Most colourful small plants for late winter and early spring show.
Spiloxene capensis	Sun			●	Has most attractive flowers in late winter and early spring.
Tritonia species and hybrids	Sun			●	Hardy little plants which make a colourful show in spring.
Tulbaghia fragrans	Part shade		●	●	Hardy, quick-growing plant; mauve flowers in late winter.
Vallota speciosa	Part shade		●	●	Attractive crimson flowers in summer.

Bulbs

Name of Plant	Sun or Shade	LARGE	MEDIUM	SMALL	Remarks
Veltheimia viridifolia	Shade	●	●		Most decorative in late winter. Long-lasting.
Zantedeschia species	Sun or part shade	●	●	●	Yellow, white and pink arums are decorative indoors and outside.

Succulents

Name of Plant	Sun or Shade	LARGE	MEDIUM	SMALL	Remarks
Aloe (small species)	Sun	●	●	●	Unusual leaves through the year. Flowers at different seasons.
Carpobrotus muirii	Sun	●	●		Very quick-growing with cyclamen-mauve flowers in October.
Cephalophyllum species	Sun	●	●	●	Some are bushy and some are trailing. Flowers in spring.
Conicosia pugioniformis	Sun		●	●	Attractive fleshy leaves. Flowers in spring.
Crassula species	Sun	●	●	●	Some are bushy and some trailing. See text.
Delosperma species	Sun	●	●		Succulent which stands drought and frost. Very showy in spring.
Dorotheanthus species	Sun	●	●	●	Hardy little annuals which produce luminous flowers of many colours in late winter and early spring.
Drosanthemum species	Sun	●	●	●	Fleshy leaves and scintillating flowers in late winter and early spring.
Euphorbia caput-medusae	Sun		●	●	Plant of unusual growth for hot, dry places.
Lampranthus species	Sun	●	●	●	Most colourful for late winter to mid-spring. Some bushy, some sprawling.

Succulents

Name of Plant	Sun or SHADE	LARGE	MEDIUM	SMALL	Remarks
Malephora crocea	Sun		•	•	Pretty succulent grey-green leaves and bronze to cyclamen flowers.
Semnanthe lacera	Sun	•	•		Prostrate succulent with amethyst flowers.
Senecio haworthii	Sun		•	•	Silver-grey leaves and yellow flowers.

PLANTS WHICH PROVIDE MATERIAL FOR ARRANGEMENTS

Name of Plant	Material
Agapanthus	Blue and white flowers for large arrangements or posies. (Summer)
Albuca species (SENTRY-IN-THE-BOX, GELDBEURSIE)	Unusual flowers coloured mostly yellow/white/green. (Spring and summer)
Aloe species	Red, orange, yellow; for large and small arrangements. (Mostly autumn and winter)
Amaryllis belladonna (BELLADONNA LILY)	Pink and white lily-like flowers. (Late summer and early autumn)
Arctotis species and hybrids (ARCTOTIS, GOUSBLOM, NAMAQUALAND DAISY)	Daisies which remain open only during the daylight hours. (Late winter and early spring)
Asparagus species (SMILAX, ASPARAGUS FERN)	Decorative leaves which last well. (All months of the year)
Babiana species (BABIANA, BOBBEJAANTJIE)	Mauve, cyclamen, cerise, cream, purple. (Late winter and early spring)
Bulbinella species (BULBINELLA, KATSTERT)	Yellow flowers on long stems. (Late winter and early spring)
Clivia miniata (CLIVIA, BUSH LILY)	Rounded heads of tawny-orange to flaming apricot. (Late winter to mid-spring)
Cotyledon orbiculata (COTYLEDON, PLAKKIES)	Apricot to orange-red flowers on long stems. (Late winter to mid-summer)
Crassula falcata (RED CRASSULA)	Long stems ending in crimson to scarlet flowers. (Summer-autumn)
Crassula multicava (FAIRY CRASSULA)	Short stems of tiny pink and white flowers. (Winter and spring)
Crassula portulacea (PINK JOY)	Heads of small pink flowers. (Winter)
Crinum species (VLEI LILY, CRINUM)	Heads of large, lily-like pink and white flowers on long stems. (Mostly late spring to mid-summer)

53

Name of Plant	Material
Crocosmia aurea (CROCOSMIA, FALLING STARS)	Bright marmalade-orange flowers on tall stems. (Summer)
Dicoma zeyheri (DICOMA, JAKHALSBOS)	Green and brick-red heads like thistles. (Spring and summer)
Dierama pendulum (HAIRBELL)	Very slender stems with nodding mauve flowers. (Spring and summer)
Dilatris species (ROOIWORTEL)	Rounded heads of lavender-blue flowers on stems of 30 cm. (Mid- to late spring)
Eucomis clavata and E. punctata (PINEAPPLE FLOWER)	Long stems of green and wine flowers which last for weeks. (Summer)
Freesia species and hybrids (FREESIA, KAMMETJIE)	Many colours; some species have a delightful scent. (Late winter to mid-spring)
Gerberis jamesonii and hybrids (BARBERTON OR TRANSVAAL DAISY)	Daisy-like flowers of many colours. (Spring and early summer)
Gladiolus species (MANY DIFFERENT COMMON NAMES)	Most species have small flowers of subtle pastel shades. (Spring and summer)
Gloriosa superba (FLAME LILY)	Unusual flowers of yellow/orange/red. (Summer)
Haemanthus katherinae (BLOOD FLOWER, BLOEDBLOM)	Fairly small flowers in large, rounded heads. Rose and red. (Summer)
Helichrysum species (EVERLASTINGS OR STRAWFLOWERS)	Strawlike flowers which last almost indefinitely. Mostly pink, white, yellow. (Spring and summer)
Ixia species (IXIA, WAND LILY, KALOSSIE)	Slender stems; flowers are yellow, orange, mauve, rose and green. (Spring)
Kniphofia species (RED-HOT POKERS)	Tall robust stems of flowers of orange and red. (Spring, summer, late winter)
Lachenalia species (CAPE COWSLIP, VIOOLTJIE)	Small plants with lovely, gleaming flowers of misty mauves or blues, or yellow or red. (Winter and early spring)
Limonium perigrinum (STATICE, SEA LAVENDER, STRANDROOS)	Tall stems on which are papery pink flowers. (Spring)
Nemesia strumosa and hybrids (NEMESIA)	Flowers of many colours on stems 30 cm high. Ideal for mixed bowls. (Early spring)
Nerine species (NERINA, GUERNSEY LILY)	Bear rounded heads of very pretty flowers. (Late summer or early autumn)
Ornithogalum species (CHINCHERINCHEE)	White, cream, yellow and orange. (Early to late spring)
Orphium frutescens (ORPHIUM)	Very pretty cyclamen-pink, waxy flowers, (Late spring and early summer)
Pelargonium species (VARIOUS COMMON NAMES)	Flowers are mostly mauve, pink and coral. (Late winter and early spring but some flowers in other seasons too)
Phoenocoma prolifera (PINK EVERLASTING)	Glistening pale to deep pink flowers. Very long-lasting. (Spring)

Name of Plant	Material
Rochea subulata (KLIPBLOM)	Short stems of ivory/pink flowers which give off a faint scent at night. (Spring)
Satyrium coriifolium (EWWA-TREWWA)	Marmalade coloured flowers on 30 cm stems. (Spring)
Schizostylis coccinea (RIVER LILY, KAFFIR LILY)	Scarlet flowers with gleaming petals. (Summer)
Sparaxis species and hybrids (SPARAXIS, HARLEQUIN FLOWER FLUWEELTJIE)	Many colours. Funnel-shaped. 30 cm stems. (Spring)
Strelitzia reginae and S. juncea (CRANE FLOWER, BIRD OF PARADISE FLOWER)	Large flowers on long stems. Orange/yellow/blue. (Winter and spring)
Tritonia species (TRITONIA, BLAZING STAR)	Very decorative salmon and orange flowers. (Spring)
Tulbaghia fragrans (SWEET GARLIC)	Mauve flowers in rounded heads. Sweet scent. (Late winter and early spring)
Vallota speciosa (GEORGE LILY, KNYSNA LILY, SCARBOROUGH LILY)	Scarlet to crimson flowers on stems 30 cm tall. (Late spring and early summer)
Veltheimia viridifolia (FOREST LILY)	Dusty-pink flowers on stems 45 cm tall. (Winter)
Watsonia species (WATSONIA)	Most have tall stems of flowers, of pink, mauve, purple, rose or white. (Spring or summer)
Zantedeschia species (ARUM OR CALLA LILY)	Flowers are large or of medium size on stems 45-60 cm tall. Colours are white, yellow or pink. (Late winter to early summer)

FLOWER COLOUR THROUGH THE SEASONS

In order to be able to create a garden which is colourful throughout the year it is important to know *when* different plants flower or, if the flowers are insignificant, when they are most colourful because of their foliage or fruits, and, in order to group plants effectively one should know the *colours* of the flowers, leaves or fruits.

In the charts which follow plants are listed according to the season when they are most colourful. Sometimes the same plant appears in two seasons. This is because it may start flowering at the end of one season and continue to be colourful into the next season, or it may be due to the fact that, because of climatic differences between different zones, a plant which flowers in winter in one zone may not flower until spring in another zone. It will therefore appear in the chart under both winter and spring.

Climatic conditions in Southern Africa vary because of latitude, elevation, proximity to the sea, hours of sunshine and rainfall. The dates when the seasons begin and end therefore appear to differ from place to place. The following dates are used in this book to cover the different seasons:—

Spring . . . September to November;
Summer . . . December to February;
Autumn . . . March to May;
Winter . . . June to August.

In the Northern Hemisphere, because of the cool weather in spring, many of the plants which flower in spring in Southern Africa are grown for summer colour there.

Dividing flowers into eight basic colours—yellow, orange, red, pink, blue, mauve, purple and white—presented many problems because of the infinite differences of shades found in these colours. For example, red includes scarlet, crimson, wine-red, blood-red, cherry-red, tomato-red, coral-red and flame-red. Plants are listed under the colour nearest the shade of the flower. A plant with apricot flowers might be listed under yellow, orange or pink, depending upon which of these three colours appears to predominate in the flower. Similarly a plant with cyclamen or carmine flowers may be listed under pink, mauve or purple. In many cases where a plant is listed under three different colours, such as yellow, orange and pink, it does not necessarily mean that it bears flowers of these three different colours; it may be that the flowers are shaded in these three colours, without any one of them being predominant. More exact definitions of the colours of the flowers are given in the individual descriptions in the text. The colours refer only to the species described in this book.

Annuals and Perennials

Name of Plant	Height	YELLOW	ORANGE	RED	PINK	BLUE	MAUVE	PURPLE	WHITE
Anchusa capensis (CAPE FORGET-ME-NOT)	45–60 cm					●			
Anemone capensis (CAPE ANEMONE)	45 cm				●				
Arctotis species and hybrids (BUSHY ARCTOTIS, GOUSBLOM, NAMAQUALAND DAISY, VENIDIUM)	20–40 cm	●	●	●	●		●	●	●
Arctotis leiocarpa (KAROO DAISY)	45 cm								●
Arctotis stoechadifolia (TRAILING ARCTOTIS)	15–30 cm	●	●	●	●		●	●	●
Arctotis venusta (FREE STATE DAISY)	40–60 cm								●
Castalis spectabilis (CASTALIS)	20 cm						●		
Charieis heterophylla (HEAVENLY BLUE DAISY)	20–30 cm					●			
Chrysocoma coma-aurea (YELLOW EDGING DAISY)	30 cm	●							
Coleus neochilus (LOBSTER FLOWER)	30 cm						●		
Cotula species (BUTTON FLOWERS)	8–30 cm	●	●						
Diascia species (TWINSPUR, BRIDE'S SADDLE)	20–45 cm				●				
Dimorphotheca species (AFRICAN DAISY, NAMAQUALAND DAISY)	20–60 cm	●	●						●
Felicia species (KINGFISHER DAISY, FELICIA)	20–60 cm					●	●	●	●
Gazania species and hybrids (GAZANIA, WILD MARIGOLD, GOUSBLOM)	15–30 cm	●	●	●	●				

Annuals and Perennials

Name of Plant	Height	YELLOW	ORANGE	RED	PINK	BLUE	MAUVE	PURPLE	WHITE
Geranium incanum (CARPET GERANIUM)	20 cm						●		
Gerbera jamesonii and hybrids (BARBERTON OR TRANSVAAL DAISY)	30–60 cm	●	●	●	●		●		●
Grielum grandiflorum (YELLOW SATIN FLOWER, BOTTERBLOM)	10 cm	●							
Helichrysum species (EVERLASTINGS, STRAWFLOWERS)	15–60 cm	●			●				●
Heliophila sonchifolia (BLUE FLAX)	45 cm					●			
Heterolepis aliena	30 cm	●							
Limonium perigrinum (SEA LAVENDER, STRANDROOS)	60 cm				●				
Lobelia species and hybrids (LOBELIA)	20–30 cm					●			●
Monsonia speciosa (LADY MONSON'S FLOWER, SNAKE FLOWER)	20–30 cm				●				
Nemesia strumosa and hybrids (NEMESIA, LEEUBEKKIE)	30–45 cm	●	●	●	●		●	●	●
Osteospermum species (WILD DAISY, DAISY BUSH)	20–60 cm						●	●	●
Pelargonium species (VARIOUS, SEE TEXT)	30–90 cm			●	●		●	●	●
Pentzia grandiflora (MATRICARIA)	30–40 cm	●							
Phoenocoma prolifera (PINK EVERLASTING)	60–90 cm				●				
Psilothonna species (EDGING DAISY)	20–30 cm	●	●						

Annuals and Perennials

Name of Plant	Height	YELLOW	ORANGE	RED	PINK	BLUE	MAUVE	PURPLE	WHITE
Roella ciliata (BLUE ROELLA)	20–30 cm					●	●		
Scabiosa africana (WILD SCABIOUS)	30–60 cm						●		●
Selago serrata (TOOTH-LEAFED SELAGO)	60 cm						●		
Selago spuria (CAPE BLUE HAZE)	60 cm						●		
Selago thunbergii (SELAGO)	45 cm						●		
Senecio arenarius (EDGING SENECIO)	30 cm						●		
Senecio elegans (PURPLE SENECIO, WILD CINERARIA)	60 cm						●		
Senecio glastifolius (LARGE SENECIO)	1.25 m						●		
Sutera revoluta (SUTERA)	30–60 cm						●		
Ursinia species (URSINIA)	30–45 cm	●	●						
Ursinia chrysanthemoides var. geyeri (CORAL URSINIA)	30 cm			●					
Ursinia sericea (LACELEAF URSINIA)	60 cm	●							
Wahlenbergia capensis (CAPE BELLFLOWER)	30 cm					●	●		
Zaluzianskya villosa (DRUMSTICKS)	20 cm						●		●

Bulbs and Bulblike Plants

Name of Plant	Height	YELLOW	ORANGE	RED	PINK	BLUE	MAUVE	PURPLE	WHITE
Albuca canadensis (SENTRY-IN-THE-BOX)	40–60 cm	•							
Anapalina revoluta (ANAPALINA)	45 cm			•					
Anomalesia cunonia (ANOMALESIA)	30–40 cm			•					
Aristea species (ARISTEA)	40–120 cm					•			
Babiana species and hybrids (BABIANA, BABIAANTJIE)	10–45 cm	•		•		•	•	•	
Boophane disticha (SORE EYE FLOWER, RED POSY)	10–20 cm				•				
Bulbine species (BULBINE—VARIOUS)	20–45 cm	•							
Bulbinella species (BULBINELLA, KATSTERT)	30–90 cm	•	•						
Chasmanthe floribunda (FLAMES, PENNANT FLOWER, SUURKNOL)	60 cm			•					
Clivia miniata (CLIVIA, BUSH LILY, ST. JOHN'S LILY)	45 cm		•						
Clivia nobilis (CAPE CLIVIA)	45 cm		•						
Crinum bulbispermum (ORANGE RIVER LILY)	60–90 cm				•				•
Crinum campanulatum (WATER CRINUM, VLEI LILY)	45–60 cm				•				•
Crinum graminicola (GRASS CRINUM)	30 cm				•				•
Crinum macowanii (CAPE COAST LILY, SABIE CRINUM)	60–90 cm				•				•

Bulbs and Bulblike Plants

Name of Plant	Height	YELLOW	ORANGE	RED	PINK	BLUE	MAUVE	PURPLE	WHITE
Cyrtanthus species (FIRE LILY, INANDA LILY, IFAFA LILY)	20–30 cm	•	•	•	•				•
Dierama species (HAREBELL, HAIRBELL, WAND-FLOWER)	1–2 m						•		
Dietes species (WILD IRIS, UILTJIE)	30–60 cm	•					•		•
Dilatris species (ROOIWORTEL)	30–40 cm						•		
Engysiphon pictus	30 cm				•				
Freesia species and hybrids (FREESIA, KAMMETJIE, FLISSIE)	15–45 cm	•	•		•	•	•	•	•
Geissorrhiza species (SEQUINS, WINE CUPS, SYSIE)	10–30 cm	•		•				•	
Gladiolus species (PAINTED LADY AND OTHERS)	20–60 cm	•		•	•		•		•
Haemanthus amarylloides (PINK HAEMANTHUS)	30 cm				•				•
Haemanthus magnificus (PAINT BRUSH)	30–45 cm			•					
Ixia species (IXIA, CORN LILY, KALOSSIE)	15–45 cm	•	•	•	•			•	green
Kniphofia caulescens (BASUTO TORCH LILY, RED-HOT POKER)	1.25 m	•		•					
Lachenalia species (CAPE COWSLIP, LACHENALIA, VIOOLTJIE)	15–40 cm	•	•	•		•	•	•	
Lanaria lanata (COTTONWOOL FLOWER, KAPOKBLOM)	60–90 cm			•					•
Lapeirousia laxa (SMALL RED IRIS)	20–30 cm			•					

Bulbs and Bulblike Plants

Name of Plant	Height	YELLOW	ORANGE	RED	PINK	BLUE	MAUVE	PURPLE	WHITE
Moraea species (MOREA, TULP)	15–60 cm	●			●		●	●	
Nymphoides indica (YELLOW POND LILY)	water plant	●							
Ornithogalum species (CHINCHERINCHEE)	15–60 cm	●	●						●
Oxalis species (SORREL, SURING)	10–25 cm	●			●		●	●	●
Pterygodium acutifolium (MOEDERKAPPIE)	20–30 cm	●							
Romulea species (ROMULEA, SATIN FLOWER. FRUTANG)	10–20 cm	●			●				
Satyrium species (EWWA-TREWWA)	15–30 cm		●	●	●				
Scilla natalensis (WILD SQUILL, BLOUSLANGKOP)	60–90 cm					●	●		
Sparaxis species and hybrids (SPARAXIS, HARLEQUIN FLOWER, FLUWEELTJIE)	15–45 cm	●	●	●	●		●	●	●
Spiloxene capensis (STARS, STERRETJIE)	15–30 cm	●							●
Strelitzia reginae (CRANE FLOWER, BIRD-OF-PARADISE FLOWER, KRAANVOËLBLOM)	1.25 m	●	●						
Synnotia variegata (SYNNOTIA).	30 cm						●		●
Tritonia species and hybrids (TRITONIA, BLAZING STAR)	30–45 cm	●	●	●	●				●
Tulbaghia fragrans (SWEET GARLIC)	30–45 cm						●		
Tulbaghia violacea (WILD GARLIC)	20–30 cm						●		

Bulbs and Bulblike Plants

Name of Plant	Height	YELLOW	ORANGE	RED	PINK	BLUE	MAUVE	PURPLE	WHITE
Veltheimia viridifolia (FOREST LILY)	30–60 cm				•				
Watsonia species	30–90 cm			•	•		•	•	•
Zantedeschia species (ARUM LILY, CALLA LILY, PIG LILY)	30–120 cm	•			•				•

Succulents

NAME OF PLANT	HEIGHT	YELLOW	ORANGE	RED	PINK	BLUE	MAUVE	PURPLE	WHITE
Aloe africana (UITENHAGE ALOE)	2–2.5 m	•	•						
Aloe ciliaris	3 m			•					
Aloe comptonii (COMPTON'S ALOE)	60–90 cm			•					
Aloe ferox (BITTER ALOE)	2–3 m		•	•					•
Aloe hereroensis (HERERO ALOE)	1 m	•	•	•					
Aloe plicatilis (FAN ALOE)	2–3 m			•					
Aloe polyphylla (BASUTOLAND ALOE, SPIRAL ALOE)	45 cm			•					
Aloe saponaria (SOAP ALOE)	45 cm	•	•	•	•				
Aloe speciosa	3–4 m			•					•
Aloe tenuior (FENCE ALOE)	2 m	•		•					

Succulents

Name of Plant	Height	YELLOW	ORANGE	RED	PINK	BLUE	MAUVE	PURPLE	WHITE
Carpobrotus species (SOUR FIG, GOUNA, GOUKUM, HOTTENTOT FIG)	10–20 cm	●					●	●	
Cephalophyllum species (VYGIES, MESEM)	10–60 cm	●	●	●	●		●	●	
Cotyledon species (PIG'S EAR, PLAKKIES AND OTHERS)	20–60 cm			●	●				
Delosperma species (VYGIE, MESEM)	10–25 cm				●			●	
Didelta carnosa var. tomentosa (DIDELTA)	20-45 cm	●							
Dorotheanthus species (BOKBAY VYGIE, MESEM)	8–20 cm	●	●	●	●		●	●	●
Drosanthemum species (VYGIE, MESEM)	10–60 cm	●	●	●	●		●	●	●
Euphorbia species (SPURGE, MELKBOS, NABOOM)	8 cm–8 m	●							
Lampranthus species (SANDVYGIE, MESEM)	8–60 cm	●	●	●	●		●	●	●
Ruschia species (CUSHION MESEM., VYGIE)	4–30 cm						●	●	
Semnanthe lacera	30–45 cm						●		
Senecio haworthii (GREY-LEAFED SENECIO)	30 cm	●							

Annuals and Perennials

Name of Plant	Height	YELLOW	ORANGE	RED	PINK	BLUE	MAUVE	PURPLE	WHITE
Arctotis venusta (FREE STATE DAISY)	60 cm								●
Chironia species (CHRISTMAS BERRY, BITTERBOS)	30–45 cm				●				
Diascia integerrima (DIASCIA)	45 cm				●				
Geranium incanum (CARPET GERANIUM)	20 cm						●		
Gerbera jamesonii and hybrids (BARBERTON OR TRANSVAAL DAISY)	30–60 cm	●	●	●	●		●	●	●
Helichrysum species (EVERLASTINGS, STRAWFLOWERS)	15–60 cm	●			●				●
Lobelia species (LOBELIA)	20–30 cm					●			
Monopsis luteus (YELLOW LOBELIA)	30 cm	●							
Orphium frutescens (ORPHIUM)	30–60 cm				●				
Plectranthus species (PLECTRANTHUS)	30–60 cm						●		
Roella ciliata (BLUE ROELLA)	20–30 cm					●	●		
Selago capitellata (SPIKY BLUE HAZE)	45 cm						●		
Selago natalensis (NATAL BLUE HAZE)	60 cm						●		
Selago wilmsii (SELAGO)	45 cm						●		
Sutera grandiflora (WILD PHLOX)	60–90 cm						●		

Annuals and Perennials

Name of Plant	Height	YELLOW	ORANGE	RED	PINK	BLUE	MAUVE	PURPLE	WHITE
Ursinia sericea (LACELEAF URSINIA)	60 cm	●							

Bulbs

Name of Plant	Height	YELLOW	ORANGE	RED	PINK	BLUE	MAUVE	PURPLE	WHITE
Agapanthus species (AGAPANTHUS, BLOULELIE)	1–1.5 m					●			●
Albuca circinata (COASTAL ALBUCA)	15–40 cm								●
Amaryllis belladonna (BELLADONNA LILY, MARCH LILY)	30–50 cm				●				●
Anapalina nervosa (ANAPALINA)	30 cm			●					
Anapalina triticea (ANAPALINA)	20–35 cm			●					
Babiana hypogea (BABIANA)	25 cm						●		
Brunsvigia species (BRUNSVIGIA, CANDELABRA FLOWER)	20–45 cm			●	●				
Crinum moorei (CAPE COAST LILY)	1.25 m				●				●
Crocosmia aurea (CROCOSMIA)	45 cm		●						
Cybistetes longifolia (MALAGAS LILY)	45 cm				●				
Cyrtanthus sanguineus (KEI LILY, NAHOON LILY, INANDA LILY)	30 cm			●					

Bulbs

Name of Plant	Height	YELLOW	ORANGE	RED	PINK	BLUE	MAUVE	PURPLE	WHITE
Eucomis species (PINEAPPLE FLOWER, WILDEPYNAPPEL)	1–2 m	green						•	
Galtonia candicans (SUMMER HYACINTH, BERG LILY)	1.25 m								•
Gladiolus carmineus (CLIFF GLADIOLUS)	30 cm			•					
Gladiolus cruentus (RED GLADIOLUS)	60–90 cm			•					
Gladiolus platyphyllus	60 cm		•						
Gladiolus salmoneus (SALMON GLADIOLUS)	60 cm				•				
Gladiolus saundersii (SAUNDERS GLADIOLUS)	60 cm			•					
Gloriosa superba (FLAME LILY, GLORIOSA)	1–1.25 m	•		•					
Haemanthus incarnatus (MARCH FLOWER)	30 cm			•	•				
Haemanthus coccineus	20 cm			•					
Haemanthus natalensis (NATAL PAINT BRUSH, BLOOD FLOWER, SNAKE LILY, SEEROOGBLOM, POEIERKWAS)	30–60 cm			•					
Kniphofia linearifolia (RED-HOT POKER)	90 cm	•							
Kniphofia triangularis subsp. triangularis (DWARF RED-HOT POKER)	45 cm			•					
Kniphofia uvaria (RED-HOT POKER, VUURPYL)	90 cm	•	•						
Littonia modesta (CLIMBING LILY, BUTTERLILY, GEELKLOKKIE)	60–90 cm	•							

Bulbs

Name of Plant	Height	YELLOW	ORANGE	RED	PINK	BLUE	MAUVE	PURPLE	WHITE
Nerine species (NERINA, GUERNSEY LILY)	25–45 cm			●	●				
Nymphaea capensis (BLUE WATER LILY, BLOUBLOM)	water plant				●	●			
Sandersonia aurantiaca (CHRISTMAS BELLS, CHINESE LANTERN)	50 cm		●						
Schizostylis coccinea (RIVER LILY, KAFFIR LILY)	45 cm			●					
Tulbaghia violacea (WILD GARLIC)	20–30 cm						●		
Vallota speciosa (GEORGE LILY, KNYSNA LILY, SCARBOROUGH LILY, BERG LILY)	30–45 cm			●					
Watsonia beatricis and hybrids (BEATRICE WATSONIA)	1.25 m	●	●	●					
Watsonia densiflora (NATAL WATSONIA)	60 cm				●				●
Watsonia galpinii	60 cm				●				
Watsonia longifolia	1.25 m				●				●
Zantedeschia tropicalis (SPOTTED-LEAFED YELLOW ARUM)	60 cm	●							

Succulents

Name of Plant	Height	YELLOW	ORANGE	RED	PINK	BLUE	MAUVE	PURPLE	WHITE
Aloe ciliaris	3 m			●					

Succulents

Name of Plant	Height	YELLOW	ORANGE	RED	PINK	BLUE	MAUVE	PURPLE	WHITE
Aloe comptonii (COMPTON'S ALOE)	60–90 cm			●					
Aloe cooperi	1 m				●				
Aloe karasbergensis (KARASBERG ALOE)	45 cm			●	●				
Aloe reitzii	1 m	●		●					
Aloe saponaria (SOAP ALOE)	45 cm	●	●	●	●				
Aloe speciosa	3–4 m			●					●
Aloe tenuior (FENCE ALOE)	2 m	●		●					
Aloe thompsoniae (THOMPSON'S ALOE)	25 cm		●						
Aloe verecunda	30 cm			●					
Cotyledon mucronata (WILLOWMORE COTYLEDON)	30 cm				●				
Cotyledon orbiculata (PLAKKIES, HONDEOOR)	60 cm			●	●				
Crassula falcata (RED CRASSULA)	60 cm			●					
Crassula perfoliata (POINTED-LEAF CRASSULA)	60 cm			●	●				●
Crassula vaginata (YELLOW CRASSULA)	60 cm	●							
Portulacaria afra (ELEPHANT'S FOOD, SPEKBOOM)	3 m				●				
Rochea coccinea (RED CRASSULA, KLIPBLOM)	45 cm			●					

Annuals and Perennials

Name of Plant	Height	YELLOW	ORANGE	RED	PINK	BLUE	MAUVE	PURPLE	WHITE
Chironia baccifera—berries (CHRISTMAS BERRY, BITTERBOS)	30–45 cm			● berries					
Coleus neochilus (LOBSTER FLOWER)	30 cm						●		
Helichrysum adenocarpum (PINK EVERLASTING)	20 cm				●				
Helichrysum argyrophyllum (GOLDEN GUINEA EVERLASTING)	20 cm	●							
Hypoestes aristata (RIBBON BUSH)	1.25 m						●		
Leonotis leonurus (WILD DAGGA, WILDE DAGGA)	1.5 m		●						●
Plectranthus species (PLECTRANTHUS)	10–20 cm						●		
Selago capitellata (SPIKY BLUE HAZE)	45 cm						●		
Selago wilmsii (SELAGO)	45 cm						●		
Sutera grandiflora (WILD PHLOX)	60–90 cm						●		

Bulbs

Name of Plant	Height	YELLOW	ORANGE	RED	PINK	BLUE	MAUVE	PURPLE	WHITE
Amaryllis belladonna (BELLADONNA LILY)	30–50 cm				●				●
Cybistetes longifolia (MALAGAS LILY)	45 cm				●				

Bulbs

Name of Plant	Height	YELLOW	ORANGE	RED	PINK	BLUE	MAUVE	PURPLE	WHITE
Gladiolus psittacinus (PARROT GLADIOLUS)	1.25 m	●	●						
Haemanthus albiflos (APRIL FOOL, POEIERKWAS)	45 cm								●
Kniphofia multiflora (BULRUSH POKER)	2 m	●							
Kniphofia splendida	1.25 m	●	●						
Lachenalia rubida	15 cm			●					

Succulents

Name of Plant	Height	YELLOW	ORANGE	RED	PINK	BLUE	MAUVE	PURPLE	WHITE
Aloe aculeata	1–1.25 m	●	●						
Aloe arborescens (TREE ALOE, KRAALAALWYN)	2–3 m			●					
Aloe bainesii (TREE ALOË, BOOMAALWYN)	7 m				●				
Aloe ciliaris	3 m			●					
Aloe cryptopoda	1–2 m	●		●					
Aloe ferox (BITTER ALOE)	2–3 m		●	●					
Aloe fosteri	1–1.5 m	●	●	●					
Aloe marlothii	4–5 m	●	●	●					
Aloe microstigma	60 cm	●		●					

Succulents

Name of Plant	Height	YELLOW	ORANGE	RED	PINK	BLUE	MAUVE	PURPLE	WHITE
Aloe thraskii (COAST ALOE)	2–3 m	•	•						
Aloe vanbalenii	1 m	•							
Aloe wickensii	1.5 m	•		•					
Crassula falcata (RED CRASSULA)	60 cm			•					
Crassula multicava (FAIRY CRASSULA)	20 cm				•				
Crassula perfoliata (POINTED-LEAF CRASSULA)	60 cm			•	•				•

Annuals and Perennials

Name of Plant	Height	YELLOW	ORANGE	RED	PINK	BLUE	MAUVE	PURPLE	WHITE
Anchusa capensis (CAPE FORGET-ME-NOT)	45–60 cm					•			
Anemone capensis (CAPE ANEMONE)	45 cm				•				
Arctotis species (KAROO DAISY, GOUSBLOM, TRAILING ARCTOTIS)	15–40 cm	•	•	•	•		•	•	•
Castalis spectabilis (CASTALIS)	20 cm						•		
Cotula species (BUTTON FLOWERS)	8–30 cm	•	•						
Diascia species (TWINSPUR, BRIDE'S SADDLE)	20–45 cm				•				
Dimorphotheca species (AFRICAN DAISY, NAMAQUALAND DAISY)	20–60 cm	•	•						•
Felicia species (KINGFISHER DAISY, FELICIA)	20–60 cm				•	•	•		•
Gazania species and hybrids (GAZANIA, WILD MARIGOLD, GOUSBLOM)	15–30 cm	•	•	•	•				
Grielum grandiflorum (YELLOW SATIN FLOWER, BOTTERBLOM)	10 cm	•							
Heliophila sonchifolia (BLUE FLAX)	45 cm						•		
Hypoestes aristata (RIBBON BUSH)	1.25 m						•		
Leonotis leonurus (WILD DAGGA, WILDE DAGGA)	1.5 m		•						•
Nemesia strumosa and hybrids (NEMESIA, LEEUBEKKIE)	30–45 cm	•	•	•	•		•	•	•
Psilothonna species (EDGING DAISY)	20–30 cm	•	•						

Annuals and Perenials

Name of Plant	Height	YELLOW	ORANGE	RED	PINK	BLUE	MAUVE	PURPLE	WHITE
Ursinia species (URSINIA)	30–45 cm	●	●						
Zaluzianskya villosa (DRUMSTICKS)	20–30 cm						●		●

Bulbs and Bulblike Plants

Name of Plant	Height	YELLOW	ORANGE	RED	PINK	BLUE	MAUVE	PURPLE	WHITE
Babiana species and hybrids (BABIANA, BABIAANTJIE)	10–45 cm	●		●	●	●	●		
Bulbine species (BULBINE)	20–45 cm	●							
Bulbinella setosa (BULBINELLA, KATSTERT)	30–90 cm	●	●						
Chasmanthe floribunda (FLAMES, PENNANT FLOWER)	60 cm			●					
Cyrtanthus mackenii (IFAFA LILY)	20–30 cm	●	●						
Dipidax triquetra (STAR OF THE MARCH, HANEKAM)	45 cm			●					●
Freesia species and hybrids (FREESIA, KAMMETJIE, FLISSIE)	15–45 cm	●	●	●	●		●	●	●
Geissorrhiza species (SEQUINS, WINE CUPS, SYSIE)	10–30 cm	●		●				●	
Gladiolus carinatus (MAUVE AFRIKANDER, SANDPYPIE)	30 cm							●	
Homoglossum hollandii (FLAMES, RED AFRIKANDER)	60 cm			●					

Bulbs and Bulblike Plants

Name of Plant	Height	YELLOW	ORANGE	RED	PINK	BLUE	MAUVE	PURPLE	WHITE
Homoglossum merianellum (FLAMES)	30–60 cm			•					
Homoglossum watsonium	30–45 cm			•					
Lachenalia species (CAPE COWSLIP, VIOOLTJIE ETC)	15–40 cm	•	•	•		•	•	•	•
Lanaria lanata (COTTONWOOL FLOWER, KAPOKBLOM)	60–90 cm				•				•
Lapeirousia speciosa (SPRINGBOK PAINTED LADY)	10 cm						•	•	
Melasphaerula ramosa (FAIRYBELLS, BRUIDJIES)	60 cm								•
Moraea species (MOREA, TULP)	10–40 cm	•			•		•		
Oxalis species (SORREL, SURING)	10–25 cm	•			•		•	•	•
Satyrium species (EWWA-TREWWA)	15–30 cm		•	•	•				
Scilla natalensis (WILD SQUILL, BLOUSLANGKOP)	60–90 cm					•	•		
Sparaxis species and hybrids (SPARAXIS, HARLEQUIN FLOWER, FLUWEELTJIES)	15–45 cm	•	•	•	•		•	•	•
Spiloxene capensis (STAR, STERRETJIE)	15–30 cm	•							•
Strelitzia reginae and parvifolia (CRANE FLOWER, BIRD-OF-PARADISE FLOWER, KRAANVOËLBLOM)	1–1.25 m	•	•						
Tritonia species and hybrids (TRITONIA, BLAZING STAR)	30–45 cm	•	•	•	•				•
Tulbaghia fragrans (SWEET GARLIC)	30–45 cm						•		

Bulbs and Bulblike Plants

Name of Plant	Height	YELLOW	ORANGE	RED	PINK	BLUE	MAUVE	PURPLE	WHITE
Veltheimia viridifolia (FOREST LILY)	30–60 cm				●				
Zantedeschia aethiopica (WHITE ARUM LILY, CALLA LILY, PIG LILY)	45–120 cm								●

Succulents

Name of Plant	Height	YELLOW	ORANGE	RED	PINK	BLUE	MAUVE	PURPLE	WHITE
Adenium obesum var. multiflorum (IMPALA LILY, SABIE STAR)	1.5–3 m				●				
Aloe aculeata	1–1.25 m	●	●						
Aloe africana (UITENHAGE ALOE)	2.5 m	●	●						
Aloe arborescens (TREE ALOE, KRAALAALWYN)	2–3 m			●					
Aloe bainesii (TREE ALOE)	7 m				●				
Aloe brevifolia (MINIATURE ALOE, KLEINAALWYN)	45 cm			●					
Aloe candelabrum (CANDELABRA ALOE)	2–4 m			●					
Aloe chabaudii	60–90 cm	●	●	●					
Aloe ciliaris	3 m			●					
Aloe dichotoma (TREE ALOE, KOKERBOOM)	3–5 m	●							
Aloe ferox (BITTER ALOE)	2–3 m		●	●					

Succulents

Name of Plant	Height	YELLOW	ORANGE	RED	PINK	BLUE	MAUVE	PURPLE	WHITE
Aloe globuligemma (Knoppiesaalwyn)	1 m			•					
Aloe hereroensis (Herero aloe)	1 m	•	•	•					
Aloe humilis (Dwarf hedgehog aloe, Krimpvarkieaalwyn)	25 cm			•					
Aloe khamiesensis	2.5 m		•	•					
Aloe krapohliana	45 cm			•					
Aloe longibracteata	1 m			•	•				
Aloe longistyla (Karoo aloe)	30 cm			•	•				
Aloe marlothii	4–5 m	•	•	•					
Aloe melanacantha (Blackthorn aloe)	60–90 cm	•		•					
Aloe microstigma	60 cm	•		•					
Aloe mutabilis	1 m	•		•					
Aloe petricola	1 m		•	•					
Aloe plicatilis (Fan aloe)	2–3 m			•					
Aloe saponaria (Soap aloe)	45 cm	•	•	•	•				
Aloe sessiliflora	1 m	•							
Aloe speciosa	3–4 m			•					•
Aloe thraskii (Coast aloe)	2–3 m	•	•						
Aloe vanbalenii	1 m	•							

Succulents

Name of Plant	Height	YELLOW	ORANGE	RED	PINK	BLUE	MAUVE	PURPLE	WHITE
Aloe variegata (PARTRIDGE-BREAST ALOE, KANNIEDOOD)	30 cm			●	●				
Aloe wickensii	1.5 m	●		●					
Carpobrotus species (SOUR FIG, GOUNA, HOTTENTOT FIG)	10–20 cm	●					●		
Cephalophyllum species (VYGIES, MESEM.)	10–60 cm	●	●	●	●		●	●	
Conicosia pugioniformis (CONICOSIA)	20–30 cm	●							
Crassula arborescens (PLAKKIES)	2–3 m				●				●
Crassula portulacea (PINK JOY, PLAKKIES, BEESTEBUL)	2 m				●				●
Dorotheanthus species (BOKBAAI VYGIE, MESEM.)	8–20 cm	●	●	●	●		●	●	●
Euphorbia mauritanica (YELLOW MILKBUSH, JACKAL'S FOOD)	1–1.5 m	●							
Ruschia species (CUSHION MESEM., VYGIE)	4–30 cm						●	●	

A magnificent cultivar
of our Belladonna Lily
(*Amaryllis belladonna*)
created by a New
Zealand
horticulturalist.

Drumsticks
(Zaluzianskya villosa)
is a charming plant
for the front of a border

79

IV

PART IV
Annuals and Perennials

◁ Namaqualand Daisy (Arctotis hybrid)

Annuals and Perennials

WHAT IS AN ANNUAL?

An annual is a plant which completes its life cycle within a year or less. From seed-sowing to flowering takes approximately three to five months. The plants die off after setting seed and do not re-appear the following year, unless seed which falls happens to germinate on its own, as it sometimes will. Generally it is necessary to sow seed again at the correct time of the year to produce new flowering plants.

All plants have a specific season of the year when they flower—a spring-flowering plant always flowers in spring, a summer-flowering one in summer, and so on. In countries of the Northern Hemisphere, however, where the climate is very different from that of Southern Africa, some of the annuals which flower naturally in spring in their homeland are grown for early summer flowers there. Where, in the pages that follow, it is recommended that annuals be sown in late summer or early autumn for spring bloom, gardeners in Europe and the northern states of America should sow seeds in early spring for summer flowers. Those in southern California and the warmer states of America and in countries of the Southern Hemisphere should follow the seasonal instructions as given for Southern Africa.

An important point which should be remembered when planning where to plant South African annuals and perennials, is that many of them open only when the light is strong and that they turn their faces towards the sun as it moves across the sky. Because of this they should be planted so that they turn towards the house or patio so as to be seen to best advantage.

Some of the most decorative of garden flowers are annuals and perennials which grow wild in the difficult climate of Namaqualand and parts of the Karoo. These plants tolerate poor soil, drought and frosts to 5° below freezing, and the beautiful hybrids developed from plants such as dimorphotheca and gazania are also fairly hardy. Although they tolerate harsh growing conditions, it will generally be found that they produce more flowers on longer stems if planted in reasonably good soil and watered fairly regularly during their growing period. On the other hand, soil which is too rich results in some of them producing an abundance of leaves and few flowers. A few packets of seed of South African annuals and perennials can transform a patch of dry, barren earth into a ravishing spectacle of colour.

Sowing seed

Seeds of spring-flowering annuals, most of which

are from the winter-rainfall region of the Cape Province, should be sown in late summer and early autumn (i.e. February-April) except when grown in the Northern Hemisphere where spring sowing is preferable. Sowing in late summer or early autumn gives the seedlings a chance to develop before the cold weather comes and inhibits further growth.

When planting a large area of ground along a drive or roadside, one can scatter the seed, cover it lightly and water it, but as the soil has to be kept damp until the seeds have germinated, which is some cases may be two weeks or more, it is generally easier to sow seeds in boxes or beds of specially prepared soil and to transplant the seedlings when they are about 2-3 cm (1 in) high.

Seeds of most South African annuals germinate very well and quickly, and raising plants from seed does not present any problem other than seeing that the seeds are kept moist until germination has taken place and the plants have had a chance to make roots. In areas which are dry it may be necessary to water the seed beds or boxes more than once or twice a day. To reduce the amount of water required it is advisable to sow the seeds in boxes and to cover the boxes with a sheet of glass which helps to keep in the moisture. Once germination has taken place the glass must be removed as it would cause scorching of the seedlings if left in place. When sown in a bed, a mulch of straw, and shading the bed will reduce the amount of water required until germination takes place. Shading is seldom necessary in coastal gardens but desirable inland.

The most important points to remember when sowing seeds are the following:
1. Sow in friable ground—i.e. ground which crumbles easily, and not in clay which is made up of tiny particles and which tends to pack hard when wet. A mixture made up of compost, vermiculite, and soil in equal quantities is a good one for seeds.
2. Sow in rows so that you will be able to tell more easily, when shoots appear, which are weeds and which your plants.
3. Sow seeds at the right time of the year. Some plants like to grow during the cool months of the year and flower in late winter and early spring and, if they are sown in spring in Southern Africa (or countries with a similar climate) they will not produce a good show in summer, as it is then too hot for their best development.

4. Cover the seeds lightly. Only a sprinkling of soil should be put over fine seeds and a thin layer of 3-6 mm ($\frac{1}{8}$ to $\frac{1}{4}$ in) should be spread over larger seeds.
5. Water sufficiently often to keep the soil damp, or cover to obviate the necessity of frequent watering.
6. Use a fine spray on the watering can when watering as a coarse one is likely to displace both soil and seeds and so spoil germination. Some seeds are as fine as dust, and when such fine seeds are sown even gentle watering may move them. It is advisable to sow seed of this kind in flower pots, so that watering can be done from the bottom. Fill the pot with sieved compost or leaf mould, soil and vermiculite, and stand the pot in a bowl of water until the soil is quite wet right to the top. If clay pots are used it is no use merely watering the soil initially, because clay pots which are dry absorb the moisture in the soil and may cause the seeds to dry out soon after they are sown. Standing the pot in a bowl of water will ensure that it, too, is soaked.

Remove the pot from the bowl of water and sow the seeds. It is not necessary to cover very small seeds with soil, but the pot should be covered with a piece of glass to keep the moisture in as long as possible. As soon as the top soil shows signs of drying out stand the pot in a bowl of water once more to soak up the water from below.

Where to plant annuals:
These colourful plants can be used to highlight any part of the garden. Low-growing ones can be sited at the front of a mixed border, along the path or drive, or they can be planted in colonies to brighten a rock-garden, or else planted in tubs or window boxes to add colour to the patio or terrace. Tall ones may be interplanted with perennials or grouped with low-growing shrubs.

WHAT IS A PERENNIAL?

A perennial is a plant which does not die after its flowering time, but grows on from year to year, flowering in its due season every year. They take longer than annuals to reach their flowering stage. The latter usually start flowering within three to five months of the seeds being sown, but perennials need nine or more months of growth before they flower. Some perennials become dormant, usually in winter, and their top-growth dies down after they have flowered and gone to seed. They send up new growth again after a month or more of dormancy. Other perennials have top-growth which is evergreen.

Perennials are useful plants because they continue to brighten the garden in their flowering season for many years and so make gardening easier. They can be grown from seed, but as it takes a year or two before some of them reach flowering size when grown this way, it is advisable to buy established plants from a nursery, or else to raise new plants from cuttings or root divisions.

The best time of the year for sowing most perennials is just after their flowering season. If they flower in spring, sow seeds in late spring or summer, and if they flower in summer, sow seeds in late summer or early autumn. Although most seeds retain their fertility for a long time, a few, notably the Barberton or Transvaal daisy (Gerbera jamesonii), lose viability quickly unless properly stored, and seeds of this plant should be less than three months old when sown.

If perennials are being grown from seed the same suggestions about watering and soil should be observed as have been outlined with regard to annuals. When transplanting perennials, however, it is advisable to transplant them to nursery beds when they are about 2-3 cm (1 in) high, spacing them about 10-20 cm (4-8 in) apart to allow them to grow to a larger size before planting them in their permanent place in the garden. It is easier to care for and water the perennials when young, if they are grown in this way in nursery beds, than if they are immediately planted out in the garden when they are only just large enough to transplant.

Dividing perennials:

It is often necessary to lift and divide perennials when they have been growing in one place for several years, as otherwise the plants become overcrowded and fail to flower well. This is a very simple process. First, cut back the top growth, if any, to within a few inches of the ground. Then dig up the plants and, with a sharp knife or spade, cut the whole mass of roots into sections which can then be replanted in soil which has been properly prepared. Generally the root sections on the perimeter are the best to replant, as they are the youngest and most vigorous. Although in most cases perennials are left in the ground for

several years, some gardeners who like to have the garden full of colour all the time, prefer to move the perennials after they have flowered in order to fill the space they occupied with annuals for quick colour. If this is to be done, the roots of the perennials may be lifted and planted in an out-of-the-way corner of the yard for three to five months, after which they can again be transferred to the garden.

When plants have to be divided, this operation should be done when they are dormant or, if they are evergreen plants, four to six months before they are due to flower. Dividing them shortly before their flowering time may inhibit their flowering that season, or else lead to their producing inferior flowers.

Watering:

Whilst they are young, perennials should be watered regularly and often, particularly when they are making new growth and flowers. If they are of the kind which become dormant during certain seasons of the year, watering can be reduced at that season, but they should not be left completely dry even when dormant. Many plants flower poorly through having insufficient water, so if in doubt about the progress of the plant, water it liberally, particularly during its most active growing period which is usually the three to six months before it flowers, and whilst it is in flower.

Where to plant perennials:

This will depend upon the size to which the plants grow. Those which are small or of medium size may be planted in beds in which annuals are to be grown, or in a rock-garden; whilst those which are tall may be used as background plants to beds of annuals and smaller perennials, or they may be planted with shrubs in a shrub border. Some of the prostrate-growing ones make good ground covers.

Preparing the soil:

As perennials remain in the same position for many years, it is advisable to improve the soil to a depth of about 15-45 cm (6-18 in) before they are planted. Should the soil in your garden be poor, dig holes this depth and diameter, and fork in humus, in the form of compost and manure, with some of the soil previously removed from the hole, or else make trenches and improve the soil in the trench in the same way. The importance of improving the soil *before* planting cannot be over-emphasized, as one cannot easily improve the quality of the soil in the root-zone later unless one goes to the trouble of lifting the plants and starting the planting process all over again. This not only adds to the labour, but it delays flowering, as very often perennials refuse to flower well until they have settled in, which may take some months. Many South African perennials grow remarkably well in soil which is not particularly good, but those which are to remain in one place for several years will benefit from the improved soil. Generally, South African perennials appear to do better in soil which drains readily than in an impermeable clay.

ANCHUSA CAPENSIS   ANCHUSA, CAPE
(A. riparia)   FORGET-ME-NOT

DISTRIBUTION: An attractive flower which grows wild in the south-western and eastern Cape and further north into the eastern Orange Free State.

DESCRIPTION: The plants grow to about 60 cm (2 ft) in height and are much branched. They bear flowers like forget-me-nots of a beautiful shade of azure blue. This is an ornamental and sturdy plant with rough hairy leaves 7-10 cm long, broader at the base than the apex. It looks striking when massed behind flowers of yellow or orange. The flowering time is late winter and early spring.

CULTURE: Sow the seeds in December or January for flowers in spring, and transplant them when about 2-3 cm (1 in) high, to stand 45 cm (1½ ft) apart. They endure moderate frost, but in hot, inland gardens some shade during the hottest part of the day will result in better flowers. They should be watered regularly and well during their growing period. Although this plant is a perennial it seldom flowers well after the second year and it should therefore be pulled up and new ones planted every two years.

ANEMONE CAPENSIS   CAPE ANEMONE
DISTRIBUTION: Grows wild in the south-western Cape.

DESCRIPTION: It bears charming little flowers of delicate shades of mauve, or pink and white on stems 45 cm (1½ ft) high. The flowers, which are daisy-like in form with narrow pointed petals, measure about 6 cm across. The leaves are light-green and delicately cut, giving them a rather fernlike appearance. The flowering time is from July to September.

CULTURE: Sow the seeds in summer and transplant the seedlings to stand about 15 cm (6 in) apart. They do well in partial shade, particularly when grown inland, and should be planted out into soil in which there is some humus. This is not a plant for hot, dry gardens.

APTOSIMUM INDIVISUM   KAROO VIOLET
DISTRIBUTION: Occurs in dry parts of the Karoo and the north-western Cape.

DESCRIPTION: This low-growing plant is no relation of the violet. It grows to only a few centimetres in height and bears masses of little funnel-shaped flowers of royal-blue, about 18 mm in length. They make a splendid show in early spring.

CULTURE: This plant would make a most effective show massed along the front of a border or when grown in colonies in a rock-garden. It tolerates dry air and fairly severe frost. Unfortunately seed is not yet available. The time to sow seeds is late summer for flowers in late winter and early spring.

ARCTOTIS   NAMAQUALAND DAISY, GOUSBLOM
DISTRIBUTION: The species described can be seen growing wild in many of the dry areas in the north-western Cape, the Karoo, near Cape Town, and north into the Orange Free State.

DESCRIPTION: Arctotis include annuals and perennials all of which produce masses of charming daisy-like flowers varying in colour from white through shades of yellow, pink, rose, cyclamen, mauve, lilac, burgundy, rust, terra-cotta, old rose, crimson and claret. The flowers open only when the sunlight is bright and they close at night, but they are nevertheless delightful in arrangements for the daylight hours. The leaves of arctotis show great variation in form and size. Most species flower in late winter and early spring. Many hybrids have arisen in nature, and some have been the result of planned pollination. These are splendid plants for dry banks and walls, and for gardens where the soil is sandy. They are low-growing and make an excellent ground cover.

CULTURE: Arctotis grow well in poor soil but produce better flowers and more of them if the soil is improved by the addition of a little compost. They grow remarkably well in seaside gardens

Arctotis grow
well in poor soil
and dry places.
The pictures
show some of
the beautiful
colours of the
flowers.

and at high elevations, too. They should be watered regularly during autumn and until their flowering time in spring. Sow the seeds in beds or boxes in March or April and transplant the seedlings to stand 30 cm (1 ft) or more, apart. The perennial species can be kept for a second year, but if the ground is required for summer-flowering plants they should be forked up, as the plants are very easy to raise from seeds and they can also be multiplied by cuttings. Most species tolerate moderate to severe frost.

A. acaulis   BUSHY ARCTOTIS,
(A. speciosa)   GOUSBLOM
This plant has been widely grown all over the world and well merits its popularity. Although a perennial it is best treated as an annual and discarded after its flowering period is over. The leaves are rough, rather large and greyish-green in colour, often deeply indented. The daisy-like flowers measuring 7-10 cm across are carried on strong stems 30 cm (1 ft) or more long. The plants hybridize so freely that it is doubtful if anyone can now decide what the colours of the original species were. The flowers are richly coloured and make a really splendid show. They are often banded at the centre with contrasting colours which make them all the more spectacular. For example, those of orange are banded with chocolate; terra-cotta with ochre; ivory with golden-

yellow; lavender with lilac; and cyclamen with burgundy. Sow the seeds in March or April for flowers from August to October. Set plants 30 cm (1 ft) apart for a dazzling carpet of colour.

A. fastuosa   VENIDIUM, NAMAQUALAND
(Venidium fastuosum)   DAISY, GOUSBLOM
This gay flowering plant thrives in the barren countryside of the northern Cape, where it grows in fields beside the roads. It is a robust annual reaching a height of 60 cm (2 ft) with large daisies up to 7 cm across. The flowers are usually a glowing orange or gold with a shining purplish-black marking at the base of each petal, making a ring around the centre. Occasionally a white form can be found. This is a showy plant, particularly useful for making a quick and colourful scene in gardens where growing conditions are difficult. It is a fine plant to naturalize along our national roads as it stands a good deal of frost and drought and it does well in poor soil.

A. hirsuta   NAMAQUALAND DAISY,
(Venidium hirsutum)   GOUSBLOM
This hardy plant thrives in regions where there is little rain and where the soil is not particularly good. It grows quickly from seed and produces a bold show of colour in late winter and early spring when it bears its bright orange or cream flowers on stems 45 cm (1½ ft) high.

Namaqualand Daisy,
Gousblom *(Arctotis hirsuta)*

More plants for hot dry situations

Venidium,
Namaqualand
Daisy
(Arctotis fastuosa)

Arctotis species and hybrids make a bright show of colour on a bank.

A. laevis   CURLY ARCTOTIS
(A. squarrosa)
A good plant for the rock-garden. It grows wild on dry hillsides near Clanwilliam. It is shrubby in growth to 90 cm (3 ft) or more and has orange flowers which make a bold show of colour in spring. It stands moderate frost. Set plants 60 cm (2 ft) apart.

A. leiocarpa   KAROO DAISY
This hardy annual is also worth a place in gardens where growing conditions are difficult. It grows to about 45 cm (1½ ft) and bears flowers of glistening white with a yellow centre. The green leaves are covered with silvery hairs. It can be seen along the roadside in the Karoo in September.

A. stoechadifolia   TRAILING ARCTOTIS
The trailing arctotis is an ideal plant to make a lovely show of colour in spring. Being of spreading habit, it drapes itself over walls and banks and hides the bare earth very quickly with its grey-green leaves, which are incised in different ways, some with small indentations and some with large ones. The flowers are like those of *A. acaulis* in colour range. Sow the seeds in March or make cuttings of the plant in spring. Although the plant is a perennial, better flowering is to be had from new plants, so it is not worthwhile keeping the old ones for more than a season except for the ground cover provided by the leaves. It stands moderate frost.

90

A. venusta   FREE STATE DAISY
(A. grandis)
This is an annual which grows wild in parts of the Orange Free State. It is bushy in habit, grows to about 60 cm (2 ft) and bears flowers about 7 cm across, of glistening white with a yellow ring at the middle circling the bluish-mauve centre. The leaves are greyish-green and covered with fine white hairs. It is able to stand hot, dry conditions and is a useful plant to have in the flower or shrub border to add sparkle to the garden in dry areas. Sow seed in spring for summer flowers, and in autumn for flowers in spring.

ASPARAGUS   ASPARAGUS FERN
DISTRIBUTION: Found mostly in the eastern Cape, Natal, the Transvaal and Rhodesia.

DESCRIPTION: These are perennial plants which are decorative, not because of the flowers they bear but because of the beauty of their foliage. They can be grown in the garden, in tubs on a patio or in containers indoors.

CULTURE: They do not stand severe frost but generally grow up again quickly after being frosted, and, if given some protection against a wall or hedge they will often survive severe winters. Plant them in good soil in a position where they have high shade all day, or at least for the afternoon. They tolerate fairly long periods with little water but do best if watered regularly. Plant them or sow seeds, in spring.

A. asparagoides

Has been popular in Europe for many years where it is known by its old name of *Medeola*. It grows wild in many parts of Southern Africa. It is a charming plant for the garden, as an indoor plant, and for use in arrangements. The plant is of a scrambling, twining nature and it bears numerous pretty leaves about 2-3 cm long. The stems of leaves are a fine addition to bouquets or arrangements. It can also be used as an indoor climber or outside on a shady terrace. The Bantu use the root for sore eyes and as a charm to increase fertility in their cattle.

A. densiflorus   BASKET ASPARAGUS
(A. sprengeri)

A scrambling plant from Natal with stems of bright little leaves rather like those of a yew. They are most decorative. The leaves measure only about 12 mm in length and are carried in tufts all along the arching stems. In summer it bears clusters of tiny, dainty flowers which are pink in the bud and white when open. These are followed by red berries. The stems are armed with small prickles. This is a splendid plant to grow in hanging baskets or to have cascading down over a ledge or tub on a shady patio. It also looks effective as a ground cover under trees.

A. setaceus   ASPARAGUS FERN
(A. plumosus)

This plant, which grows wild in the eastern Cape, Natal and the Transvaal, is very popular for floral arrangements. It bears dark green leaves like the finest lace on stems which twine and climb. Grow it in a fairly shady position and provide it with some support. This species does well when grown in containers indoors or on a shady patio.

BRACHYCARPAEA JUNCEA

DISTRIBUTION: Grows in the west and south-west Cape.

DESCRIPTION: This is a perennial with rush-like stems to 60 cm (2 ft). The leaves are about 2-3 cm long and 3 mm wide and are sparsely carried along the stem, usually standing erect. The flowers are rather fragile-looking, composed of four obovate petals of pale to deep mauve. They measure about 2-3 cm across. Massed or interplanted with diascia, which bears pink flowers at the same time, they make a fine show. The flowering time is August and September.

CULTURE: This plant seems able to tolerate poor growing conditions, but undoubtedly produces finer flowers for a longer period when the soil is improved. It stands drought and moderate frost. Sow the seeds in spring or summer and set plants about 15 cm (6 in) apart.

CASTALIS   CASTALIS,
                              OX-EYE DAISY, WIT MAGRIET

DISTRIBUTION: Occurs in the Transvaal and in the Cape.

DESCRIPTION: The species mentioned are perennials with daisy-like flowers measuring up to 7 cm across. The flowers appear in spring at the ends of stems 30-45 cm (1-1½ ft) long. The leaves are slender. Castalis make an effective show when massed or when planted in pots or window boxes. *Castalis nudicaulis* (Ox-eye Daisy or Wit Magriet) has white flowers with a burgundy flush on the backs of the petals and in the centre of the flower. *C. spectabilis*, which is to be found in the Transvaal, has lilac petals with a centre of deeper hue.

CULTURE: Sow seeds in spring and transplant when 2-3 cm (1 in) high to their permanent place in the garden, setting the plants about 20 cm apart.

Castalis *(Castalis nudicaulis)* has flowers of great charm

Christmas Berry (Chironia) bears glistening red berries in late summer

CHARIEIS HETEROPHYLLA

(New name is *Felicia heterophylla*) HEAVENLY BLUE DAISY

DISTRIBUTION: A charming little plant from the south-western Cape. The pronunciation of the first name is: "care-e-us".

DESCRIPTION: Is an annual with flowers measuring 2-3 cm across. The flower is daisy-like in form, with petals of sky or cornflower blue with a centre of deeper blue. It opens up properly only on bright days and when the sun is high in the sky. The foliage is of a soft shade of green carried near the ground, whilst the flower stems grow to about 30 cm (1 ft). It flowers in August and September and makes a sparkling show when massed in front of orange or yellow flowers, such as ursinia or gazanias.

CULTURE: This little daisy makes a gay bedding plant, but it is not easy to grow in cold gardens as it succumbs to frost. Keep it well watered throughout autumn and winter. Sow seeds in March or April and transplant the seedlings to stand 15 cm (6 in) apart.

CHIRONIA

CHRISTMAS BERRY, WILD GENTIAN, PILES BUSH, TOOTHACHE-BERRY, BITTERBOS, PERDEBOSSIE

DISTRIBUTION: There are fifteen species of chironia widely distributed from the Transvaal, through Natal, the Orange Free State, the Eastern Province and the south-western Cape. They belong to the same family as the Alpine gentian.

DESCRIPTION: Different species are to be found in the wild, growing under diverse conditions— some on dry plains, some in vleis and marshy places, and some along the coast. Some species are annuals and others are perennials. The most decorative ones are 30-45 cm (1-1½ ft) tall, and erect or shrubby in habit of growth. They bear small cyclamen-pink, star-like flowers with five slender petals. In some the petals are pointed whilst in others they are not. The flowers make a fine show in late spring and early summer, and the best-known species remain decorative right through to autumn.

CULTURE: They do not seem to mind poor soils, but the addition of some humus to the soil will produce better results. Most species tolerate moderate frost. Some species do not mind being allowed to become fairly dry, whereas others need a good deal of moisture to encourage their best development. Sow seeds in spring or summer.

C. baccifera
CHRISTMAS BERRY, BITTERBOS

This species, which is fairly well-known in cultivation, is an evergreen perennial which develops a shrubby form, with slender, graceful stems bearing little leaves 2-3 cm long and only 3 mm in breadth. They are carried in pairs opposite each other. In early summer it becomes covered with small cyclamen-pink flowers about 2 cm across. When the flowers fade it is wreathed in bright red berries which remain decorative through autumn. It can be found growing along coastal sand dunes and inland. In hot, inland gardens plant it where it is shaded during the hottest hours of the day. It is interesting to note that the name *Chiron* refers to a centaur who, according to Greek legend, was connected with medicine and botany. This particular species of chironia has been widely used medicinally in South Africa, not only by Bantu tribes but also by the early European settlers. An infusion made from the plant and its roots was used by the former for diarrhoea and leprosy, and by the latter for various skin afflictions, such as boils and veld sores, and for haemorrhoids. The plant is thought to be toxic to sheep.

C. krebsii   Mountain Chironia

Is generally found in marshy or damp places at fairly high altitudes, from 600 m to 1800 m. It flowers abundantly in summer on the higher slopes of the Drakensberg. The plant grows to a height of 45 cm (1½ ft).

C. palustris   Marsh Chironia

This species is widely distributed, and it is variable in manner of growth in different habitats. It occurs along water-courses or marshy areas near the coast and inland, on the highveld. The flowers with their lustrous petals of pinky-mauve are extremely attractive and make a wonderful show in summer. The silvery leaves are attractive at any time of the year.

CHRYSOCOMA COMA-AUREA   Yellow Edging Daisy

DISTRIBUTION: Is widespread in the western and south-western Cape.

DESCRIPTION: This is a bushy little perennial which grows happily in uncultivated soil along the roadsides and makes a dazzling show in September when it is in full flower. It grows to about 30 cm (1 ft) and is rounded in form. The leaves are small, similar to those of an erica, and in spring it becomes studded with myriads of tiny golden-yellow flowerheads which look like the centre of a daisy without petals. Plant it behind charieis or in front of anchusa, both of which have blue flowers which show up well against the yellow. A species common in dry areas of the Karoo is known as *C. tenuifolia* (Bitterbossie). They are excellent plants to make a gay and colourful show in spring.

CULTURE: It grows very readily from seed which should be sown in spring or summer and stands a good deal of frost. Although tolerant of poor and sandy soil, it does better when given some attention. Set plants about 20 cm (8 in) apart in the front of the flower border or along a path.

Yellow Edging Daisy *(Chrysocoma coma-aurea)*, which can be seen along many a roadside, is a delightful garden plant

Button flowers,
Gansekos (*Cotula
turbinata*) make a
brilliant show when
massed

COLEUS NEOCHILUS — LOBSTER FLOWER, COLEUS

DISTRIBUTION: A quick-growing, spreading plant which grows wild in the Transvaal, South West Africa, Rhodesia, Natal and the eastern Cape.

DESCRIPTION: This is a good perennial to use where growing conditions are difficult, as it will cover the ground fairly quickly. It makes a pretty show for most months of the year, even although the soil be dry and uncultivated. It is a decorative plant to have hanging over a bank, in tubs on a stoep, or under trees. It has pale green leaves with serrated edges, almost as broad as they are long. In spring it sends up spikes of jacaranda-blue to mauve flowers with two lips, the top one recurved and shorter than the bottom one. The plant has a pungent smell when handled. If, as the flowers fade, they are cut off with a good length of stem, new ones will appear by summer.

CULTURE: The roots can be planted out at any time of the year. In regions which have severe frost, it should be planted where it has some protection. It grows in full sunshine at the coast. In inland gardens it will grow in full sun or partial shade. It grows readily from seeds sown in spring and autumn, but as this takes much longer to produce flowering plants, gardeners are advised to plant roots or make cuttings. It grows well in any soil or situation and is a useful ground cover in light shade.

COTULA — BUTTON FLOWERS, GANSOOGIES

DISTRIBUTION: These charming little plants, seldom more than 10-30 cm high, are to be seen growing by the million in fields in the northern Cape, and in dry and damp places in the south-western Cape.

DESCRIPTION: Each flower looks like a button, or the centre-piece of a daisy without petals. The leaves are slender and graceful. To look effective they should be planted very close together. The flowering time is late winter to mid-spring.

CULTURE: Sow the seeds in March or April and prick the little seedlings out when they are about 12 mm ($\frac{1}{2}$ in) high, setting them in their permanent place in the garden about 10 cm (4 in) apart. They do well in porous sandy soils, and some species thrive in marshy ground. A pretty ribbon border of blue, yellow and orange can be made by planting charieis alternately with cotula, with felicia behind them and ursinias behind the felicia.

C. barbata

Grows to only about 10 cm (4 in) in height, is bushy in habit, with slender, lacy leaves and masses of golden-yellow flowers in late winter and early spring. The flowers, which are only about 6 mm across, sometimes exude an unpleasant odour, but this in no way detracts from their usefulness as edging plants. They look particularly attractive when grown in front of blue flowers.

C. leptalea

This species has feathery, grey-green foliage which forms a little bush near the ground and golden-yellow, button-like flowers on stems 10 cm (4 in) high. The flowers are about 12 mm across. It flowers in spring.

C. turbinata   GANSEKOS
(Cenia turbinata)

Has yellow or white flowers only 12 mm (or less) in diameter, on stems 20-30 cm high. The foliage is feathery. This plant makes a gay show in front of a rock-garden or planted between paving stones of a path or patio.

DIASCIA   TWINSPUR, BRIDE'S SADDLE

DISTRIBUTION: Most of the species mentioned are to be found in the western and eastern Cape extending up into the highlands of Pondoland.

DESCRIPTION: These plants bear small flowers which make a colourful show, despite their tiny size. Diascias may be annuals or perennials, but it is the perennials which are the most decorative. They are somewhat shrubby in growth. The flowers are made up of a broad, rounded basal petal flanked by two smaller petals at the top, with twin spurs pushing out from the back of the flower. The colours are usually from pink to rose.

The leaves are pointed with serrated edges. Because of their habit of growth they are excellent plants to fill in where a bed of rigid plants is being grown. For example, they make a good ground cover planted between watsonias.

CULTURE: They seem to grow readily in almost any soil and situation and some species will stand quite severe frost. Sow seeds, or set out the plants, in spring or summer.

D. aliciae

A little trailing plant which makes a brave show in a hanging basket or tub where it can cascade down over the edge. It has pale pink flowers with rose markings. The flowering time is summer.

D. capsularis

This perennial species grows in districts which have cold winters and bears its pink to rose flowers on stems about 30 cm (1 ft) high. It flowers in late spring and early summer.

D. cordata

A perennial which grows wild in districts that have cold winters, such as the foothills of the Drakensberg. It has more rounded leaves than the other species mentioned here and pink flowers in spring and summer.

Twinspur *(Diascia integerrima)* is a charming plant for the flower border

D. integerrima

This is the most popular of the diascias and is a fine plant to have in a mixed border, particularly between plants of rigid growth, such as gladioli. It is a perennial and stands fairly severe frost and a certain amount of dryness, but it performs much better if it is watered regularly. It grows to 45 cm (1½ ft) and flowers from September through summer.

D. moltenensis

Is a little plant from the eastern Cape near Barkly East and Molteno. It grows to about 30 cm (1 ft) and is bushy with supple stems. The leaves are 2-3 cm long and 6 mm wide at the base, tapering to the apex. They have minute serrations along the margins. The flowers are carried in little clusters. They are about 18 mm across and coral-pink in colour.

D. rigescens

Grows in the eastern Cape, the Transkei and parts of Natal. It is a perennial with erect stems to 45 cm (1½ ft) which come up from the base of the plant. The leaves are sessile, clasping the stem, and considerably broader at the base than the apex. They have sharp little serrations along the margins. The flowers, carried in loose clusters, are from pink to rose with pronounced shading of deep rose in the throat. The flowering time is from summer through to autumn.

DICOMA ZEYHERI DICOMA, JAKHALSBOS

DISTRIBUTION: An unusual plant in appearance, to be found growing wild in the Transvaal and parts of Natal.

DESCRIPTION: Dicoma is a perennial with flowers which last for a long time when picked, and it is therefore useful in the picking garden. Each flowerhead is carried on a stem 30 cm (1 ft) or more high, and looks rather like a thistle with sharply pointed bracts arranged in a whorl. The bracts which enclose the flowers are green, suffused with mauve, terra-cotta or brick-red. The slender, oval leaves are felted white beneath and green on top.

D. anomala is larger but very similar to the species described. Bantu tribes make use of the powdered roots in treating stomach disorders in their animals or themselves.

CULTURE: Sow seeds in spring or late summer and water the plants regularly during the growing period. It dies down in winter and is not affected by frost. This plant grows well in any kind of soil.

DIMORPHOTHECA AFRICAN DAISY, NAMAQUALAND DAISY, BOTTERBLOM

DISTRIBUTION: Although dimorphothecas grow in all parts of the country, the most decorative species are to be found in the drier parts of the south-western and north-western Cape.

African Daisy (Hybrid Dimorphotheca) sparkle in the sunlight

The flowerheads of Dicoma are attractive in arrangements

DESCRIPTION: These daisies can be considered one of the most attractive, and at the same time one of our hardiest spring-flowering plants, for some species tolerate fairly severe frost and they all grow well even where the air is dry and the soil rather parched. Some of them are annuals and some are perennials. They are first-class plants to provide a quick carpet of colour in spring in hot sunny gardens where the soil is poor and frosts are not very severe. They grow well in coastal gardens and at a high elevation.

CULTURE: Sow the seed in March and April and transplant the seedlings when 2-3 cm (1 in) high to stand 20-45 cm (8-18 in) apart, depending on the size of the species grown. They do not demand good soil but they do best when planted in sandy or friable soil, and they like to be watered during autumn and winter. They should be planted in full sunshine as the flowers open only under strong sunlight and they turn in the direction of the sun.

D. chrysanthemifolia
(Calendula chrysanthemifolia)
This is a shrubby species which grows to about 60 cm (2 ft) and has fairly large leaves, similar to those of a chrysanthemum. They are of a metallic green and spotted with glands. The yellow daisies which appear in spring measure up to 7-8 cm across. It is not a tidy-looking plant but it is certainly worth growing in districts where scanty rainfall and intense sunlight with cold nights makes the growing of more tender subjects difficult. It grows very readily from cuttings.

D. cuneata
This, like the above, is a useful plant for difficult gardens. It, too, is a perennial with a shrubby habit of growth to 60 cm (2 ft) and more. In this case the flowers are glistening white daisies, the backs of which are suffused with biscuit shadings. The leaves are small. New plants are neat and decorative, but older plants become woody and

97

Shrubby Felicia *(Felicia amelloides)*. The shrubby Felicia enhances the garden for many weeks of the year.

Rain Daisy *(Dimorphotheca pluvialis)*. Rain Daisy provides a scintilating carpet in late winter and early spring

African or Namaqualand Daisy *(Dimorphotheca sinuata)* produces a mass of vivid flowers

leggy and it is advisable therefore to raise fresh plants each year.

D. pluvialis   CAPE DAISY, RAIN DAISY, WITBOTTERBLOM

Is a little annual which paints the slopes of Table Mountain and many parts of the surrounding countryside white, in late winter and early spring. It grows to about 30 cm (1 ft) in height and bears scintillating white flowers with yellow centres. A variety of this has white flowers with a band of deep purple around the central disc. Sometimes this band is so narrow that it is hardly noticed and sometimes it is clearly defined. The backs of the petals are flushed with mauve. The leaves are long and slender, widely toothed and pointed, with a well defined midrib. It makes a fine carpeting plant or edging to a long drive. It grows very readily from seed which should be sown in March or April. It seems to flourish equally well in sandy soil and in a heavy soil.

D. sinuata   NAMAQUALAND DAISY, AFRICAN DAISY

An easy-to-grow annual, 30-45 cm tall, which bears vivid orange flowers up to 8 cm across, with centres which are also orange. Around the centre at the bottom of the petals is a narrow, greenish-mauve ring. Natural hybrids of many other shades have resulted, producing flowers from pale cream to yellow and salmon. The leaves of this species are slender, about 5 cm long, and have widely toothed edges. The flowering time is mid-winter to mid-spring. Seed sown in February or March will produce a charming display by August.

FELICIA   FELICIA

DISTRIBUTION: Felicias grow wild in different parts of the country but most of those which are of decorative value in the garden are native to the Cape.

DESCRIPTION: They have daisy-like flowers usually of a beautiful azure or pale blue shade with yellow centres. Some of them are annuals and others are perennials. Both types can be considered good garden plants; the annuals for the front of a border and the perennials to group with other perennials, or to plant in the rock-garden or as a border in front of shrubs. Some authorities believe that the felicias should be known as "asters", but as opinion on this is divided, I have listed them under the names by which they have been previously described.

CULTURE: The annuals are grown from seed sown in March or April. Plant them out 10-20 cm (4-8 in) apart when they are 2-3 cm (1 in) high. The perennials can be grown from seed sown in spring, but much quicker results will be had by planting roots or by making cuttings during spring. Most of them are not resistant to severe frost and need protection in cold gardens. They grow in sandy or clay soil. Water them from autumn to spring.

F. adfinis
(New name is *F. dubia*)
A dwarf annual growing to about 20 cm (8 in) in height. To look effective in the garden they should be massed together, planted only 10 cm (4 in) apart. Their blue flowers look most attractive if planted alternately with groups of yellow cotula.

F. amelloides   SHRUBBY FELICIA
(*F. aethiopica*)
Can be seen growing wild in parts of the south-western and eastern Cape where it often occurs in gravelly soils on hillslopes.

It is a shrubby perennial reaching a height of 30-45 cm (1-1½ ft) with leaves about 3 cm long. It bears masses of sky-blue and darker blue daisies with yellow centres. They measure about 3 cm across. The flowers are carried well above the shrubby foliage and make a bright show in spring. If cut back after flowering, it will generally produce another crop of flowers later on in the summer. This is a fine plant for the rock-garden, the flower border, and the front of a shrub border.

F. bergerana   KINGFISHER DAISY
This is one of the most attractive of the indigenous spring-flowering annuals. It grows to only about 20 cm (8 in) in height and has charming little daisy-like flowers with narrow petals of sky-blue, and yellow or black centres. The little leaves are 3 cm long and 6 mm wide. It needs full sunshine to induce the flowers to open. For an effective show space them only 10 cm (4 in) apart. They make a fine edging in front of ursinias. Sow seeds from February to April.

F. echinata var. **paralia**   PRICKLY FELICIA
(New name is *Polyarrhenia reflexa*)
This perennial species grows to about 60 cm (2 ft) and is bushy, with little oval leaves only 12 mm long and 3 mm broad. It becomes covered with

Prickly Felicia (*Felicia echinata* var. *paralia*) is a useful plant for large gardens (New name is *Polyarrhenia reflexa*)

daisy-like flowers 18 mm wide with narrow, mauve petals and canary-yellow centres. The flowering time is August and September. Set plants 45 cm (1½ ft) apart.

F. elongata
(F. tricolor)
This perennial, best treated as an annual, grows to about 20 cm (8 in) and has flowers 3-4 cm across. The flowers are white, pale pink or mauve with a yellow centre surrounded by a cyclamen band, which gives them a gay appearance. The leaves are small and slender. It is not hardy to severe frost but will tolerate the moderate frost experienced in many parts of the highveld. Sow the seeds in March or April and transplant the seedlings to stand 20 cm (8 in) apart.

F. petiolata
A little perennial which bears flowers of mauvy-pink about 2-3 cm wide on slender stems which rise above the foliage. The centre of the flower is yellow. It is bushy in growth and flowers in spring and early summer. The leaves and stems are hairy. This is a fine plant to have on a dry bank or along the edge of a wall or tub. It is hardy to frost. Sow seed in spring or late summer and set the plants 30 cm (12 in) apart. After the main flowering period is over shear off the tops and the plants will usually come into flower again within a

100

couple of months.

F. tenella
This delicate-looking felicia is an annual growing to about 20 cm (8 in) in height, with pale-blue flowers with yellow centres. The leaves are very fine, slender and hairy. To make an effective show it should be mass-planted as a border in front of a background of dark green leaves or with a shrub with yellow flowers (e.g. euryops) as the backdrop. Sow seed in March and set plants 15 cm (6 in) apart.

GAZANIA
GAZANIA, GOUSBLOM, WILD MARIGOLD

DISTRIBUTION: Is widespread in the north-western Cape and can be found in the other provinces too.

DESCRIPTION: Of all our native flowers few produce as glorious a show of colour year after year, under the most adverse circumstances, as does the gazania. Despite its many attributes, it is only within the last few years that one has seen it in South African gardens, and even now it is not widely grown throughout the country. In Australia and New Zealand our gazanias have been widely grown for many years and lovely hybrids developed. Some of them have double flowers and others have single.

How rich is the sheen and colour of this gazania hybrid ▷

Gazanias
flourish in hot,
dry places

Pictures show
the rich range
of colours of
hybrid gazanias

Gazanias can be used anywhere in the garden–as a ground cover to hide dry, hard earth; in the rock-garden, on dry banks and walls, or in pots and window-boxes in sunny places. It is, furthermore, a most decorative plant to use along highways and railway embankments to help hold the soil and prevent erosion. Gazanias are splendid plants for seaside gardens, too.

They hybridize so readily in nature that botanists are having a difficult time trying to decide which are original species and which are hybrids. Names are therefore likely to be changed from time to time.

The size of the flowers varies according to species, from those with flowers less than 3 cm across to the more showy ones with flowers measuring 6-8 cm across. In some species and hybrids the flowers are like velvet in texture and of the most glorious range of colours—glowing yellows, orange, tawny-gold, flame, cyclamen and wine-red. The leaves vary considerably from species to species. They flower most prolifically in late winter and spring, but bear some flowers at other seasons as well.

CULTURE: Gazanias grow readily from seed sown in March or April and some of them can be grown from root divisions or cuttings too. Increase of particular ones should be made by dividing the roots or making cuttings. This is best done in spring or autumn, but gazanias do not mind being moved at any time of the year. They grow well in poor soil and tolerate frost and long periods without water; but, to have the best results, start them off in soil which is friable and water them regularly from autumn to spring. When the plants become overcrowded, lift and divide the roots.

G. krebsiana

Grows wild in different parts of the eastern Cape and northwards into the Transvaal.

This is a perennial plant commonly seen along roadsides making a bold splash of colour during the autumn to spring period. The leaves are variable in shape, often long and slender, green on the upper surface and felted ivory on the underside. The flowers are carried on stems up to 30 cm (12 in) high. They are deep glowing orange, with markings of chocolate and cinnamon at the centre. It flowers most in late winter and early spring, and can be grown from seed which should be sown in spring to summer. Many colourful hybrids of this species are now available.

G. leiopoda (G. pinnata)
PEACOCK GAZANIA, WILD MARIGOLD, GOUSBLOM

So many hybrids have occurred naturally that there is some confusion as to whether or not this is now a legitimate name. Together with G. krebsiana, this is presumed to have given rise to the most beautiful of all the hybrids with flowers most gloriously marked with contrasting patterns of colour, like those on a peacock's tail.

The leaves vary considerably in shape when young, but the mature leaves are generally divided and are dark green on the upper surface and felted with white underneath. The flowers of the hybrids vary in colour from all shades of yellow and orange to terra-cotta, burgundy and russet.

It will flower in early spring from seeds sown in summer. It tolerates quite severe frost, and grows in dry situations but should be given some water in winter to encourage growth and flowering.

G. linearis
WILD MARIGOLD, GANSBLOM

This is a sturdy plant which can be seen growing along the roadsides in the eastern Cape in winter. It has daisy-like flowers measuring about 5 cm across, of a clear yellow hue with deeper yellow centres. The leaves are long and slender with rounded ends, dark green on the upper side and felted white on the underside, with a prominent green rib. The Xhosas peel off this white felting, twist it and use it as thread on which to string their beads. It can be grown from seed sown in summer or from cuttings. It is a perennial which needs no encouragement to make it grow, and it will stand fairly severe frost.

G. rigens var. uniflora (G. uniflora)
TRAILING GAZANIA

Although this species does not have flowers which are as spectacular as some of the others, it is one of the most useful perennials to have, especially in the large garden where growing conditions are difficult, and in seaside gardens. It grows well in dry districts and it tolerates quite severe frost. The leaves hug the ground and hide the bare earth very quickly. They are long and slender and of a pleasant silvery colour. The flowers measure 2-3 cm across and are bright yellow. The flowering time is mostly spring and summer. This gazania is a fine plant to have growing over dry banks and walls or cascading down over the edge of a

The silver leaves of this Gazania are a fine foil to its yellow flowers

tub or a patio. It is also a useful plant to edge a lawn, for its silver leaves make an effective colour contrast against the green of the lawn. On the Canary Islands it is used to make scroll bedding effects. To do this the plants must be clipped to shape.

Grow it from root sections planted at any time of the year. Another decorative species with silver leaves and yellow flowers is known as *G. rigens* var. *leucolaena*.

GERANIUM INCANUM Carpet Geranium, Vrouebosse

DISTRIBUTION: A charming edging or carpeting plant which grows wild in the south-western Cape, parts of the eastern Cape and the Transvaal.

DESCRIPTION: Most gardeners the world over refer to both geraniums and pelargoniums as "geraniums", a term which should be applied to very few of the plants commonly called by this name. Most of the plants called "geraniums", which are used for garden show and for pot culture are, in fact, pelargoniums.

The flowers are quite different. They both have flowers with five petals, but those of the geranium are arranged in an even manner, usually in a saucer or bowl shape, whereas the petals of a pelargonium are irregularly arranged—two together at the top and three at the bottom.

Geranium incanum is a true geranium with flowers of a soft shade of mauve, sometimes almost pink, which measure about 2-3 cm across. The petals are rounded at the ends with a slight indentation. They are carried on slender stems about 20 cm (8 in) high just above the lacy foliage which carpets the ground.

In addition to being a fine plant at the edge of a bed or to carpet the ground, this little geranium is an excellent one to plant in crevices between paving stones or in a rock wall, or to have in pots on a window ledge. The flowering time is spring and summer.

CULTURE: It grows very easily but as it is a perennial the soil in which it is to be planted should be improved by adding compost or leaf mould. If the soil is good and it is watered regularly it will generally seed itself. Sow seeds or set out new plants in spring or summer. Plants should stand about 20 cm (8 in) apart to make a compact show. After flowering, cut the plants back and they will usually reward you with fine new green growth and another crop of the flowers within six weeks. In regions which get sharp frost the plants may be frosted to the ground but they usually grow up quickly again in spring if watered regularly towards the end of winter. Where frosts are severe, cover the ground where they are growing with a mulch of straw as this helps to protect the roots from frost damage.

105

GERBERA JAMESONII   BARBERTON DAISY, TRANSVAAL DAISY

DISTRIBUTION: This daisy first found in the Transvaal near Barberton was hybridized many years ago.

DESCRIPTION: The newest hybrids are spectacular, with flowers of enchanting colours measuring 12-15 cm across on stems 60-90 cm (2-3 ft) in length. They are produced by the million under glass in Europe for sale as cut flowers during winter and early spring.

The flowers of the original species vary from pale to bright coral-red. They have long slender petals radiating from the centre. When grown in good soil the flowers may be as much as 7 cm across on long, strong stems, but usually one sees much smaller specimens both in nature and in gardens. The new hybrids are of many different shades and colours—pale cream, tawny old gold, yellow, peach, apricot, claret, cyclamen, rust and flame, with red or yellow centres. Double ones have also been produced. Some of these are bi-coloured, with the outer petals a lighter shade than the inner ones. The leaves are large, long and deeply indented. Because of its long-lasting quality when picked, this is an admirable flower for arrangements, but it is also a splendid garden flower when grown in clumps in a well arranged border, or on a rockery. The main flowering time is from September to November.

CULTURE: Barberton daisies do not like to be kept dry but they do like to be planted in soil from which water drains away fairly readily. They do much better in porous soil than in clay. If your garden is of heavy clay, make holes fairly wide and deep and put in some small stones and gravel at the bottom and compost on top before planting. They should be grown in full sunshine, although shade for part of the day does not deter them from flowering. They grow naturally in a region which has a fairly mild winter, but they have been grown out of doors in the south of England planted against a south wall. In highveld gardens the plants should be mulched during winter and planted where they will benefit from the reflected heat of a north-facing wall.

Set the plants about 30 cm (1 ft) apart and leave them in the same place for several years. When the flowers appear to be getting smaller lift the plants and divide them, discarding the old, woody central portion and planting sections of the remainder. They can also be grown from seed which should be sown when it is fresh (less than three months old) as otherwise it may not germinate. It takes a year or two for plants grown from seed to reach flowering size.

Transvaal or Barberton Daisy make a pretty show in the garden and in arrangements

Carpet Flower (Geranium incanum) looks effective both in the garden and in window-boxes

Yellow Satin Flower (*Grielum grandiflorum*) with its fragile flowers thrives in hot, dry areas

GRIELUM GRANDIFLORUM YELLOW SATIN FLOWER, BOTTERBLOM

DISTRIBUTION: Can be found in sandy soil from Namaqualand south to Worcester.

DESCRIPTION: This is a prostrate-growing annual which is exceptionally lovely. It has dainty fern-like foliage of a pleasing shade of greyish-green, and colourful flowers with five rounded petals which look as though they have been made of gleaming, yellow satin. It is usually found growing in sandy soil. This is a fine plant for the front of a border or to have in drifts in a rock-garden or edging a path.

CULTURE: I have not been able to glean any facts about the cultivation of this charming plant, and seed is as yet not procurable from any source. One hopes, however, that this will soon become available for this is one of the prettiest of flowers. It obviously does best in sandy soil and it endures hot dry growing conditions very well.

HELICHRYSUM EVERLASTING, STRAWFLOWER,

DISTRIBUTION: Helichrysums occur in nature in different parts of the world, and there are some 200 species in South Africa, distributed all over the country, and in Rhodesia.

DESCRIPTION: Most of them are not particularly showy and only those of some garden merit are described here. Many of the helichrysums are used medicinally by the Bantu. The leaves are applied to cure festering sores, and sometimes a decoction is made to relieve menstrual pain, cure diarrhoea or ward off a magic spell.

The flowers are often used for flower pictures, dried arrangements or wreaths, as they last indefinitely. In earlier days they were used as the stuffing for mattresses and cushions. They look as though they have been made of shiny straw, and are of soft colours, mostly pinks, white and yellows. The leaves are from green to grey or silver. They do well in coastal gardens as well as inland.

CULTURE: Everlastings grow naturally in dry places and are fine plants to have in a large rock-garden. Not all of them are hardy to sharp frost. They can be grown from seed sown in spring or late summer. They thrive in porous, sandy soil.

H. adenocarpum PINK EVERLASTING

Can be seen in fields in the eastern Cape and Natal. It reaches a height of 20 cm (8 in) and has silvery leaves in rosettes at the base, and pink to rose flowers which make pretty dried posies. It flowers in late summer and autumn.

This Everlasting *(Helichrysum argenteum)* does well in poor soil.

H. argenteum   Everlasting

Grows into a spreading mound about 30 cm (1 ft) across and has slender, oval, silver leaves on silver stems which are very decorative. In late winter and early spring it bears glistening, white flowers like little double daisies with white papery petals and golden centres. It makes a good ground cover for dry sandy soil. The flowers are useful for small posies.

H. argyrophyllum   Golden Guinea Everlasting

Is one of the most decorative of this genus for garden show, but in certain parts of the eastern Cape it has become a noxious weed, as it grows to the detriment of the grazing land.

This perennial everlasting grows in a low mat across the ground, covering the soil with its masses of little shiny, silver leaves only about 6 mm long. The foliage is decorative throughout the year, and in summer and autumn it becomes covered with bright yellow flowers on stems 10-

The Golden Guinea Everlasting *(Helichrysum argyrophyllum)* makes a fine show anywhere in the garden

20 cm (4-8 in) high. It makes a fine carpet for dry banks and for walls. If it is cut down by severe frost it usually grows up again as soon as spring comes.

H. calocephalum

The flowers of this species from the eastern Cape are carried on stems about 45 cm (1½ ft) tall, each stem holding a single flower with papery petals of bright yellow. The leaves are grey and clustered together at the base of the plant. The flowers close in dull weather and at night, but open again next day. The flowering period is summer.

H. felinum

A shrubby little plant which gives rise to silvery stems of flowers of palest pink carried in rounded heads. The little flowers are charming for small posies. It is native to the south-western Cape.

H. foetidum EVERLASTING, MUISHONDBLAAR

This species from the eastern Cape and Natal grows to 60 cm (2 ft). The leaves are coated with silvery hair and the colour of the flowers is bright yellow. It flowers in spring.

H. kraussii STRAW EVERLASTING

This species is not particularly showy but as it stands both drought and frost it can be considered a useful plant for gardens where growing conditions are difficult. It grows in a shrubby fashion to about 90 cm (3 ft) in height and spread. It has small green leaves and clusters of tiny, tawny-yellow flowers in spring. It can be seen growing wild on the Transvaal highveld.

H. paniculatum

A species seen in the south-western and eastern Cape with grey stems rising to bear flowers about 60 cm (2 ft) above the ground. The oval, pointed leaves which hug the stem are silvery-grey and the papery flowers have white pointed petals and bright yellow centres. The flowering time is spring.

H. sesamoides

This species is very similar to the above. It grows to 45 cm (1½ ft) and has minute leaves which hug the stem, and flowers about 4 cm across with a whorl of papery, pointed, white, pink or yellow petals surrounding a yellow centre. The flowering time is spring and early summer.

H. vestitum FELTED EVERLASTING

This perennial can be found in many parts of the south-western Cape. Tapering, slender silver-grey leaves hug the silvery stems which grow out to about 60 cm (2 ft) and bear flowers with little pointed petals of silvery-white opening up to a flower measuring about 4 cm across. It flowers in late spring and summer. Like the others it is splendid for long-lasting arrangements.

HELIOPHILA CORONOPIFOLIA BLUE FLAX
(H. sonchifolia)

DISTRIBUTION: A dainty annual which grows wild along the roadsides and in fields in the south-western Cape. Although referred to as blue flax, it is not related to the true flax at all.

DESCRIPTION: Its flowers are of the blue of summer skies—a beautiful shade which shows up well against any other colour. It reaches a height of about 45 cm (1½ ft) and bears its loose clusters of little flowers at the ends of the fragile stems. Each flower is about 12 mm across and has four rounded petals with white markings ending off the blue at the centre. The slender leaves are carried mostly along the bottom sections of the stems. Massed, it makes an enchanting show. It flowers in late winter and early spring.

CULTURE: It is not hardy to frost and should be kept watered well during the autumn to spring period. It grows very readily from seed sown in March or April. The little plants should be set out only 5-8 cm (2-4 in) apart as this flower makes a spectacular show only when massed. It looks very effective growing next to or amongst yellow and orange flowers such as ursinias.

HETEROLEPIS ALIENA

DISTRIBUTION: Is to be found on lower mountain slopes near the sea and on coastal plains within 50 kilometres of Cape Town.

DESCRIPTION: This is a perennial of great charm. It is a low-growing plant and has sprawling stems with tiny leaves hardly 12 mm long and only 3-4 mm broad, with sharp tips edged with red. The flowers are daisy-like in form and measure 2-3 cm across. They have a few broadly oval petals and a centre of a bright, pure yellow. This is a pretty little plant to have growing over a wall or bank, or in crevices between paving stones.

109

Helichrysum sesamoides (Everlasting) ▷

Heterolepis aliena is a charming plant for the rock-garden

CULTURE: It appears to be difficult to raise from seed or cuttings, but once established it grows for several years. It stands moderate frost and quite considerable drought.

HYPOESTES ARISTATA　RIBBON BUSH
(H. antennifera)

DISTRIBUTION: Is widespread in parts of the eastern Cape, the Transkei and lowlands of Natal.

DESCRIPTION: It is a perennial of bushy habit of growth, reaching a height of about 1.25 m (4 ft). The flowers emerge along the stems from the axils of the leaves. Each flower is made up of a narrow tube opening up into a two-lipped face with the lips curving backwards. The flowers are of a mauve or pinky-mauve with darker spots on the upper segments of the flower. The leaves which

112

come off from the stem opposite each other, are broad at the base, pointed at the end, 2-5 cm in length, and clearly veined. It flowers in May and sometimes later, where frosts are not severe. It should be cut back in spring to keep it in shape and to encourage new growth.

CULTURE: In its natural habitat it grows mostly in fairly moist places and at the edges of forests. When planted in the garden it is advisable to see that it is watered regularly, and that it is planted in soil rich with leaf mould. It is tender to severe frost but can be grown in cold areas if sheltered. When frosted it generally grows up again quickly. Ribbon bush makes a splendid show in autumn.

LEONOTIS LEONURUS　WILD DAGGA, WILDE DAGGA

DISTRIBUTION: This plant is widespread over large areas in the eastern Cape, Natal, the Orange Free State, the Transvaal and Rhodesia.

DESCRIPTION: It derives the name of Wild Dagga because of the similarity of its leaves to real dagga (Indian Hemp, *Cannabis sativa* var. *indica*). Some African tribes use the juice of the roots as nose drops to treat sinus conditions and the leaves are chewed to cure stomach aches. The leaves were used by the Hottentots as tobacco but have no narcotic effect. They also made a tea of the leaves to be used as a purgative. Early colonists used it medicinally, too. In the garden it makes a colourful background plant.

This is a tall, rangy perennial with stems reaching 1.5 m (5 ft) and more, with tubular flowers of bright orange carried in whorls coming out from the axils of the leaves at intervals along the top sections of the stems. The leaves are slender and tapering. There is also a white form of this species. Another species, *L. leonitis*, grows readily too but it is not as showy. The main flowering time is autumn to mid-spring, but it bears some flowers at other seasons as well.

CULTURE: Wild dagga grows like a weed and tolerates cold winters and fairly dry conditions. It may be cut down by severe frost but the stems grow quickly again and flower in due season. In regions where frosts do not cut down the growth it is advisable to trim the plants back to keep them from becoming too leggy. The quickest way to establish plants is by planting roots, which can be done at any time of the year, but preferably in

◁ *Helichrysum sesamoides* (Everlasting)

spring. It can be grown from cuttings or seeds, too. It does well in poor soil.

LIMONIUM PERIGRINUM
(L. roseum, Statice rosea)
STATICE, SEA LAVENDER, STRANDROOS, PAPIERBLOM

DISTRIBUTION: A perennial found growing in sandy places along the coast north of Cape Town.

DESCRIPTION: This is a decorative plant for the garden and for floral arrangements as the flowers last for weeks when picked. It bears its papery flowers in wide, spreading panicles, on stems 60 cm (2 ft) tall. Each flower is less than 12 mm across, composed of a pale pink calyx and slender petals of darker pink. The pink calyx remains decorative even after the petals have faded. The leaves are oval and leathery and carried on the bottom part of the plant. It is an excellent plant for coastal gardens.

CULTURE: This plant is a perennial but it is not an easy one to establish as it resents being transplanted. It can be grown from cuttings or seeds, but the cuttings do not root easily, and the seed falls so quickly from the flowers that it is difficult to collect. It does not like wet feet, but on the

Leonotis leonurus (Wild Dagga)

Wild Dagga
(*Leonotis leonurus*)
with its orange or
white flowers shows
up well at the back of
a border

Statice,
Sea Lavender
(*Limonium
perigrinum*) is
decorative in the
garden and in
arrangements

other hand, it also likes to be watered moderately throughout the year, and particularly in winter. Once established it will endure cold winters, but not very severe frost. Plant it in well-drained, sandy soil to which compost has been added. Seeds should be sown in spring or late summer.

LOBELIA   LOBELIA

DISTRIBUTION: These little plants are widely distributed in all provinces and Rhodesia.

DESCRIPTION: Some species make splendid edging plants and the hybrids have been grown widely for this purpose in many countries of the world. They are also decorative when grown in pots or hanging baskets.

Most species grow to about 20 cm (8 in) in height and bear flowers which are blue. Each flower is made up of a squat tube opening to a face with two slender segments close together at the top, and three broader ones near each other at the bottom. The leaves are small and generally clustered along the bottom part of the stem. The flowering time depends upon when the seed is sown.

CULTURE: These plants are not difficult to grow from seed, which may be sown in late summer or in spring. In regions with cold winters and summer rains they are best grown for a summer display, whilst in the winter-rainfall region it is advisable to sow them in early autumn for spring flowers. Prick out the little seedlings when they are 2-3 cm (1 in) high and plant them about 10 cm apart, so that they make a compact show of colour. After flowering cut the plants back slightly and they will generally produce more flowers. They do well in loose soil.

L. caerulea
Grows in such masses in some districts of the eastern Cape that the veld appears to be painted blue. As a rule the flowers are a deep azure blue but sometimes variations with white or mauve flowers are found. This is a perennial species worth a place in the garden and in hanging baskets. It flowers in summer.

L. coronopifolia
A decorative perennial lobelia which is taller than the other species mentioned. The plant is not as floriferous as other species but it is a good one for interplanting with other low-growing flowers. The flowers are deep blue carried on stems about 30 cm (1 ft) high. Sow seeds in spring for flowers in summer.

L. decipiens   BUTTERFLY LOBELIA
This is a charming little perennial species with a woody underground stem. It is found in the

114

Lady Monson
(*Monsonia speciosa*)
is a pretty flower for
the front of a border

Transvaal, Natal and the eastern Cape, usually in damp places. It grows to about 15 cm (6 in) and bears dainty flowers with lower segments of deep blue marked with a yellow spot, and upper ones of purple. The leaves are tiny and slender. The flowering time is late spring and early summer.

L. erinus   Edging Lobelia

This is the annual species which is grown in many parts of the world as an edging plant and the one from which named hybrids have been developed. It grows to only a few centimetres in height and has flowers of pale to deep blue. It is an attractive species for edging a small bed.

MONOPSIS LUTEA   Yellow Lobelia
(*Parastranthus luteus*)

Distribution: The natural habitat of this little perennial is the Cape Peninsula.

Description: It grows to about 30 cm (1 ft) in height and bears bright yellow flowers about 12 mm across. The leaves are small, broad at the bottom and pointed at the ends, with serrated margins. In nature it is usually found in marshy places. The flowering time is summer. To make an effective display this plant should be massed at the front of a border or in a rock-garden.

Culture: It grows from seed which should be sown in March or April. For good results water the plants regularly, particularly during autumn and winter.

MONSONIA SPECIOSA   Lady Monson,
                    Snake-flower, Slangblom

Distribution: This perennial plant can be seen in many districts of the south-western Cape. Other species, not as decorative, occur in the Transvaal and Natal.

Description: It bears very pretty flowers made up of five broad petals varying in colour from pale pink to cyclamen, often faintly striped with a darker hue. Occasionally a white one may be found. The flowers measure about 5 cm across and are carried on slender stems about 20 cm (8 in) in height. The foliage is fine and feathery and grows near the ground. The flowering time is September.

Culture: Sow seed in spring and summer and set the plants 7-10 cm (3-4 in) apart, or plant them between other low-growing plants at the front of a border. In districts which have frosts it is advisable to plant them under a tree which will protect them from the early morning winter sun. They should be watered regularly particularly in autumn and winter.

115

NEMESIA STRUMOSA

NEMESIA, LEEU-
BEKKIE

DISTRIBUTION: This colourful plant used to grow in vast fields in the sandy veld around Darling.

DESCRIPTION: As the years pass and more ground is put under the plough one sees fewer and fewer nemesias growing wild. Fortunately, however, about eighty years ago seeds of this species were sent to a large firm of seed-merchants in England who cultivated the plants and hybridized them too, and today there are many very beautiful hybrids available.

It is an annual which grows to 30-45 cm (12-18 in). The flower is made up of a short tube opening up to a face composed of two lips—the upper one indented and the lower one ruffled. The colours of the flowers are shades of yellow or orange, misty blues and mauves, russet, cream and white. The flowering time is early spring. This nemesia is a splendid plant for bedding on its own, and for window boxes and hanging baskets. *Nemesia versicolor* is another pretty species. Its flowers are much smaller and coloured mainly mauve or yellow and white.

CULTURE: Sow the seed in February or March and set the plants out about 20 cm (8 in) apart. They are very accommodating as regards soil, but tall plants with large flowers will result if the soil is improved by the addition of plenty of humus in the form of compost or old manure. They should be watered in autumn and until they finish flower-ing. Nemesias are tender to frost, but where frosts are severe they may be induced to grow if planted against a wall which reflects at night the heat absorbed during the day. They do best where winters are fairly mild.

ORPHIUM FRUTESCENS

ORPHIUM

DISTRIBUTION: Occurs in the south-western Cape, along parts of the coast and in certain areas near Cape Town, and further afield towards Clan-william.

DESCRIPTION: Orphium is one of the prettiest of our native perennials and also one of the most effective for a display in the garden and in arrangements during late spring and early summer. Planted in front of blue agapanthus it will keep the garden bright and colourful throughout the Christmas season. Plant it in the flower border with other perennials and annuals, or in groups along the front of a shrub border.

Orphium is variable in manner of growth, and in the size and shape of the leaves. One form which grows naturally in sandy soils near the coast, tolerating salt-laden air and soil, is an ideal plant for seaside gardens. It has sturdy, erect stems and leaves which are elliptic to spatulate and 2-3 cm long and 1 cm broad. It attains a height of 60 cm (2 ft). The form which can be found on the Cape Flats and further inland is shrubby in growth with slender, gracefully spreading stems. Its leaves are long and narrow,

Nemesia hybrids are charming plants for hanging baskets or the garden

A close-up of the flowers of Orphium. *(Orphium frutescens)*

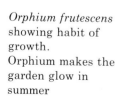

Orphium frutescens showing habit of growth.
Orphium makes the garden glow in summer

being 3-4 cm in length and 2-3 mm wide. They are arranged in pairs on slender stems.

At Christmas time the plants are covered with beautiful clusters of flowers. Each flower measures 2-4 cm across and has five petals, broader at the end than in the middle. They are sticky to the touch, waxy in texture, and of a lovely, luminous pinky-mauve to cyclamen-pink colour, fading to biscuit as they age. The bright yellow stamens enhance the beauty of the flowers. The flowers persist on the plant for three to four weeks and they make a show in a vase for two weeks. New buds keep opening as the older flowers in the clusters fade.

CULTURE: This is not a difficult plant to grow, and, once established, it stands a good deal of frost. When cut down by frost it usually grows up again quickly and flowers again in summer. Although it grows naturally in areas which are extremely arid in summer, it appears to do better if planted where it can be watered fairly regularly throughout the year. The places where it grows naturally are marshy during the winter months. Set the plants out about 45 cm (18 in) apart to create a compact show of colour at the back of a flower border or in front of large perennials or shrubs. Seeds may be sown in summer for flowers by Christmas, or in spring, for flowers the following year.

OSTEOSPERMUM　　　　WILD DAISY

DISTRIBUTION: Different species are to be found in the different provinces.

DESCRIPTION: They all have daisy-like flowers which are yellow, mauve or white in colour. Some are annuals whilst others are perennials. They all grow easily and the species mentioned below are most decorative plants which can be used anywhere in the garden—as ground covers to hide dry banks, in front of a border of shrubs, in tubs on a terrace or patio, or in hanging baskets.

CULTURE: They can be grown from seed sown in March or April but perennial types are easier to grow from root sections or from cuttings. They are hardy to moderate frost and tolerate dry growing conditions, but most species are native to the western Cape and require some water from autumn to spring. They need an abundance of light to make the flowers open.

O. ecklonis　　　　WHITE DAISY BUSH
(*Dimorphotheca ecklonis*)
Is a perennial of bushy habit of growth with a height and spread of 90 cm (3 ft). In late winter and spring it becomes covered with large, glistening, snow-white daisies with petals which are flushed with mauve on the underside. The deep metallic-blue centre of the flowers makes a won-

derful contrast to the snowy-whiteness of the petals. The leaves measure 7-10 cm in length, are obovate and 2-3 cm broad at the apex. The flowering time is from August to October. This is a spectacular flower and very easy to grow from cuttings made during the warmer months. In very cold gardens it needs some protection against frost.

O. fruticosum   MAUVE AND WHITE
(Dimorphotheca fruticosa)   DAISY BUSH
This perennial species grows in the south-western Cape and eastwards to Natal. Its flowers are very similar to those of the above species except that the centre is lavender instead of blue, and the plant is not shrubby in growth but sends up individual stems which tend to sprawl. It makes a good ground cover or border to a drive.

O. jucundum   TRAILING
(Dimorphotheca jucunda)   MAUVE DAISY
This perennial is to be found in parts of the eastern Transvaal, the Orange Free State and Natal. It bears mauve daisy-like flowers 3-5 cm across. The leaves are fairly long and slender, with slight points along the margins. It is hardy to average frosts and, once established, it endures long periods without water. *O. barberae,* common near the coast in the eastern Cape, has flowers which are similar.

The Trailing Mauve Daisy is a most decorative garden plant thought to be a hybrid of the above.

It grows almost flat along the ground, sending up numerous stems to about 20 cm in height. On the ends of these are attractive daisies carried in profusion in late winter and early spring. They vary in colour from palest mauve to a deep rich shade which is very pleasing. This is a useful plant for growing in a large tub or hollow wall, to hang down over the edges. It is also a useful plant for hiding a dry bank or to plant as a ground cover anywhere in the garden. It grows very easily from slips and root sections.

PELARGONIUM   PELARGONIUM
DISTRIBUTION: There are more than two hundred species of pelargonium growing wild in different parts of South Africa. They vary tremendously in manner of growth, and in their leaves and rootstock, as well as in the size and colours of the flowers.

DESCRIPTION: Unfortunately the wrong name is still being used for these plants. Most gardeners refer to them as geraniums, which are quite different although belonging to the same family. The difference between the two is quite apparent. In the true geranium the five petals are of equal size and arranged in a regular fashion making a cup-shaped or saucer-shaped flower, whereas in the pelargonium the petals are of unequal sizes and they are arranged in an irregular way. The two upper petals are close together, separated from the three lower ones which are usually smaller. Most pelargoniums are perennials with

The Trailing Mauve Daisy makes a good ground cover

an aromatic smell. Many species are used by the Bantu for chest troubles. They infuse the leaves and drink the tea or burn the leaves for the relief of asthma.

More than 200 years ago specimens of our wild pelargoniums were taken to Europe and from these thousands of hybrids of spectacular beauty have been evolved. It is estimated that millions of plants are propagated annually for bedding out in gardens in Europe, the United States and Australia where hybrids of our wild pelargoniums are one of the most popular of summer bedding plants. They are excellent plants for pots or tubs on a patio, as well as being useful plants for any part of the garden e.g. banks, walls, borders, or beds. They do well in seaside gardens as well as inland at higher elevations.

CULTURE: Pelargoniums grow very readily from cuttings and this is the quickest way to make new plants, but they can be grown from seed, too. They generally prefer full sun but some of them do well in part shade. Most of them are hardy to moderate frost and, even if frost does cut back the top growth, they send up new shoots very quickly. They are tolerant of poor soil and arid growing conditions.

P. angulosum
Grows to 45 cm in height and spread and is shrubby but tends to become leggy at the base if it is not cut back. The flowers are of a pretty shade of mauve and are very like those of *P. cucullatum* in shape and colour. It is very quick-growing and useful for seaside gardens.

P. burtonae　　　　BURTON'S PELARGONIUM
Comes from the eastern Cape. It is a robust plant to about 60 cm (2 ft) which bears a mass of cerise flowers in spring.

P. capitatum　　　　ROSE GERANIUM
This species is abundant from the south-western Cape up to Natal, and is often found in sandy soil. The plants grow to about 60 cm (2 ft) in height and across, and the flowers are carried in clusters at the ends of stems. They are pale pink to deep rose in colour, sometimes streaked. The velvety leaves give off a sweet scent when bruised. This species is one of those cultivated in the south of France and elsewhere for the production of oil of geranium for the perfume industry.

P. cordatum
(*P. cordifolium*)
Its natural habitat is the eastern Cape. This is a shrubby and robust species growing to about 1.25 m (4 ft) in height and spread. It produces flowers varying in colour from pale pink to deep purple, with darker veinings on some of the petals. The foliage is soft and hairy. The main flowering time is spring.

P. cucullatum　　　　WILDEMALFA
A rangy and attractive pelargonium of shrubby habit which grows to about 1 m (3 ft) in height and more in spread. In spring it bears large mauve flowers, the upper petals being marked with darker veinings. The leaves are velvety and round. It is a useful plant for coastal gardens and for those inland where dry air and cold make gardening difficult.

P. incrassatum　　NAMAQUALAND PELARGONIUM
This little pelargonium grows from a tuber which keeps it alive during the long dry period experienced in its native habitat. It has deeply indented leaves and stems about 20 cm (8 in) long, with clusters of dainty flowers of a cyclamen hue.

P. inquinans　　　　SCARLET PELARGONIUM
A large species growing to 1.25 m (4 ft) and more, even in dry districts of the eastern Cape where it gets little water. It is one of the parents of the hybrid zonal pelargoniums. This species was cultivated in glass-houses in Europe more than 250 years ago. The pink to scarlet flowers are carried in clusters on fairly long stems. The large velvety leaves measure 10 cm across. It does well in high shade.

P. (hybrid)　　　　'MORE'S VICTORY'
An attractive hybrid known as More's Victory is well worth growing. It reaches a height of about 60 cm (2 ft) and flowers in spring, and on and off during the year. It has crinkled leaves which give off a lemon scent when crushed, and dainty light-red flowers with maroon marks on two petals.

P. multicaule
Is a shrubby pelargonium which reaches a height of about 60 cm (2 ft). It has flowers of a soft mauve shade with darker markings on the top petals. The flowering time is summer.

121

◁ *Pelargonium angulosum* is a fine plant for the garden or for planting in containers

Pelargonium cucullatum
in a flower border or
the front of a shrubbery

Matricaria *(Pentzia suffruticosa)* thrives in any soil

'More's Victory' *(Pelargonium)* has flowers of a
delightful colour.

P. peltatum   IVY-LEAFED PELARGONIUM

A perennial which grows from the south-western Cape through the eastern Cape up to Natal. It is a sprawling plant which can be trained up a stake or tree trunk. It is a fine one to have hanging over a wall or dry bank or the edge of a tub. The colour of the flowers is pink with deeper markings on the two upper segments. The fleshy leaves have five points rather like those of the ivy, which accounts for its common name. It can be regarded as one of the parents of the modern popular hybrids which go under the name of "ivy-leafed pelargoniums". It was introduced into Holland by Adriaan van der Stel in about 1700.

P. salmoneum   SALMON PELARGONIUM

A decorative species from the eastern Cape which grows into a bush of about 60 cm (2 ft) in height and spread. It has big heads of bright, salmon-pink flowers measuring about 4 cm across. The leaves are rounded and indented along the edge.

P. scabrum

This species is upright in growth and has pretty leaves rather like those of an ivy in form, with deep veins. The flowers carried in little clusters are of cyclamen-pink. They are not showy but the plant is worth growing because of the pleasant lemon-scent which the leaves give off when crushed. It is quick-growing and a good background plant for gardens large and small.

P. zonale   ZONAL PELARGONIUM

A species native to the south-western Cape. This one is distinctive in the dark brownish-purple markings on the leaves. The flowers are of pretty shades of pink to carmine. It is one of the progenitors of the "zonal geraniums" which became popular in Europe many years ago.

PENTZIA GRANDIFLORA   MATRICARIA
(Matricaria grandiflora)

DISTRIBUTION: Can be seen growing along the roadsides in the western and south-western Cape.

DESCRIPTION: These plants, which grow with the cheerful abandon of a weed, make a striking show when they flower in September and October. They grow to 30-45 cm ($1\frac{1}{2}$ ft) and have feathery foliage and golden-yellow, button-like heads of flowers which look like the centre of a daisy without petals. Massed in the flower border they make a gay show, and they are also decorative when planted as a foreground to shrubs. *P. suffruticosa* is another bright species which is inclined to grow too easily, and which may therefore become a nuisance in the garden. They are, however, good plants for dry gardens where it is difficult to grow many other plants.

CULTURE: Sow the seed in March or April, and transplant the seedlings to stand about 30 cm (12 in) apart. They stand fairly severe frost.

Matricaria *(Pentzia grandiflora)* is a good plant for the dry garden

PHOENOCOMA PROLIFERA   Pink Ever-
lasting, Sewejaartjie

DISTRIBUTION: A decorative perennial plant which can be seen growing on plains and lower mountain slopes from the Cape Peninsula eastwards to Mossel Bay.

DESCRIPTION: The common name of Everlasting is very apt because the plant looks very like the everlastings. It belongs to the family of *Compositae* which embraces the daisies. The petals, which are really bracts, are papery in texture like those of the everlastings, normally pink to deep rose in colour, but occasionally white. It grows to a height of 60 cm (2 ft) and has minute dark green leaves tightly packed all along the stem. The flowers are about 4 cm across and appear mainly in spring but it produces some flowers in summer, too. This is a charming flower for long-lasting arrangements and for seaside gardens.

CULTURE: Sow seeds in spring and set the plants out about 30 cm (1 ft) apart. To look effective grow this plant in clumps in a mixed border of flowers or in front of a shrubbery. It likes a loose soil from which water drains easily and grows well even in poor soils. It stands fairly severe frost but in gardens where frosts may be very severe it should be planted so that the first rays of the winter sun do not strike the plant. It should be watered during the winter and allowed to become somewhat dry in summer.

PLECTRANTHUS   SPURFLOWER

DISTRIBUTION: Widely distributed in the four provinces of South Africa.

DESCRIPTION: The name is derived from the Greek *plectron* meaning a spur. Plectranthus belongs to the same family as the salvia. The plants have tubular flowers which end in two lips. Generally the flowers are arranged in spikes. The plants are robust in growth and need to be cut back occasionally to keep them within their allotted place in the garden. They include shrubs and herbaceous perennials. The main flowering time is summer and autumn. The species described here are good ground covers for shady places.

CULTURE: All the plectranthus are quick-growing and easy to propagate from root sections or from cuttings which root very readily. They can also be grown from seed but this is a slow way of reproducing them. They like some compost in the soil and they do best in shady places, although near the coast they do not mind full sunshine. They are tender to frost but often, if the top is frosted to the ground, the plants will come up rapidly again in spring.

P. ciliatus

This is a charming plant to use as a ground cover in the shade of trees or a building. In a mild climate its leaves cover the ground throughout the year but, in cold areas, the top-growth may be frosted back. Generally, however, the plant shoots up rapidly again in spring. The stems grow to 20-30 cm and are thickly clothed with leaves with serrated margins—green on the top surface and purple on the underside. They are 5-7 cm long and almost as broad, rough in texture with prominent veins on the underside. In late summer and early autumn the dainty spikes of flowers appear in profusion, making a misty cloud of mauve under trees where they grow.

P. nummularis   GOSSIP PLANT

This species, which occurs in the eastern Transvaal and Natal, was probably given its common name because it spreads so rapidly. It is similar to the species described above and makes an excellent ground cover in shady places.

P. verticillatus

Although when in flower this species is not as showy as the two mentioned above, it is a better plant to use as ground cover in the small garden for its leaves are smaller and neater than the others mentioned. They are only about 3 cm in length and almost the same across, with a somewhat fleshy texture and neatly serrated margins. The stems of leaves grow close to the ground and cover it completely. It roots easily and grows quickly, and generally comes up again after frost. In warm areas it is evergreen. Like the others it does best in shade or partial shade.

PSILOTHONNA   EDGING DAISY
(Gamolepis)

DISTRIBUTION: Charming little annuals native to the south-western Cape.

DESCRIPTION: They seldom grow more than 10-30 cm (4-12 in) in height and bear tiny daisies in great profusion. The colour of the flowers varies from yellow to orange, and when massed together they make a carpet of colour which is quite spectacular. The leaves are fine and feathery.

Pink Everlasting (*Phoenocoma prolifera*) does well in coastal gardens. ▷

They look particularly effective when interplanted with low-growing flowers of blue or with blue flowers behind them. The flowering season is spring.

CULTURE: They grow readily from seeds sown in March or April. Plant the seedlings about 15 cm (6 in) apart in full sunshine. They do best in friable soil and they are hardy to fairly severe frosts.

P. speciosa
Grows to about 20 cm (8 in) and bears masses of orange flowers about 18 mm across.

P. tagetes
This is a bushy little plant which reaches a height of 20-30 cm (8-12 in) and has flowers of golden-yellow. The flowers measure only 18 mm across and make a wonderful show when massed. It is a fine edging plant to a bed of blue flowers such as charieis, heliophila, anchusa or felicia.

ROELLA CILIATA   BLUE ROELLA
DISTRIBUTION: This very attractive perennial is a member of the campanula family. It grows in a few districts of the south-western Cape.

DESCRIPTION: The cup-shaped flowers measure about 5 cm across and have five broad pointed petals of a soft shade of lilac with beautiful contrasting colours half-way down the petals. First comes a narrow white band, then a broad dark blue one, and edging it on the lower side, a band of very dark blue. The flowers are carried on stems 20 cm (8 in) high clothed with many minute, needle-like, hairy leaves. Occasionally the flowers may be white or pink. Planted close together in a bed it makes a fine show but it is so beautiful that it should be grown as a pot plant where its beauty can be better appreciated. The flowering time is late spring and early summer.

CULTURE: Roella grows either from seed or root sections. The difficulty in raising plants from seed is that it takes a long time to germinate, and if it dries out during this period the seed may never germinate. It is advisable to soak the seeds for a few days, starting them off in warm water. Much quicker results will be had by planting root sections. Plant them in well-drained soil as they do not like being too wet during the summer months, and water the plants well from autumn until they have finished flowering.

126

SALVIA   SALVIA
DISTRIBUTION: These plants are widely distributed in South Africa and Rhodesia as well as in the warmer countries of the other continents.

DESCRIPTION: They include perennials for the flower border and small shrubs. The upper part of the two-lipped flower is hooded and the lower lip is sometimes the same length as the upper, sometimes shorter, and occasionally longer. The leaves vary according to the species. Our native species are not showy plants but useful for dry gardens, where it is difficult to grow many other plants.

CULTURE: They grow readily either from seed or from cuttings. Seed can be planted in spring or late summer and cuttings made in summer. Plants grown from seed may not flower for a year whilst those grown from cuttings will flower in about six months. They like full sunshine and do not demand anything special in the soil. They need to be trimmed back occasionally to keep them shapely.

S. aurea   BEACH SALVIA,
(S. africana-lutea)   STRANDSALIE
This is a shrubby plant to 90 cm (3 ft) found growing naturally in sandy places near the coast in the south-western Cape. It produces flowers of most unusual shades of terra-cotta to brown. The two-lipped flowers are carried in terminal clusters from late winter to early spring. The calyces of the flowers are shaded lime-green and dusky maroon and persist for quite a long time after the flowers drop, and are really more attractive than the flowers. They last well in water and make effective arrangements. The leaves are oval, of greyish green and carried opposite each other all the way up the stem. They give off a pleasant aromatic smell when crushed. S. africana-coerulea has flowers of pale and deep mauve.

SCABIOSA   WILD SCABIOUS
DISTRIBUTION: Are to be seen in many parts of the country. The name refers to the fact that some species were once used to relieve the irritation caused by scabies.

DESCRIPTION: These are annuals or perennials growing to about 30-60 cm (1-2 ft) in height. The flowerhead, which is referred to as the flower, really consists of numerous small flowers arranged in a disc. The flowers vary in colour from pale mauve to lavender, and occasionally white.

Wild Scabious
(Scabiosa africana) is a pretty flower for arrangements as well as the garden

Edging Daisy *(Psilothonna tagetes)* is an excellent plant for the rock garden or the front of a border

The leaves differ according to species and so does the flowering time. The species are not as pretty as the hybrids which have been evolved, but some of them are quite attractive in the garden when massed. They do well in coastal gardens.

CULTURE: They grow very readily from seed sown in spring or autumn and flower within a year. They like full sunshine and should be watered regularly, particularly during winter. They stand cold, but in districts which have severe frost they should be planted where they will be protected from the early sun in winter.

S. africana

Is a perennial which is shrubby in growth reaching a height of about 90 cm (3 ft) with flowers carried well above the foliage. The plants should be trimmed back after flowering as otherwise they are apt to become leggy.

S. angustiloba
(S. buekiana)

A perennial from the eastern Cape and further north with flower stems about 30 cm (1 ft) high. The leaves are hairy and crowded at the base of the plant. The flowering time is spring.

Tooth-leafed Selago
(*Selago serrata*)
produces its pretty
flowers in spring

SEBAEA EXACOIDES SEBAEA

DISTRIBUTION: Occurs on plains and lower mountain slopes in the south-western Cape.

DESCRIPTION: This is a dainty annual which grows to about 30 cm in height. It has few leaves and they are rounded in shape, sometimes pointed at the tip, and sometimes not. They are arranged in pairs opposite each other. The flowers are carried in dainty clusters at the ends of stems. Each flower consists of a slender tube opening to a charming face about 20 mm across, composed of five oval petals of a bright canary-yellow colour, prettily marked with two short orange lines at the centre. Massed this plant would make a delightful show in a rock-garden or at the front of a border. Two other pretty species which can be found in the Transvaal and the eastern Cape are *S. grandis* and *S. macrophylla*. They flower in late winter and spring.

CULTURE: The plants appear to do best when planted where they have some shade and a good deal of moisture. They are not suitable for hot dry gardens. Sow the seed in late summer or early autumn and transplant them to stand about 10 cm apart.

SELAGO SELAGO, BLUE HAZE

DISTRIBUTION: Perennials native to different parts of the country.

DESCRIPTION: They grow from 30-60 cm (1-2 ft) in height, and have flowers which vary in colour from white to misty mauves and lavender. The flowers are very small but carried in elegant spikes or flat clusters which are showy. Each tiny flower consists of a slender tube opening to a starry face with five petals. They are decorative plants for any part of the garden.

CULTURE: Species from the summer-rainfall region should be watered well in summer, when grown at the Cape. Those from the winter-rainfall region are tender to frost and, if grown in the summer-rainfall region, they should be planted where they are shaded for part of the day, and watered well in winter. Improve the soil by the addition of compost before planting them. They grow from seed which should be sown in spring and early summer.

S. capitellata SPIKY BLUE HAZE
A wild flower from Natal and the Transvaal which grows to 45 cm (1½ ft) and which makes a fine

128

show. In late summer it bears long plumes of minute flowers of a misty mauve hue. The leaves are tiny and needle-like, hugging the stem all the way up to the flowers. It stands moderate frost. Massed, this species makes a pretty show and it is a good plant to grow between plants of more rigid growth, such as watsonias.

S. natalensis   NATAL BLUE HAZE
Is shrubby in habit up to 60 cm (2 ft) in height and bears flat clusters of mauve flowers in summer. The tiny, needle-like leaves cover the stem thickly.

S. serrata   TOOTH-LEAFED SELAGO
A perennial which can be seen on mountain slopes in the south-western Cape, growing to a height of 60 cm (2 ft). Its little tubular flowers of lavender are closely crowded in flat heads measuring 6 cm across. The leaves are 1-2 cm in length and only 3-6 mm wide, with edges like a saw. The flowering time is mid-spring.

S. spuria   CAPE BLUE HAZE
A native of the south-western Cape with rigid stems 60 cm (2 ft) high covered with tiny, linear leaves which are larger at the base of the plant than near the top. The flowers are carried in flat clusters and are generally mauve, but they may be pink or white. The flowering time is mid-spring. These pretty flowers last well when picked.

S. thunbergii   BLUE HAZE
A charming species from the winter-rainfall area. This plant should be treated as an annual and re-grown from seed or cuttings each year. It grows to 45 cm (1½ ft). The tiny leaves, rather like those of a heath, are carried in little tufts all along the stems. It bears its flowers all along the top part of the stem in most decorative plumes which are shaded from lilac to lavender. The flowers appear in early spring and make a charming show. After flowering cut the plants back to encourage new growth or remove them after making cuttings.

S. verbenaceae
Grows to about 45 cm (1½ ft) and has dark green, oval, pointed leaves about 2.5 cm long, with sharply serrated margins. The stem is quadrilateral and deeply grooved. The little flowers are carried in flat clusters and are of a pretty shade of deep mauve.

Blue Haze *(Selago thunbergii)* has graceful plumes of flowers of misty mauve

S. wilmsii
This species is from the summer-rainfall region. It is hardy to frost and in summer it bears flat clusters of mauve flowers on rigid stems 45 cm (1½ ft) tall. The leaves are small and oval.

SENECIO   SENECIO, WILD CINERARIA
DISTRIBUTION: Includes a vast number of species distributed all over the world. There are more than 250 in South Africa.

DESCRIPTION: Some are weeds but others are worth growing in the garden. They vary in height from annuals of a few inches to climbing and twining plants. They have daisy-like flowers, usually of yellow or mauve. The leaves vary considerably according to species. The species described are all quick-growing and very showy when in flower.

CULTURE: Senecios, both annuals and perennials, grow easily from seeds, and the perennial types are also very readily propagated from cuttings. They are not particular as to soil but like an abundance of sunshine. Sow seed of spring-flowering annuals in March or April, and the summer-flowering annuals and the perennials in spring; or purchase established plants from a nursery.

S. arenarius — EDGING SENECIO

A cheerful annual which makes a colourful border. It grows to 30 cm (12 in) in height and bears heads of flowers of pinkish-mauve with yellow centres. Each flower is 2-3 cm across. The leaves are deeply indented. It is a plant of the winter-rainfall region and will stand quite severe frost. The flowering time is spring.

S. elegans — .PURPLE SENECIO, WILD CINERARIA, JACOBAEA

This very decorative species shows great variation in its habit of growth and leaves according to where it grows in nature. Near the sea, where it grows in sand, the leaves are much fleshier than when found inland. It is a perennial growing to 60 cm (2 ft) with characteristic daisy-like flowers of rosy-mauve measuring 2-3 cm across and carried in flat clusters. This species grows wild in many parts of the country and in both the summer- and winter-rainfall regions. It flowers in late winter and early spring and stands fairly severe frost. Grown close together this species makes a fine show. The best time to sow the seed is in spring to summer. It can be seen in September making sheets of colour in the sand of the Cape Flats.

This senecio *(Senecio elegans)* grows with cheerful abandon in poor soil

S. glastifolius — LARGE SENECIO

A perennial from the south-western Cape which flowers in spring; it grows to about 1.5 m (5 ft) and bears flat heads of pinky-mauve flowers with yellow centres, in masses. The individual flowers measure about 2-3 cm across. The leaves are up to 7 cm long, oval, dark green on the upper side and pale underneath, and unequally indented. This is a plant which becomes untidy at the bottom as it ages, and it should therefore be planted behind small shrubs or perennials. In large gardens it looks effective when grown in massed beds. It stands moderate frost. Sow seed or make cuttings in November to December and set plants in nursery beds for six months before planting in their permanent place in the garden. Cut plants back after their flowering season is over to keep them neat.

S. rigidus — TALL SENECIO

Is a quick-growing, tall and rangy species which is useful as a background plant or stop-gap in the large garden. It bears its yellow flowers in showy clusters in late spring and early summer.

STREPTOCARPUS — CAPE PRIMROSE

DISTRIBUTION: Most of the attractive species of

Streptocarpus is a charming plant for a shady corner

this genus grow naturally in damp places in forests, from George through the eastern Cape, and up into Natal, the eastern Transvaal and Rhodesia. The name is derived from *strepto* (twisted) and *karpos* (fruit) because the seed-pod forms a spiral.

DESCRIPTION: Some species are exceptionally beautiful when well-grown and it is worth going to some trouble to see that their requirements are satisfied. There are two different types of streptocarpus. The one kind bears a single large leaf which grows from a few centimetres to 60 cm (2 ft) or more in length. These bear many flower stems usually with small flowers. The other type has a rosette of leaves, similar to those of a primrose plant, and these usually give rise to larger individual flowers. The leaves are rough and hairy, and the flowers are tubular, opening to five broad segments of unequal size. The colour varies through shades of mauve to purple, blue, white and brick red. They have been grown in Europe for about one hundred and fifty years and many beautiful hybrids are now available.

CULTURE: It is easier to grow these plants in pots than in the open garden, as they resent being dried out by hot winds. If grown in the garden,

Large Senecio *(Senecio glastifolius)* is a stately plant

The Tall Senecio
(Senecio rigidus)
makes a gay show in
spring

plant them in leaf mould in a shady place or under trees where they are protected from drying winds, and water them well, particularly during the flowering period. They have a very shallow root-system and during periods of dry winds it is advisable to mulch the plants with leaf mould.

Most species are dormant during winter and come into active growth again in spring, to flower in summer. During their dormant period they need less water than when actively growing. They can be grown from seed sown in spring. It takes about eighteen months to produce flowering plants. As the seed is very fine it should have hardly any soil covering, but care must be taken when watering to see that the seed is not displaced by the spray or a heavy jet of water. The best way to raise them is in pots covered with a pane of glass which keeps moisture and heat in. Watering can be done by standing the whole pot in a basin of water until the soil is soaked to the top, when the pot should be taken out again. Watering in this way must be done regularly so that the soil does not dry out. When the little seedlings are 2-3 cm (1 in) high, prick them out into boxes or pots which can stand in a shaded and sheltered place.

They can also be grown from division of the roots or from the leaves. Slit the veins of the leaves on the underside, place the leaf on a bed of compost and pin it down with hairpins. Shade and water it well until roots develop.

S. dunnii RED NODDING BELLS

This species is unusual in that the colour of the flower is different from the more usual mauve. The small pendulous flowers carried in clusters are terra-cotta to brick-red on stems 30 cm (1 ft) high. The single leaf is large—about 20 cm wide and up to 45 cm in length. It is to be found near Barberton in the eastern Transvaal.

S. grandis

Can be seen in the warm forests of Natal where it gives rise to a single huge, hairy leaf which grows to about 60 cm in length and about 20 cm in width. The flowers appear in mid-summer on stems about 45 cm ($1\frac{1}{2}$ ft) tall. They are carried in clusters and are of deep mauve with darker markings in the throat.

S. primulifolius

Grows wild in forests and ravines in the eastern

Cape and north-east into the Transkei. Its flowers measure 5-6 cm across and 6-8 cm in length and are very pretty. They appear in summer and are of a deep shade of mauve, with maroon markings at the throat.

S. rexii

Grows from George eastwards into Natal, in forests or shady places. The leaves are arranged in a rosette and are hairy and rather rough and thick. The flowers are about 5 cm wide at the mouth and are jacaranda-blue in colour, with maroon streaks in the throat. The flower stem is about 15 cm (6 in) high and bears one or two flowers. The flowering time is late spring, but it may carry flowers at other seasons too. It is recorded that the leaves and roots are used by young Xhosas as love charms.

S. vandeleurii

This species grows on slopes of mountains in the eastern Transvaal, usually on rocks on shady ledges. It has a solitary leaf about 30 cm long and very broad, with a hairy and deeply furrowed surface. It bears large ivory-white flowers on stems 30 cm tall.

S. wendlandii GIANT STREPTOCARPUS

This handsome plant grows wild in Zululand. It has a huge leaf measuring about 60 cm in length and almost 30 cm in breadth, deep green on the top surface and maroon underneath. The flower stems grow to about 30 cm (1 ft) and bear as many as twenty flowers at a time. Each flower is nearly 5 cm in length and of a deep mauve-blue shade with white streaks on the bottom lobe.

SUTERA SUTERA, WILD PHLOX

DISTRIBUTION: Decorative species can be seen in different parts of the country.

DESCRIPTION: These are perennials, often shrubby in growth, with flowers somewhat like those of a phlox, and leaves which vary according to species.

CULTURE: Sutera grow easily from root sections, cuttings or from seed, which should be sown in spring or summer. When the little plants are 2-3 cm (1 in) high, plant them in nursery beds, transferring them to their place in the garden when they are about 10 cm high. For an effective show, grow them in groups in a border or in front of shrubs. They are hardy to moderate frost.

Ursinia cakilefolia
growing in rock

S. grandiflora

This species flowers in summer and autumn. The plant gives rise to flat clusters of mauve flowers, each one 2-3 cm across. The leaves are greyish-green and aromatic. It grows to about 90 cm (3 ft) and should be cut back each year after flowering to keep it from becoming untidy and to encourage new flowering stems. The flowers are pretty in arrangements. It can be raised from seed sown in spring, or from division of the roots.

S. revoluta

Is a bushy little perennial growing to about 30 cm (1 ft) with a mass of little mauve flowers measuring less than 12 mm across. The leaves are shiny, 2-3 cm long and 6 mm wide. Its natural habitat is the winter-rainfall region. Sow the seed in spring or summer.

URSINIA   Ursinia

DISTRIBUTION: Although species of ursinias are to be found growing wild in other parts of South Africa, most of the decorative ones are from the south-western Cape.

DESCRIPTION: This genus includes both annuals and perennials. All of them grow as readily as weeds and they make a gay show for weeks in late winter and early spring. With these bright little flowers only too anxious to grow, nobody should complain about not being able to have a colourful garden at this time of the year. They endure cold, drought, poor soil and neglect. Most of them bear orange or yellow daisy-like flowers and have attractive feathery fern-like foliage.

CULTURE: Although ursinias grow readily in any soil, sturdier plants with finer flowers will be produced in gardens where the soil has been improved by the addition of some humus. Seed should be sown in March or April to produce a brilliant display from July to September. Although these hardy plants will tolerate rather dry growing conditions they will produce far more flowers if they are watered fairly regularly during their growing period. They should be grown in full sunshine as the flowers do not open properly in a shady place. Because the flowers turn their faces towards the sun, it is advisable to set the plants out in the garden so that the flowers can be viewed from the direction towards which they turn. Some species stand quite considerable frost.

U. anethoides

Is a shrubby annual growing to about 45 cm (1½ ft) with flowers measuring 2-3 cm across and sometimes more. The flowers have a chocolate to purple blotch at the base of each petal, forming a ring around the orange centre of the flower.

U. anthemoides

Is a handsome little annual growing to 30 cm (1 ft) or a little more, with flowers about 5 cm across. The petals are orange at the top with a brownish blotch at the base. Their backs are tinged with brown on the underside.

U. cakilefolia

This is a gay annual which grows to about 45 cm (1½ ft) and has flowers 2-3 cm across, coloured bright orange, with gleaming centres like dark green buttons. It is decorative and very easy to grow. It flowers from late July to September. This species stands considerable frost.

U. calenduliflora

Although it is small in stature this is one of the showiest of the ursinias. The flowers are a gleaming orange and stand well above the foliage at a height of about 30 cm (1 ft) from the ground. The flowers seldom measure more than 2-3 cm across. Massed, it makes a fine border or bedding plant.

U. chrysanthemoides var geyeri   CORAL URSINIA

This charming little perennial grows to 30 cm (1 ft) and bears flowers of a delightful and unusual shade of coral-red. They make a lovely show when massed in front of blue flowers such as anchusa. It flowers from August to October. Although this is a perennial it seldom bears many flowers after the second year, and it is therefore advisable to raise new plants each year. Sow the seed in late spring or summer and transplant the seedlings to stand 10-15 cm apart.

U. crithmoides

Is a robust and decorative perennial which reaches a height of 60 cm (2 ft) and bears masses of bright yellow flowers 2-3 cm across, in September. It is sensitive to severe frost.

U. sericea   LACELEAF URSINIA

This ursinia is a perennial with most attractive lacy, silvery foliage and canary-yellow flowers. It grows to 60 cm (2 ft) in height and is a splendid edging plant for a long drive. Its pleasing grey foliage makes it a good plant to use anywhere to highlight the garden. The flowers which appear in September are pretty, and stand well above the leaves.

Ursinia crithmoides bears gay yellow flowers in masses

Coral Ursinia (*Ursinia* ▷ *chrysanthemoides* var. *geyeri)* has flowers of a charming and unusual shade

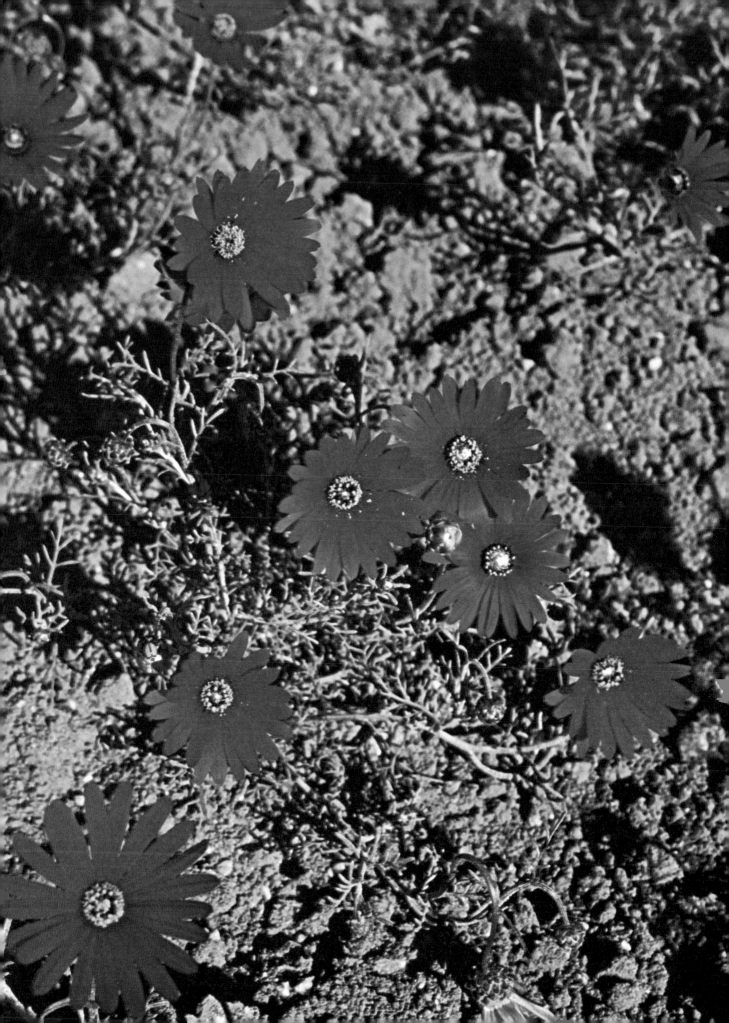

Laceleaf Ursinia (*Ursinia sericea*) is a shrubby and decorative plant

U. speciosa

Is an annual which makes the garden bright in late winter and early spring. It reaches a height of 30 cm (1 ft) and has flowers of different colours, but the predominating shades are yellow to orange. The flowers are 2-4 cm across.

VELLOZIA RETINERVIS   MONKEY'S TAIL
(New name is *Xerophyta retinervis*)

DISTRIBUTION: Can be found in parts of the Transvaal, from Pretoria to the north and east.

DESCRIPTION: When not in flower the plants have curious blackened-looking stumps of no decorative value. From the tops of these stumps arise slender, grass-like leaves about 25 cm in length, and, in November, when the flowers appear, the plant becomes decorative for a short time. The six-petalled flowers carried on short-wiry stems are of a charming shade of lilac and give off a faint scent of vanilla.

CULTURE: They stand fairly sharp frost and drought and do not seem to mind poor soil.

136

VERNONIA   WILD HELIOTROPE

DISTRIBUTION: These can be seen in many parts of the country except the Karoo and the south-western Cape.

DESCRIPTION: They include annuals, perennials and shrubs, often of straggly growth. Only two or three species are worth a place in the garden.

CULTURE: Sow seed in spring or late summer, or make cuttings of the perennial types in summer. They stand a fair amount of frost and lack of water, but should be watered regularly during their growing and flowering periods.

V. capensis
(*V. pinifolia*)
Grows to about 60 cm (2 ft) in height and has greyish-green leaves. Clusters of tiny mauve to purple flowers appear at the ends of the stems in late spring. Certain Bantu tribes are said to burn the plant, believing that the smoke can divert hailstorms!

V. hirsuta
This species reaches a height of 60 cm (2 ft) and bears small clusters of purple flowers in late spring. The leaves are oval and pointed. It is a good background plant for the flower border.

V. natalensis
Bears trailing stems covered with silvery leaves about 7 cm long and 2-3 cm wide. The tiny deep mauve flowers are carried at the ends of the stems in little clusters. This is a good plant for the rock-garden.

WAHLENBERGIA   WILD BLUEBELL
DISTRIBUTION: These plants grow naturally from the western Cape eastwards into Natal and in the Transvaal. Few are worth a place in the garden.

DESCRIPTION: They are dainty plants—members of the campanula family—and bear little flowers of cup or bell-like form, often with a widely open face. The leaves vary according to species.

CULTURE: Species from the western Cape should be watered well in autumn and winter when they are coming into flower. Plant them where they are shaded from the heat of the day and give them additional protection in gardens where frosts are severe, as they are not hardy to cold.

W. capensis   CAPE BELLFLOWER
This is a charming little annual with flowers

carried on stems 30 cm (1 ft) high. The cup-like flower has five petals. They are jacaranda-blue in colour with dark markings at the centre. The small, slender, oval leaves are finely toothed. Sow the seed in March for flowers in August and September.

W. rivularis   BELLFLOWER
Is a tall-growing perennial to 60 cm (2 ft) which, if left in one place, will form dense clumps. It grows naturally in the shade at the edge of forests where there is a good deal of light, but little direct sun. The flowers, which open wide to five oval pointed petals, are a delightful shade of mauvy-blue in colour. The leaves are small, oval and pointed at the tips. It flowers in summer and can be raised from seed sown in spring, or from root sections.

W. zeyheri
Occurs from near the coast in the eastern Cape to high mountain slopes of the Drakensberg. The flowering time varies according to habitat. Near the coast the flowers appear in late winter, whilst on cold mountain slopes they appear in summer. It is hardy to sharp frost and bears pretty flowers of lavender-blue.

WALAFRIDA CINEREA
DISTRIBUTION: Can be found growing in fields in the eastern Cape.

DESCRIPTION: This is a perennial plant growing to 1.25 m (4 ft) in height. It bears dense clusters of tiny flowers, each one composed of a slender tube opening to a starry face. The colours of the flowers are usually lilac, but occasionally white. The leaves are short and needle-like and carried in little whorls up the stem. The main flowering time is winter, but some flowers appear at other seasons, too.

CULTURE: Sow the seed in spring. This plant stands drought but it is not hardy to much frost, and in inland gardens it should be planted where it gets some shade during the hottest part of the day.

ZALUZIANSKYA   DRUMSTICKS
DISTRIBUTION: Grows naturally in the south-western Cape and east into Natal, and in the Transvaal.

DESCRIPTION: It is a pity that these charming little flowers have such a forbidding botanical name. They are named after a Polish botanist of the sixteenth century. The most decorative species is worth a place in the garden as the flowers, although they are tiny, make a beautiful show when massed. The flowers which are less than 12 mm across, are composed of a slender tube opening to a flat face with five petals, each of which is deeply notched at the tip. The colours of the flowers are mauve, lilac, white or yellow. Often they have a centre stained yellow or orange. They flourish in sandy soil and are excellent for coastal gardens.

CULTURE: This depends upon the area of their origin. The species from the western Cape should be sown in March or April and watered regularly until flowering time, which is late winter and early spring. Species from other parts of the country require more water in summer. They can be raised from seed sown in spring. The plants grow in friable soil and in their natural habitat they can be found growing in abundance in sandy soil.

Z. maritima
This is a perennial which grows wild in the eastern Cape, the Transkei, Natal and the Transvaal. It reaches a height of 30 cm (1 ft) and bears flowers which give off a strong, sweet scent at night. It is worth growing near a window just for its scent, as it is of little decorative value in the garden. The flowering time is summer.

Z. villosa
Is a charming little annual growing to about 15 cm (6 in) with masses of mauve, lilac or white flowers, usually with a yellow or orange spot in the centre. The flowering time is late winter and early spring. They can be seen growing in sand near the coast in the western Cape and further inland, in dry districts. It is difficult to believe that anything so fragile and delicate in appearance can grow and flower under such harsh conditions, but they seed themselves freely and make a carpet of colour. The flowers give off a rather delightful aromatic scent.

V

Part V
Bulbs

Bulbs

GROWING SOUTH AFRICAN BULBS

Some of the easiest flowers to grow are those which develop from bulbs, and gardeners who dislike sowing seeds and transplanting and caring for seedlings will enjoy handling bulbs. Because of their size and the fact that they grow more readily and with less attention than seedlings, they make gardening very much easier. Fortunately also, some of the most beautiful of our wild flowers are those which grow from bulbs, and it is not surprising that these were among the first plants to be taken to Europe and grown there in gardens and greenhouses almost 300 years ago.

South African bulbs have now spread right around the globe, and one will find them flowering in gardens in many countries on all continents. Many of them are cultivated out-of-doors in the Northern Hemisphere, being planted there in spring for flowers in summer, whereas they would, in the Southern Hemisphere, be planted in late summer for flowers in spring.

Several species of bulbs from the south-western Cape were being cultivated in Holland by the year 1630—that is some years before the establishment of the first settlement at the Cape. In the late seventeenth century and throughout the eighteenth century what were known as "Cape bulbs" were highly prized and in great demand amongst gardeners in England, and elsewhere in Europe. At least one species of many of the genera mentioned in this section of the book were grown in England, France or Holland two hundred years ago.

In this section are included plants with fleshy or woody roots and rhizomes as well as true bulbs and corms. It is not vitally important that the gardener should know the differences between these, but some gardeners may like to have some idea as to what these different terms mean and definitions are therefore given.

A true bulb is a structure containing the immature plant surrounded by scales, which are often fleshy, and which protect it and store food for its use when it starts developing. It should not be stored out of the ground in a dry state. New bulblets develop underground from the one planted. A corm is a piece of swollen underground stem which is also a storehouse of food, but in this case the structure is solid and can be stored out of the ground in a dry state without deteriorating. New corms form on the old corms. A rhizome is a creeping thickened underground stem which is also a storehouse of food. It sends up flower and leaf stalks from growth buds on the top, and roots develop beneath it. A tuber is a fleshy underground stem which does not elongate as does a rhizome. It develops from "eyes" which can be removed with a portion of the tuber for making new plants. The most familiar examples of tubers are potatoes and dahlias. In addition many plants have fleshy or woody roots. When storing any of the bulbous plants which are not corms care must be taken to see that they do not dry out for a long period, as this will inhibit their growth.

NATURE OF ROOTSTOCK OF PLANTS IN THIS SECTION

Bulb	Corm	Rhizome, Tuber or Fleshy or Woody Roots
Albuca	Anapalina	Agapanthus
Amaryllis	Babiana	Aristea
Ammocharis	Chasmanthe	Bobartia
Boophane	Crocosmia	Bulbine
Brunsvigia	Dierama	Bulbinella
Crinum	Freesia	Clivia
Cyrtanthus	Geisshorrhiza	Dietes
Galtonia	Gladiolus	Dilatris
Haemanthus	Hesperantha	Eucomis
Lachenalia	Homeria	Gloriosa
Nerine	Homoglossum	Kniphofia
Ornithogalum	Ixia	Lanaria
Scilla	Lapeirousia	Littonia
Tulbaghia	Moraea	Satyrium
Vallota	Romulea	Schizostylis
Veltheimia	Sparaxis	Strelitzia
	Spiloxene	Tulbaghia
	Synnotia	Zantedeschia (arum)
	Tritonia	
	Watsonia	

POTS AND WINDOW-BOXES

A great many of our bulbs produce flowers which are held in great esteem as pot plants and are grown by the million for this purpose in Europe and America. It seems strange, therefore, that so few South Africans should be aware of the beauty of their wildings. Those who live in flats and have no ground for gardening can have a bright show of colour in window-boxes and pots by planting many of the bulbs mentioned in this section of the book.

When grown in containers the same remarks about when and how to plant them should be observed as if they were to be grown in the garden. If they are sun-lovers they will do well in containers only if they have adequate sun and, if they are plants which like to be planted high in the ground, they should be planted in the same way in pots. When grown in containers plants generally need to be watered more often than when grown in the open ground as there is less soil around them and this dries out more quickly than would soil in the garden. Furthermore, it must be remembered that clay pots dry out rapidly because of evaporation through their sides. Where drying winds prevail it is advisable to use pots made of plastic or asbestos, as these keep the soil damp for longer periods. When plants growing in pots become dormant, the pots can be removed from their position in the house or patio and stored in an out-of-the-way corner of the garden or a shed, where they can be watered occasionally until the next growing season. Then the bulbs may be re-planted in fresh soil or given fertilizer and watered regularly once more to encourage new growth.

As there are bulbs which flower at different seasons of the year it is possible to have a succession of plants coming into flower in containers.

141

SPRING-FLOWERING BULBS:

Most of these lovely plants are native to that part of South Africa which has its rain from autumn to spring and which is dry and hot during the summer months. They can, however, be grown very successfully in regions with a dry winter if they are watered regularly during their growing period which is from March to October. When grown in regions which are hot and dry during winter many of the spring-flowering bulbs from the winter-rainfall region do better if they are planted where they have some shade during the hottest hours of the day. Plant them where a tree, shrubs or a wall will shade them for a part of the afternoon but avoid heavy shade as some of them open their flowers properly only when the light is bright.

It is not essential to lift them when they become dormant in summer but, if the soil where they are growing does not allow of good drainage and if the rainfall is heavy in summer and the plants do not resent being moved, as some do, then lift and store them, dry, in boxes if they are corms, and under soil, with occasional watering, if they are not.

Plant the spring-flowering bulbs in February and March and water them well and regularly until the foliage has died down after flowering is over in spring.

SUMMER-FLOWERING BULBS:

Most of these, as one would expect, grow naturally in those parts of Southern Africa where the rains fall in summer and where the autumn to spring period is dry. The plants start into growth in spring, flower in summer, and many of them become dormant at the beginning of autumn and need little water from then until spring, when new growth starts. These bulbs should be planted at the end of winter or early in spring (August to October) and watered regularly until the foliage has died down after flowering. They can then be left rather dry until the following spring. Although the rainfall in the south-western Cape is fairly high in winter it does not cause damage to these bulbs from the summer-rainfall region which are dormant at this time, and they may therefore be left in the ground for several years until they become overcrowded.

HOW TO TREAT BULBS WHEN DORMANT:

Most, but not all, of the plants described in the pages which follow are dormant for a certain period of the year—some for a very short time, a month or so, and some for two or three months or more. These plants all follow the same pattern. At a certain season of the year the plants which have been dormant start into growth; many of them will do this even though the bulbs may be out of the ground. They will not, however, reach flowering stage if they are not planted. After they have flowered, the leaves of most bulbs begin to yellow. This may be a month or more after the flowers have faded and is a sign that they are going into a state of dormancy. When this happens the bulbs should be given less water, and finally, when the leaves have died down completely, the bulb can be allowed to dry off, and those with corms may be lifted and stored in boxes until the next growing season. If the ground in which the bulbs are growing is required for other plants before the foliage has died down, transplant the bulbs with their foliage into another part of the garden, taking care to remove a large chunk of earth with each plant so as not to disturb the roots too much. Water the transplanted plants regularly until the foliage has turned yellow. When it has disappeared a little water should be given occasionally until new growth starts, when more frequent watering will again be necessary.

Fleshy bulbs and roots should, however, never be allowed to dry out completely even when the top growth has disappeared. They should be left in the same place in the garden or pot, or else lifted and stored in earth in a shed or an out-of-the-way part of the garden. When plants are grown in pots it is better to be on the safe side, and if you are not certain whether the rootstock can stand being quite dry, sink the pot up to its rim in a corner of the garden which is seldom watered rather than leave it to dry out completely in a shed.

Gardeners who live in an area where the rainfall is heavy should, where possible, plant bulbs in ground which drains well, i.e. friable soil and not clay. Clay can be made lighter by the addition of compost and coarse sand, or drainage can be improved by making drainage channels beneath the bed. If this is done most bulbs will not be affected by water during their dormant season.

Lachenalia, however, seem to have a tendency to rot more quickly than many others, and it is a good idea, therefore, to plant them in large pots which can be sunk into the garden to make a show in spring, and to lift the pots after the flowers have faded, and to store them in an outhouse, watering them very occasionally during their dormant period which lasts until January.

There are few parts of Southern Africa where the rainfall is such that it is likely to cause bulbs to rot when they are left in the ground during their dormant period, and as so many bulbs multiply well and thrive only if left in the ground for several years, I feel that it is better to leave them in the ground than to move them, unless one is certain that they rot easily, or unless they are planted near other plants which need a lot of water.

PLANTS WHICH RETAIN THEIR LEAVES:

Most bulbs have a definite period of rest after the leaves have disappeared and before the new growth starts but some plants retain their leaves throughout the year. This means that they are in active growth, but it does not mean that they need the same attention throughout the year. Generally plants need more water and food when they are coming into flower than at other times. It is sometimes puzzling to know when to transplant or divide these evergreen subjects. The best rule to follow is to divide and replant them shortly after they have flowered.

BULBS WHICH DO NOT FOLLOW THE RULES:

Most bulbs produce their leaves first, and when these are well-grown they come into flower. Later, when the flowers have faded, the leaves begin to wither and finally disappear. There are, however, a few bulbs which do not follow this pattern of growth. These bulbs do not produce flowers whilst they have leaves, but send up a flower stem from the bare earth, and their leaves emerge whilst they are in flower or after the flowers have faded. The leaves persist for three or four months, or longer, and then they disappear again. The best time to divide such plants is after the leaves have died down and before the flower shoots appear. The following are some plants of this nature which should be planted in late spring or early summer (November to January), as they flower between

January and March: belladonna lily (*Amaryllis belladonna*); Malagas lily (*Cybistetes longifolia*); sore-eye flower (*Boophane guttata*); candelabra flower (*Brunsvigia orientalis*); April fool (*Haemanthus coccineus*) and nerina (*Nerine sarniensis*). Some of these bulbs, such as the belladonna lily and nerina, differ in another way, inasmuch as they produce their flowers at the end of the dry season in their natural habitat, whereas most bulbs produce their flowers during or towards the end of the rainy season.

PREPARING THE GROUND FOR BULBS:

Those who have seen our bulbous plants growing naturally in the veld must have marvelled at the beautiful flowers produced from earth often quite dry and so hard that it would require a pick-axe to dig into it. To me, one of nature's marvels is the belladonna lily. That such fragile loveliness and pure elegance can arise from hard, barren, dry earth is astonishing. Many South African bulbs will grow well and produce beautiful flowers in poor soil, but most of them produce more and better flowers if the soil is improved by the addition of compost or leaf mould. It is not essential to do anything to the soil before planting, but those who aspire to have finer plants will find that a little improvement of the soil, where necessary, will pay dividends. Improving the soil is essential in the case of those plants which do not like being moved and which should therefore grow in the same place for several years. Some of these plants do not flower for a year or two after they have been moved, and for this reason it is advisable to prepare the ground properly before planting and then to leave them to grow and multiply for several years.

In gardens where moles are a menace, it is advisable to take precautions to check their depredations in beds of bulbs. The easiest way to protect bulbs from them is to sink netting-wire with a fairly fine mesh (chicken-netting) beneath the ground, allowing the edges of the netting to project above the ground a little. This serves also to demarcate the area where the bulbs are growing and thus ensure that they are not accidentally dug up or damaged through having a fork rammed into them during their period of dormancy, when there may be no leaves above ground to indicate where the bulbs have been planted. These precautions are necessary only with some of the smaller bulbs, as moles do not eat the large bul-

bous or fleshy roots, such as those of arums, agapanthus, belladonna lily and many others.

WHERE TO PLANT BULBS:

The plants which grow from bulbs vary considerably in height and they can be used in any
part of the garden. Those with small flowers may
be planted in cracks between paving stones of the
path or patio, in a retaining wall, massed in the
front of a border, in a rock-garden, or along the
sides of a path. These small ones are also ideal
for pots or window-boxes. Tall ones make fine
background plants in the flower border and they
also look effective planted in colonies or groups
in front of, or between shrubs in a shrub border.
Many of the spring-flowering bulbs come from
the south-western Cape where the intensity of
the light is often relieved by the clouds and rain
which occur during their growing months, and
they seem to perform better in districts which
have bright hot days during autumn to spring if
they are shaded for part of the day. Partial shade
is better than full shade as some of them open
their flowers properly only when the light is
bright.

FROST:

The remarks about frost-damage on page 30
should be read by those who live in areas which
experience frost. Generally it can be assumed that
plants which are dormant in winter will not be
damaged by frost.

DEPTH TO PLANT:

When dealing with exotic bulbs there is a general
rule that they should be planted under the soil to
a depth equal to twice the diameter of the bulb.
This rule may be applied to our small bulbs, but
not to the large ones, for some of the plants with
huge bulbs do best if the bulb is planted so that
its top is either level with or just above the soil.
In a few cases they grow well when the upper
half of the bulb is exposed above the soil. In the
pages which follow the depth to plant the bulbs
is indicated.

STORING BULBS:

The only ones which can be safely stored in a
completely dry state are corms. They are listed
at the beginning of this section of the book. Also,

in the descriptions which follow, it is stated
whether the plant has a corm, bulb or fleshy root.
Plants growing from corms may be lifted when the
leaves have died down. Be careful when digging
out the corms as often there are tiny cormlets
attached to the parent ones which may be lost
in the soil when lifting. It is best to lift them with
a spade of earth and to place this in a shady place
until the earth is quite dry and crumbly. One can
then spread it out and pick out all the corms.
These may be stored in boxes until the next planting season. It is advisable to label all the boxes
clearly, as it is not easy to remember which are
which, when it comes to planting them once more.

Plants with fleshy bulbs and fibrous or fleshy
roots or rhizomes cannot be stored dry, but they
can be lifted after the foliage has died down and
then stored in soil, either in pots or boxes in a
shed or else in a corner of the garden until they
are due to start into growth once more. During
their period of dormancy they should be watered
occasionally.

Many bulbs do not like being moved and, in
the pages which follow, it is stated in the description of the plant where this is the case.

DIVIDING BULBS:

To keep plants which grow from rhizomes, tubers,
fleshy roots, bulbs or corms healthy and vigorous
it is necessary to divide them occasionally, as
each year they form additional underground
growth and they may eventually be so crowded
as to produce poor flowers. When dividing appears
to be necessary, lift the whole plant and remove
the small bulbs and corms of those which grow
from bulbs or corms. Some of them produce only
a few new ones, whilst others are prolific in their
increase and grow as many as a hundred spawn
in a couple of years. These little bulbs or corms
become detached from the parent plant very
easily and care must be taken when lifting to
ensure that they are not left in the ground.
Generally it is better to plant the small bulbs and
corms in specially prepared nursery beds or boxes
of soil where they can grow for a year or two until
they reach flowering size, when they can be
planted in the garden. Some of them produce
flowers in a year whilst others need two or three
years before they produce good flowers. Those
plants which grow from rhizomes can be in-
creased by lifting the rhizomes and cutting
through them with a sharp knife or spade to make

two or more new plants. Some rhizomes will yield several plants after three or four years whilst others are slow to increase. Plants which grow from tubers are multiplied by cutting out "eyes" with a piece of tuber and planting these, as one does with potatoes. Those with a fleshy root-stock are easily divided by cutting through the whole mass of roots with a spade or sharp knife. Each root segment or division is a plant in itself, capable of producing new flowers in its proper flowering season.

The correct time to lift and divide plants is when they are dormant, i.e. after the leaves have died down, and before new top-growth starts. There are some plants, such as some species of agapanthus, which are evergreen. Such plants should be divided after their flowering season, and six months before they are due to flower again.

GROWING BULBS FROM SEED:

Increasing your stock of bulbs from seed requires more patience than growing them from offsets (baby bulbs or corms), but by sowing seeds one can produce a much larger number of bulbs at a comparatively low cost. Plants grown from seed are not always exactly the same as their parents but the natural hybrid which may result is not necessarily less attractive. It may be even prettier.

Some of them grow very easily from seed and the same rules about sowing and care should be followed as is given in the section dealing with annuals and perennials. The important point to remember when growing them from seed is that they must be kept moist all through their growing season and allowed to become somewhat dry when the plant normally goes into a period of dormancy. If it happens to be a plant which does not have a dormant period the seedling should be watered throughout the year.

As a general rule, seeds of the bulbs which flower in spring should be sown in February or March, whilst seed of those which flower in summer may be sown in late summer or early spring. Seeds of some of the small bulbous plants, such as sparaxis and freesias, often produce flowers within eight months, but generally seeds produce flowering plants only after a full year has elapsed and after their second season of growth (roughly eighteen months after sowing). Some take two to four years from the time seed is sown until flowers appear.

During their months of active growth, the soil in the seed beds or boxes should not be allowed to dry out. If sown in beds, the addition of peat to the soil, and a light mulch of straw, will help to keep the soil moist, and, if they are being grown in pots or boxes, a sheet of glass over the box and overhead shade will keep the soil moist.

Some of the big bulbs, such as crinums, produce large seed which should be sown whilst it is green. In some cases the seed starts to grow in this state even before it has dropped from the parent plant. Such seed can be grown in nursery beds or boxes, or it can be planted in the soil next to the parent plant.

AGAPANTHUS AGAPANTHUS, BLOULELIE
DISTRIBUTION: Grow naturally in many parts of the country, from sea-level to high mountain slopes.

This is one of the many indigenous plants used by the Bantu people in magic and medicine. It was common for a Xhosa bride to wear pieces of the root as a necklace to ensure fertility and easy childbirth, and the roots are pounded up to provide medicine for various disorders.

DESCRIPTION: These handsome flowers which were once prolific and commonly found on a walk in the countryside, even a generation ago, are now seldom encountered in their natural habitat except in inaccessible places. Fortunately, however, they have been popular with gardeners for a long time and some species and hybrids can be found in gardens throughout the country. Agapanthus may be divided into two groups according to the type of flowers they bear. At the one extreme there are those with flowers having short tubes with perianth segments spreading out widely, and at the other are those with long tubes and perianth segments which do not spread much. They may also be divided according to whether they are evergreen or deciduous. The evergreen species may have their leaves killed by frost but the plant generally survives. The deciduous species lose their leaves for a short period and are more hardy to cold and therefore best suited to gardens where winters are severe.

Evergreen species occur naturally in the Cape Peninsula and east into the Transkei, whilst the deciduous ones are found from the Transkei north through Natal and Lesotho into the Transvaal. The evergreen species, with the exception of *A. walshii* have spreading perianth segments; the

deciduous ones include types with flowers having long or short tubes and narrow or open flowers.

Agapanthus vary in height considerably from 30-150 cm. (1-5 ft) and the size of the flowerheads varies too. The most handsome of them have masses of flowers on strong stems making a beautiful globular head. The flowerheads last for a long time and even when the flowers drop the heads remain decorative for some time. The leaves are smooth and blade-like and attractive at all times. The flowerheads are splendid in large arrangements and the individual flowers can be detached to make charming small table arrangements, or combined with other small flowers to make posies.

It is not surprising that this should have been one of the first South African plants to be grown in Europe. There is a reference dating back to

1679 where it is described as having flowered in a garden in Europe. It is recorded in a catalogue of plants of the Leyden Botanic Gardens dated 1687, and there is also a record dated 1692 stating that it had flowered in the Royal Garden at Hampton Court. Agapanthus are grown today not only in the south of England but in many other parts of Europe and America, Australia, New Zealand and South America. Beautiful hybrids have been raised in other countries and it is a pity that South Africans have not been more active in this field.

Recently the whole genus has been studied and re-classified and readers who wish to make a collection of agapanthus should refer to this work on agapanthus by Frances Leighton, produced as Supplementary Volume No. IV of the Journal of South African Botany. The notes on species which follow are based on this work.

CULTURE: Agapanthus are the most rewarding and adaptable summer-flowering plants. In their natural habitat they are to be found at different altitudes, but always in places where the rainfall is more than 500 mm a year. They grow from a fleshy rootstock and have masses of big fleshy roots which enable them to stand long periods without water. The roots multiply from year to year, giving rise to new plants and eventually the plants begin to suffer through being overcrowded. For this reason the clumps which they form should be lifted every few years and divided.

Agapanthus will grow in any kind of soil—clay, sand or gravel, but where the soil is poor, to have good results for several years, it is advisable to prepare the soil before planting by digging holes or trenches to a depth of 30-45 cm. (1-1½ft) and incorporating some compost and manure in the bottom with soil previously removed. Set the plants about 45-60 cm (1½-2 ft) apart. They are all hardy to frost and the deciduous ones will stand very severe frost. Although they tolerate drought, they flower better if watered during the spring and summer when they form their flowers. When they became overcrowded, lift them and cut through the root-mass with a spade or sharp knife and replant in soil to which compost has been added.

Agapanthus grow in full sunshine but they also grow and flower well in partial shade and, as they can stand the competition of the roots of trees, they are ideal plants to grow under large spreading trees, providing that they are not planted near the trunk where the shade may be too dense for them. They can be grown at the back of the flower border, in front of a shrub border, along a drive, or massed to form colonies in a large garden. They are also good plants to use in tubs on a patio or terrace. These handsome plants should also be widely planted along our national roads in districts where climatic conditions are suitable.

A. africanus AGAPANTHUS
(A. umbellatus)
Can be found growing from sea-level to near the tops of mountains in the Cape Peninsula and eastwards towards Mossel Bay. It is evergreen with flowering stems of about 60 cm (2 ft) and flowers of deep blue, although they may sometimes be rather pale. There is also a white form. *A. walshii* is very similar; it has not yet been decided whether this is indeed a separate species.

A. campanulatus BELL AGAPANTHUS
This is a hardy deciduous species native to the cold areas of the eastern Cape near Matatiele and spreading further north into Lesotho and the highlands of Natal and the eastern part of the Orange Free State. It varies in height from about 45-60 cm (1½-2 ft) and more, with flowers of pale or deep blue. The perianth segments are spreading.

A subspecies *A. campanulatus* subsp. *patens* now takes the place of the species formerly listed separately as *A. patens*.

A. caulescens AGAPANTHUS
This rather tall species occurs in the highlands of Natal, Swaziland and the Transvaal. It reaches a height of 60-120 cm (2-4 ft) and has flowers with an open face in well shaped heads, *A. coddii* is similar to the species just described.

A. comptonii
An evergreen species growing to about 60 cm (2 ft) or more which occurs in the eastern Cape near East London. Its flowerhead is not as full as that of some of the other species and it flowers a little later in the year, seldom bearing flowers before January or February.

A. dyeri
Grows wild in the Transvaal producing small heads of flowers on stems about 45 cm (1½ ft) tall, but in cultivation it may grow to a greater height. The flowers are fairly open and tend to droop over.

A. inapertus DROOPING AGAPANTHUS
This species from the mountains of the eastern and northern Transvaal is deciduous. It is very different in form from the species and hybrids usually seen in gardens but well worth including because, although the flowerhead is not as showy, the deep blue colour of the flower makes it a good addition to the garden. It is a tall-growing species reaching about 2 m (5-6 ft) with flowers which do not open widely and which hang down or droop.

A. praecox COMMON AGAPANTHUS
An evergreen species found mostly in the eastern Cape with rounded heads of flowers with spreading segments. The height is variable. The following sub-species have been noted: subsp. *praecox* (A. umbellatus) with a large rounded head of flowers on stems up to 90 cm (3 ft) and more; subsp. *orientalis (A. orientalis)* with shorter

leaves and denser heads of flowers. This is the agapanthus most commonly found in gardens all over the country. It grows to 90 cm (3 ft) and more in height and has large, showy heads of flowers of mid-blue. There is also a white form but this is known only in cultivation. Subsp. *minimus (A. longispathus)* is another species from the eastern Cape. It is much smaller both in height and in the flowerhead than the others and the flowers are of a pale colour.

ALBUCA   ALBUCA

DISTRIBUTION: Occur from the south-western Cape eastwards into Natal and further north.

DESCRIPTION: These are charming flowers for pots and window-boxes where they can be seen at eye-level. In the garden their beauty is apt to be overlooked because the flowers are often green or shaded with green which does not show up well when they are planted in a mixed border of flowers. Each flower is made up of three inner petals which are close together forming a loose tube and three outer ones which curve out and over the inner ones. The colours are pale green,

mustard, yellow and white. Each stem carries several flowers at a time.

CULTURE: Plant them in soil which drains well, as the bulbs seem to like being dry when they are dormant. They grow well even in poor soil but undoubtedly do better in soil to which some compost has been added. Set the bulbs 3-5 cm (1-2 in) below soil-level and about 10-15 cm (4-6 in) apart. The best time to plant the spring-flowering species is in February to March; summer-flowering ones may be planted in spring.

A. canadensis   SENTRY-IN-THE-BOX, GELDBEURSIE

Grows to about 45 cm (1½ ft) and bears heads of yellow flowers prettily marked with a green band down the centre of the three outer petals. The central petals are mustard-yellow. The flowering time of this species is spring.

A. circinata   COASTAL ALBUCA

Grows in sandy soil along the coast in the eastern Cape. The graceful flowers of shades of green and pale mustard are very effective and worth grow-

Sentry-in-the-box
(*Albuca canadensis*).
A dainty flower for
pots or window-boxes

Belladonna Lily
(*Amaryllis belladonna*)
is one of the most
beautiful plants of
Southern African and
one of the easiest to
grow

ing more widely in gardens. They have a faint, sweet scent. This species flowers in summer.

A. longifolia

Is common in the eastern Cape near East London. It has a large bulb from which arise long, slender leaves almost 60 cm long. The flowering stem grows to about 30 cm (1 ft) and bears a conical head of upright flowers which are white banded with green.

AMARYLLIS BELLADONNA   Belladonna Lily, March Lily

DISTRIBUTION: This lovely flower is native to the south-western Cape.

DESCRIPTION: The belladonna lily is one of the most beautiful of South African flowers and also one of the easiest to grow. Like the agapanthus, it is tolerant of very different kinds of growing conditions. It grows in deep shade under trees and in full sunlight; in hot, dry places and in cool gardens. It produces its lovely flowers even when grown in hard, uncultivated soil. The flowers emerge when the plant is bare of leaves and it is an astonishing sight to find a host of belladonna lilies where the ground was quite bare only a few days previously. Once the bud, enclosed by its sheath, emerges from the ground in February or March, the stem rises quickly to a height of about 45 cm (1½ ft). The large trumpet-shaped flowers are carried in handsome clusters and vary in colour from gleaming white through delicate shades of shell-pink to rose. Often flowers are flushed with several shades of pink. The flowers last well when cut and it is surprising that they have not been more extensively grown for florists. Beautiful hybrids have been evolved in other countries and it seems a pity that we in Southern Africa do not do more hybridizing of our lovely wild flowers.

The leaves, which are narrow and strap-shaped, appear with, or just after the flowers, and remain green through the winter, disappearing again in late spring when the bulbs become dormant. Because there is then nothing to show where the bulbs have been planted, it is advisable to mark their position clearly to obviate their being damaged, should the garden be dug over.

These lovely flowers can be grown in colonies under trees, interplanted with other flowers in the flower border, or planted in groups in front of shrubs. They also make good pot or tub plants.

They have been crossed with crinums and brunsvigias but the resulting hybrids have not yet become available in South Africa.

CULTURE: Belladonna lilies seem to do best in rather loose soil to which compost has been added. At the coast they may be grown in full sunshine but in hot, inland gardens they do better if planted where they are shaded during the hottest hours of the day. They stand cold winters and have been grown out-of-doors in England. The general rule about watering plants well for the three to four months before they flower does not apply to the belladonna lily, for it flowers well in February and March in its natural habitat, even though it may not have received much water during the previous three months. It should, however, be watered during autumn and winter when it is in leaf and actively growing. Plant the bulbs in November to January, just beneath, or with the neck showing above the surface of the soil. Once planted it is advisable to leave them in the same place for many years. They can also be grown easily from seed but this takes about three years to produce flowering plants. Collect the seed as it forms in April and plant it whilst it is still green. It is a good idea to plant the seed next to the mother plant so that it receives water at the right time of the year. When grown in gardens in the summer-rainfall region where heavy rains occur it is advisable to set them in porous ground as a heavy clay soil which holds water may cause them to rot. This is a plant which I feel should be grown in every garden and home, and together with the agapanthus and some other native bulbs, it should be naturalized on farms and by the roadsides in many parts of the country.

AMMOCHARIS CORANICA GROUND LILY
DISTRIBUTION: This plant can be found all over Southern Africa except the south-western Cape.

DESCRIPTION: It produces large, rounded heads of ten to twenty pink to rose-coloured flowers. The stem which carries the head is seldom more than 25 cm (10 in) high and leans over as the flowers open. The leaves are strap-shaped measuring up to 60 cm in length. Their flowering time is from November to January, and a mass of them in flower is a lovely sight.

CULTURE: Plant the large bulbs in late winter and early spring in a sunny place in friable soil. Set them high in the soil so that the neck of the bulb is at ground-level. As they do not like being moved they may not flower for a couple of years after planting. New plants can be grown from seed sown as soon as it is ready to fall from the plant in summer. Cover the seed with a thin layer of soil and see that it is adequately watered.

ANAPALINA ANAPALINA
DISTRIBUTION: Is to be found in the veld of the eastern Cape and in the south-western districts too.

DESCRIPTION: These plants were at one time grouped with antholyza. They are useful plants to set out in a large garden where some parts cannot be easily cultivated for they need little attention to make them grow. The flowers vary in colour from rose to scarlet and are carried in spikes on stems 30-60 cm (1-2 ft) in height. The slender leaves are usually almost as tall as the flower stems.

CULTURE: Plant the corms of spring-flowering species in friable soil in March and April and those of summer-flowering ones in spring. They need not be lifted until they appear to become overcrowded. They do best in loose, sandy soil.

A. caffra, with brick-red flowers and A. nervosa, with red or yellow ones are two decorative species from the eastern Cape. The former flowers in spring and the latter in summer. A. revoluta and A. triticea (both with brick-red flowers) are from the south-western Cape. The former flowers in spring and the latter in summer.

ANOMALESIA CUNONIA ANOMALESIA
(Antholyza cunonia)
DISTRIBUTION: Occurs in a few places, mostly on mountain slopes of the Cape Peninsula.

DESCRIPTION: This little plant grows from a corm and produces flowers on stems 30-45 cm (1-1½ ft) high. The leaves are long and slender, about 25 cm in length tapering to the tip. The flowers which are about 4 cm long are of a showy, luminous coral-red colour and unusual form, for one of the segments of the flower is long and spoon-shaped and protrudes over the anthers. It is a fine pot plant and would look effective massed in the garden or rockery.

CULTURE: Plant corms in February about 15 cm (6 in) apart and 5 cm (2 in) deep, in good soil. The plant grows rapidly and will flower by spring. In areas where frosts are severe, plant them where they will be shaded from the early morning sun in winter.

Rat's Tail
(*Antholyza ringens*)
should be planted at
the front of a rock-
garden or in a pot

Anomalesia (*Anomalesia cunonia*) is a pretty plant for
the border or flower box

ANTHOLYZA RINGENS   Rat's Tail
Rattestert, Hanekam

DISTRIBUTION: Grows naturally in sandy soil
near the coast north of Cape Town.

DESCRIPTION: This plant is grown more because
of its unusual form and colouring than for its
beauty. It is more likely to be effective when
grown as a pot plant than in the garden. It has
been grown as such in England for many years.
The flower stem always seems to grow out at an
angle. It is only about 15-20 cm (6-8 in) in length
and closely crowded all around with scarlet,
funnel-shaped flowers. The blade-shaped leaves
are about the same length, rigid and clearly
ribbed.

CULTURE: Plant it in friable soil, setting the corms
fairly deep—about 15 cm (6 in) under the soil and
20 cm apart. If it is to be grown in a container,
choose a fairly large one so that the plant has
about 5 cm of soil above it, and about 10 cm of soil
below in which the roots can develop. It should
be watered fairly regularly during autumn and
winter.

151

Plant Aristea (*Aristea major*) at the back of a flower border or between shrubs

APONOGETON DISTACHYOS CAPE POND WEED, CAPE HAWTHORN, WATER UINTJIE

DISTRIBUTION: There are several species of aponogeton growing in vleis and ponds in different parts of Southern Africa.

DESCRIPTION: When in flower in late winter and spring, it is certainly a striking plant and worth having, because at this time of the year the other water plants such as water lilies are dormant, and ponds are apt to look rather dismal. However, one must be careful to see that it does not spread all over the pool.

152

The flowerheads are about 7 cm long and of ivory colour with brownish-black anthers making an effective show against the pale background. They are said to be called Cape Hawthorn because they smell like hawthorn. For years the plants have been used in cooking and the "water-uintjie bredies" of the Western Province have been considered dishes of great merit for many generations. In the eastern Cape another species is used by Africans as a relish served with mealie-meal porridge.

Although one seldom comes across this little water plant in pools in South African gardens, it has been cultivated in England for a long time and several varieties have been hybridized there to produce larger flowers of different colours.

CULTURE: Plant the tuber in a pot of good soil and water it well until it grows, or stand the pot in shallow water until the stem has grown out well when it can be put into a deeper part of the pool.

ARISTEA ARISTEA, BLOUKNOL

DISTRIBUTION: Different species of aristea are to be found in many parts of South Africa and in Rhodesia.

DESCRIPTION: The plants vary considerably in height, most of those of garden merit being rather tall plants. They bear flowers of beautiful shades of blue. The flowers have six petals arranged in a circle and are carried in spikes. They open for only part of the day and close in the afternoon, but are nevertheless of value in the large garden when planted in groups. They look particularly effective growing between pink, white or yellow flowers.

CULTURE: Aristeas grow from a woody rootstock or fibrous rhizome. They do well even in poor soil but should be planted in some leaf mould or compost and left to multiply for several years. Near the coast they do well in full sun, but in hot, inland gardens better results will be had from plants which have some shade during the hottest hours of the day. As they do not transplant readily it is advisable to sow the seeds where the plants are to grow to maturity.

A. macrocarpa
Grows to 90 cm (3 ft) and has handsome spikes of large, pale blue flowers in late spring and early summer.

The Cape Hawthorn or Water Uintjie (*Aponogeton distachyos*) spreads rapidly in a shallow pond

A. schizolaena

This grows in the eastern Cape and reaches a height of about 60 cm (2 ft). It has flowers of deep blue in late spring.

A. spiralis

Can be found in the Peninsula and some districts of the south-western Cape. It grows to about 45 cm (1½ ft) and bears flowers 4 cm across, shaped like a flat bowl. They are either white or very pale blue in colour and are enhanced by the bright orange-yellow anthers and the blue stigma. The backs of three of the segments are beautifully marked with olive green. The flowering time of this species is September and October and, left to form clumps, it makes a fine show.

A. thyrsiflora   TALL ARISTEA
(New name is *A. major*)

This is a statuesque species reaching a height of 90-150 cm (3-5 ft) with long spikes of royal blue flowers in October and November. It makes a splendid show when interplanted with pink watsonias.

BABIANA   BABIANA, BABIAANTJIE

DISTRIBUTION: The species which are most decorative are native to the south-western and western Cape.

DESCRIPTION: The name "babiaantjie" is said to have been given to them because the baboons dig up the corms and eat them. They have sword-shaped leaves which are clearly ribbed and more or less funnel-shaped flowers carried on stems varying in length from 15-45 cm (6-18 in). They are beautifully coloured in shades of royal blue, cyclamen, mauve, purple, cream and white. Massed at the edge of a flower border they look exceptionally lovely. These are fine plants for the rock-garden and they also make splendid pot plants for a sunny position.

CULTURE: Set the corms in groups of twenty-five or more, 8-10 cm (4-5 in) apart. They should be planted deep, about 15 cm (6 in) below the surface of the soil. They need not be lifted for years and it is therefore wise to improve the soil before planting them. In areas of the summer-rainfall region which have a very high rainfall and where the soil

153

is a heavy clay, it is advisable to lift them in summer when they are dormant and to store them until the following March. Generally, however, they are unlikely to rot even if watered during their dormant season. They stand fairly severe frost and in districts where frosts are very severe they should be planted where they are protected or will be shaded from the early morning sun in winter. Plant them in January or February.

They also grow easily from seed but this takes longer to produce flowering plants. Seeds should be sown in late summer. In cold, northern climates they should be planted in spring for summer flowers.

B. disticha   BLUE BABIANA
Has scented blue flowers on stems about 30 cm (1 ft) high in late winter.

B. hypogea   AUTUMN BABIANA
(B. bainesii)
This one grows in many parts of South Africa and Rhodesia. It has spiky leaves to about 25 cm in length. These are taller than the mauve flowers which grow in clusters near the ground. The flowering time is autumn.

154

B. macrantha   CREAM BABIANA
Bears large, cream flowers with a maroon blotch at the bottom of the cup.

B. patersoniae
Grows wild in the eastern Cape and bears scented blue flowers in late summer.

B. plicata
A small species which grows to only about 10 cm (4 in) with scented flowers set between the leaves. They appear in late winter and are cyclamen, mauve or purple, often with white markings at the base of two of the petals.

B. pulchra
Reaches a height of about 25 cm (10 in) and is bright, deep blue with wine-coloured suffusions.

B. rubrocyanea   WINE-CUP BABIANA
This is an impressive little flower carried on stems only 15 cm (6 in) high. Each flower is coloured crimson at the bottom and royal blue at the top. It is very like another little native plant known as *Geissorrhiza rochensis* which also has the com-

mon name of wine-cups. The flowering period is late winter and early spring. It does well in heavy soil and needs plenty of moisture from autumn through winter.

B. stricta
Is a taller and more showy species growing to about 45 cm (1½ ft) with flowers of rich royal blue, cyclamen or mauve held high above the leaves.

B. stricta var. sulphurea
Reaches a height of 30 cm (1 ft) and has flowers of cream to pale yellow. It makes a handsome show when planted in colonies between more vividly coloured species.

B. tubulosa var. tubiflora
Is a showy little species growing to about 15 cm (6 in) with cream-coloured flowers marked with coral-red.

B. velutina var. nana   DWARF BABIANA
Grows wild in Namaqualand where it is often found in cracks between the rocks. It reaches a height of only 10-12 cm (4-5 in) and has magenta flowers which face upwards as though to make sure that they will not be overlooked. There are white markings on two of the petals.

Wine-cup Babiana (Babiana rubrocyanea) has a very lovely flower

Bobartia
(Bobartia indica)
does well in poor soil

B. villosa   CRIMSON BABIANA

Is a handsome species with cup-shaped flowers of blue, mauve or burgundy, enhanced by prominent black anthers. It grows to about 45 cm (1½ ft) and flowers in September.

BOBARTIA INDICA   BOBARTIA, BESEMBIESIE
(B. spathacea)

DISTRIBUTION: From the Cape Peninsula along the coast to Humansdorp.

DESCRIPTION: This perennial grows to 60-90 cm (2-3 ft) and is rush-like in appearance. The flowering stem is tall, round and sturdy, ending in a sharp point. The flowers appear in spring or summer and are generally more profuse after fires have burnt out the veld. They are carried in clusters coming off from one side of the stem about 12 cm from its tip. The flowers open two or three at a time and do not last long but new ones open daily. The buds are tightly ensheathed in rather leathery bracts. Each flower measures 6-8 cm across and has six oval petals of bright canary yellow or a paler shade. They are showy and would make a bright patch of colour massed in a large garden. It would look splendid also interplanted with blue aristea which flowers at the same time.

Other species very similar in growth are to be found in different areas of the western and eastern Cape, near the coast. *B. aphylla*, *B. gracilis* and *B. gladiata* are worth cultivating also. The rush-like stems have been used for many generations for making brooms.

CULTURE: Bobartia grows from a short creeping rhizome usually buried deep beneath the soil. It stands both drought and frost.

BOOPHANE   SORE-EYE FLOWER, RED POSY, GIFBOL, CAPE POISON BULB

DISTRIBUTION: Is found in all the provinces of South Africa and Rhodesia.

Description: Has large round heads of flowers measuring 15-20 cm across. In some cases the flowerhead is on such a short stem that it appears to grow directly from the bulb almost at ground level. The colours of the flowers vary but they are never very bright, ranging from dull pink to brownish-purple. The leaves emerge after the flowers fade.

CULTURE: Plant the huge bulbs so that the neck and a piece of the bulb show above the ground. They seem to be able to grow equally well in sandy soil and in hard ground, but they take a long time

The Sore-Eye Flower *(Boophane disticha)* grows wild in many parts of South Africa

Candelabra Flower
(*Brunsvigia orientalis*)
is an unusual one for
the garden and for
large pots or tubs

to flower after being moved, and the bulbs do not produce flowers until they are quite large. In areas which get severe frost the spring-flowering species should be planted in a protected spot. They can stand drought but not much cold.

B. disticha   SORE-EYE FLOWER, RED POSY, GIFBOL, CAPE POISON BULB
This species grows wild in various parts of Southern Africa. The large round heads of pink flowers measuring 20-25 cm in diameter appear in spring on very short stems only a few centimetres above the ground. The leaves are tapering, usually with a fluted edge, up to 30 cm long and about 4 cm wide, and arranged in fan-formation. This spring-flowering species will flower even though it receives little or no water during winter.

Parts of this plant are used by some Bantu tribes and also by some Europeans to cure various ailments. The outer covering of the bulb is applied to boils and abcesses and fresh leaves are used to check the bleeding of a wound. It is not certain whether the name of Gifbol (Poison Bulb) was given to the plant because the bulb is poisonous to stock or because the Bushmen at one time used it to make poison for their arrows. The name of ''Sore-eye Flower'' is apt, because if one is near the open flower in a confined space, one's eyes do become sore and one's head may begin to ache too.

B. guttata   SORE-EYE FLOWER
(*B. ciliaris*)
The flowers of this species are not attractive and the plant is grown more as a curiosity than for colour. Like the species mentioned above, the flowers are arranged in an umbel, each flower being attached to the main stem by its own stalk. The main stem is fairly tall and the flowerhead is about 20 cm across. The leaves are about 30 cm in length and about 8-10 cm wide and spread out horizontally. The flowering time is autumn, and the leaves appear after the flowers fade and persist through the winter. This species should be watered well during the winter months but can be left dry in summer.

BRUNSVIGIA   BRUNSVIGIA, CANDELABRA FLOWER, KANDELAAR
DISTRIBUTION: Different species can be found in various parts of South Africa.

DESCRIPTION: The plant is named after the house of Brunswick in Germany. In the eighteenth and nineteenth centuries many of the aristocratic families of Europe, and particularly those of England, had magnificent gardens and private parks. They vied with each other in collecting exotic plants and some even sent their own plant collectors abroad to bring home rare and unusual ones. The Duke of Braunschweig in Germany grew this brunsvigia from bulbs sent to him by Ryk Tulbagh, Governor of the Cape from 1699 to 1771.

It has huge umbels of flowers which may measure up to 40 cm across. Each flower is attached to the central stem on its own sturdy stalk. In some species the leaves lie flat on the ground while others have leaves which are fairly erect; in some the leaves appear together with the flowers, whilst in others they grow out after the flowers fade. Hybrids have been created by crossing this plant with the belladonna lily but these hybrids are not yet available in South Africa.

CULTURE: Plant the large bulbs so that their tops are at ground-level or just above, in soil which is friable and contains some leaf mould. These bulbs should be left in the same place for some years as they do not flower for a year or two after being planted. It is important, therefore, that they be planted in soil which drains fairly well, because those from the summer-rainfall area do not like to be too wet in winter and vice versa. They may be grown in full sunshine or in partial shade. They can be grown from seed which should be sown whilst it is still green. Sometimes the seed starts to send out shoots whilst still on the plant. Quicker results will be had by planting bulbs, as the seedlings take two or three years to flower.

B. gregaria
Has four broad leaves only about 10 cm in length which lie flat on the ground. They appear in winter after the flowers fade. The rosy-red flowers are carried on stems about 30 cm (1 ft) high in late summer. This species can be found in various parts of the summer-rainfall area of South Africa.

B. josephinae   EMPRESS JOSEPHINE'S BRUNSVIGIA, KONINGSKANDELAAR
Bears its coral-red flowers in late summer on stems about 45 cm (1½ ft) high. The leaves are very long, up to 60 cm and about 10 cm wide. Its natural habitat is the winter-rainfall area of the Cape.

B. natalensis   NATAL BRUNSVIGIA
Grows in Natal and the eastern part of the Transvaal. It has short, broad leaves, rounded at the ends, which lie almost flat on the ground, and a flaring umbel of flowers.

B. orientalis   CANDELABRA FLOWER,
(B. gigantea)   KANDELAARBLOM
In late summer or early autumn this species bears huge heads of flowers which may measure up to 60 cm across. The broad leaves appear after the flowers fade and lie flat on the ground. It should be watered during winter and allowed to dry out after the leaves disappear in spring.

B. radulosa   PINK BRUNSVIGIA
This hardy species grows wild in parts of the Transvaal, Natal, the Orange Free State and the dry north-western Cape. It is the most decorative of the brunsvigias and bears its flowers of clear pink on sturdy stems in late summer. The leaves which are broad and rounded, lie flat on the ground. They generally appear together with the flowers and die down in winter. It can be grown in cold gardens, but where frosts are very severe the ground should be covered with a mulch to prevent damage to the bulb.

B. undulata   RUBY BRUNSVIGIA
The flowerhead is not large but it makes quite a pretty show in February and March when it comes into flower. It grows to about 45 cm (1½ ft) and has flowers of a distinctive shade of red. The leaves which are narrow, appear with the flowers and die down in winter. It is native to Natal but stands cold winters as it is dormant during the winter.

BULBINE   BULBINE, KATSTERT
DISTRIBUTION: Different species of this flower grow wild in many parts of the country.

DESCRIPTION: The flowers are carried in tufty spikes from 5-15 cm long on stems 30-45 cm (1-1½ ft) tall. The little flowers which have six petals are very like those of bulbinella, but in the bulbine the yellow stamens have fluffy filaments, whilst those of the bulbinella have smooth filaments. The leaves are rather succulent in appearance and the plant has tuberous fleshy roots which enable it to stand long periods of drought. It is a useful plant for dry gardens and for providing flowers for arrangements. It can be grown as a ground cover on dry banks, along paths, at the front of a border, or in a rock-garden. It does well in coastal gardens and inland.

CULTURE: As they stand both drought and cold these plants should be used more in gardens where growing conditions are difficult. The roots can be planted at any time of the year or plants can be raised from seed sown in spring or summer, but this method does not produce flowering plants for two or three years. They do well in poor soil and grow in full sunshine or in light shade.

Florist's Bulbinella
(*Bulbinella floribunda*)
bears its pretty flowers
in late winter.

B. alooides   ALOE-BULBINE, ROOI WORTEL

Has thick succulent leaves, broad at the base and tapering to the tips, rather like the leaves of a small aloe, both in their shape and arrangement. The flower stem grows to about 60 cm (2 ft) in height in late winter. This plant will grow in sun or in partial shade, in a hot climate, in frosty gardens, and in poor soil. It produces fine flowers for arrangements.

B. asphodeloides   GIANT BULBINE, GEEL
KATSTERT

A large-flowering bulbine with yellow flowers on thick, fleshy stems about 45-60 cm (1½-2 ft) high. The leaves are succulent but rather grass-like in form. It flowers in spring and summer and is resistent to drought. In cold gardens it dies down in winter but shoots up again quickly in spring.

B. caulescens   STALKED BULBINE

This is one of the best for garden show, particularly in areas which have long periods of drought and cold winters. The plants send out runners from which new plants develop and it makes a good ground cover. The pencil-like leaves are short and succulent and the flower stems rise to about 45 cm (1½ ft) and bear spikes of yellow flowers which make a pretty show in mid to late spring. To keep the plants tidy cut off the flowers as they fade, and if the plants become woody, dig them up and plant root sections to produce new plants.

B. stenophylla   NARROW-LEAFED BULBINE

This low-growing type common in the Transvaal is less spreading than the other species and the flowers are carried on shorter stems seldom more than 25 cm (10 in) tall. Mass-planted, it makes a pretty show in spring. In cold gardens the succulent little grass-like leaves may die down for a short period in winter.

BULBINELLA   BULBINELLA, CAT'S TAIL,
KATSTERT

DISTRIBUTION: The most attractive species grow wild in the Cape but there are species in all the provinces.

DESCRIPTION: These are attractive plants not only for making a show in the garden but also for providing flowers for arrangements. The flowers, which appear in late winter and early spring, are somewhat like miniature red-hot pokers in form,

159

Flames, Pennant Flower *(Chasmanthe floribunda)*. This plant thrives even when neglected

coloured mainly yellow, although orange and white forms do occur. The flower should not be confused with that of the bulbine, which is very similar. In the case of the bulbine the filaments are clothed with fluff, whilst in the bulbinella they are smooth. The leaves are usually long and slender, often grooved down the centre. The roots are fibrous. Bulbinella makes a pleasing show anywhere in the garden—interplanted with other plants or set out in colonies making showy groups of plants between other plants in the border, or in front of shrubs.

CULTURE: They should be planted in summer, in well-drained soil, in sun or semi-shade, with the

roots just below the surface of the soil. They stand very dry summers and cold winters, but they should be watered regularly during autumn and winter, when they are in active growth. They seem to do best in acid soil. Seed sown in late summer will produce flowering plants in two years, whereas roots planted in January will produce flowers by July.

B. floribunda   FLORIST'S BULBINELLA,
(B. setosa)   KATSTERT
This is one of the best of the species for use in arrangements. The flower stems are about 60 cm (2 ft) in height and the little flowers are a rich shade of yellow arranged in long cylinders at the tops of the stems. The leaves are long and narrow.

B. floribunda var. **latifolia**   LARGE
    BULBINELLA
Grows wild in the western Cape in vleis which dry out completely in summer, but does well in highveld gardens and in other parts of the country. The flower stems which appear between July and September grow to 60-90 cm (2-3 ft) and bear long spikes of daffodil-yellow flowers. There is also an orange coloured form of this. The leaves are deeply grooved down the centre.

CHASMANTHE FLORIBUNDA   FLAMES,
(Antholyza prealta)   PENNANT FLOWER,
    SUURKNOL
DISTRIBUTION: Different species of chasmanthe grow in various parts of the country, but the most decorative are native to the south-western Cape.

DESCRIPTION: Chasmanthe is a good plant for the large garden. It multiplies too rapidly for the confines of the small garden. It is an excellent plant for farm gardens, to have along a drive or planted along main roads, as it requires little attention. It bears its orange-red flowers in spikes at the top of slender stems which often grow to 90 cm (3 ft) in height. The flowers are curved and hooded in appearance with projecting stamens. The flowering time is late winter and early spring.

CULTURE: They grow in full sunshine and in partial shade, and, in highveld gardens, where frosts are severe, it is advisable to plant them where they are shaded from the early morning sun in winter, or against a north-facing wall which radiates heat. They do not seem to mind poor soil but they do need to be watered during the winter months. The plants die down in early summer but it is not necessary to lift the corms. Plant corms in late summer 5-10 cm (2-4 in) deep and about 30 cm (1 ft) apart and let them grow in the same place until they appear to be over-crowded. It takes about eighteen months to raise flowering plants from seed, but bulbs planted in February will produce flowers by August.

CHLOROPHYTUM COMOSUM HEN AND CHICKENS, BRACKET PLANT, SPIDER PLANT

DISTRIBUTION: Can be found in many of the warm districts of the summer-rainfall region.

DESCRIPTION: It has slender, arching leaves about 30 cm long and only 1 cm wide. They come up from the ground to form rounded, tufty plants. The flowers are ivory-white and starry, but the plants are grown for the foliage effect rather than the flowers. A variety which is popular in many countries is known as *Chlorophytum varie-gatum*. Its leaves are prettily coloured with bands of green and white running lengthwise. New plants arise spontaneously and hang down all round the mother plant. They are excellent as edging plants or as a ground cover in shade, and they make decorative pot or patio plants.

CULTURE: They grow rapidly from the little off-sets. Plant them in well prepared soil in pots in-doors, or in the open ground in shade. They are tender to sharp frost. Set plants about 30 cm (1 ft) apart.

CLIVIA CLIVIA, BUSH LILY, ST. JOHN'S LILY, BOSLELIE

DISTRIBUTION: Most species grow wild in Natal, the eastern Cape and in forests of the eastern Transvaal.

DESCRIPTION: These attractive plants are mem-bers of the amaryllis family and are worth a place in the garden and as pot plants for the balcony or patio. One species has been grown in England as a pot plant for more than a century.

The flowers are carried in clusters on stout stems and are of apricot to tawny-marmalade in colour. The plant does not have a bulb but the base of the stem where the leaves emerge is thickened, and long fleshy roots come off from this point. The leaves are strap-shaped and some-what fleshy. Clivias are splendid plants for shady parts of the garden or to grow in pots for indoor decoration.

CULTURE: Plant the roots in late summer or in spring in soil which has been well enriched with leaf mould or compost, setting them about 5 cm (2 in) below the surface of the soil. They grow naturally in the shade provided by trees and this also prevents them from being damaged by frost when grown in gardens where frosts tend to be severe. They are however, not suitable for gar-dens where frosts are really severe. The plants should be left in the same place for years as they do not like being disturbed. They should be watered well, particularly in summer and spring. They may also be grown from seed but this method takes about three years to produce flowering plants. The seed should be sown in spring or summer, 7-10 cm (3-4 in) apart and 2-3 cm (1 in) deep in leaf mould or compost and kept watered and shaded until growth starts. In their dormant season the little plants should be allowed to dry out slightly.

C. caulescens STALKED CLIVIA

Grows wild in forests in the mountainous parts of the eastern Transvaal. It has tubular flowers arranged in round heads on stems about 45 cm (1½ ft) high. About fifteen flowers are carried in each head. They are orange with green tips and hang down in a circle.

C. miniata CLIVIA, BUSH LILY, ST. JOHN'S LILY

This is the most handsome of the clivias with large heads of flowers of glowing apricot to salmon-red, carried at the tops of stout stems. Each flower is about 6-8 cm in length and funnel-shaped. They are arranged in rounded heads measuring 15 cm and more across. The strap-shaped leaves grow to about 50 cm in length. The flowering time is from August to October. The large red berries which follow the flowers are also decorative. It grows in bush and forests of the eastern Cape, the Transkei, Natal and the Transvaal, and has been cultivated as a pot plant in England for many years. Several very hand-some hybrids have been developed from this species.

C. nobilis CAPE CLIVIA

Is distributed over a small area of the coastal part of the eastern Cape near East London, and the Transkei. It bears a whorl of drooping tubular flowers of orange or reddish-yellow tipped with green. There are about thirty flowers on one head and they are carried on stems about 45 cm (1½ ft)

tall. The leaves are long and strap-shaped. It should be planted in shade and protected against severe frost. It flowers in winter and early spring.

CRINUM   CRINUM

DISTRIBUTION: Widely distributed throughout South Africa and Rhodesia.

DESCRIPTION: Crinums are robust plants with long leaves and large lily-like flowers carried on sturdy stems. The flowers are trumpet-shaped and vary in colour from white, through pale pink to deep rose. They are carried in clusters. They are most decorative when in flower but suited more to the large garden than the small as the leaves take up a good deal of space. Some species are good plants for large containers on terraces.

CULTURE: Most crinums are waterside plants. They can be grown at the edge of a pool or dam or along a water furrow. Once established they can, however, endure long dry periods. Plant the bulbs, which are generally very large, so that the neck is just above soil-level. Once planted they should be left in the same place for years as they do not like being moved. Plant them in soil in which there is some compost or leaf mould. They grow readily from seed but it takes about four years to produce flowering plants. The seed should be sown whilst still green. It will actually start growing on the plant or if it is put on a damp piece of paper and kept moist. Set the seeds 6-8 cm (2-3 in) apart and 2-3 cm (1 in) deep in compost and keep them moist until germination has taken place and the leaves die down.

C. bulbispermum   ORANGE RIVER LILY
(C. longifolium, C. capense)
Bears up to fifteen flowers each measuring about 10 cm in length on stems 60-90 cm (2-3 ft) tall. The flowers are handsome and vary from white to pale pink. Each petal has a stripe of rose colour running down the centre. The flowering time is October. The leaves, which are about 60 cm in length and 7-10 cm broad, arch up and then fall back towards the ground again. They die down in winter and emerge again in spring. The name of Orange River Lily was given to this plant because it was first found along the Orange river but it occurs in many other parts of the country, too.

C. campanulatum   WATER CRINUM, VLEI
(C. aquaticum)   LILY
This species bears its flowers in September and October on stems about 45 cm (1½ ft) high. It grows naturally in vleis in the eastern Cape which dry up during winter. In the garden it should be planted where it can be watered well in summer, or it can be planted in a pot of soil to be sunk into a garden pond where it will be covered by 5-20 cm (2-8 in) of water. In late summer the pot can be taken out of the pond and sunk into soil in a corner of the garden until late winter, when it should be watered regularly or put back into the pond. The bulb of this species is smaller than those of other species described.

C. graminicola   GRASS CRINUM
Grows on the highveld of the Transvaal and does not need as much water as the other species. The flowers appear in October and are clear pink, or white with rose-pink stripes down the middle of each petal. They are carried on stems about 30 cm (1 ft) high. The stem tends to lean over as the flowers open. The leaves are somewhat leathery and broad.

C. lugardiae
(C. polyphyllum)
Has large trumpet-like flowers and leaves which are shorter and broader than in other species.

C. macowanii   CAPE COAST LILY, SABIE
                                              CRINUM
This species which is variable according to where it grows, is to be found from the Sabie River south through Natal to the eastern Cape. It has long, undulating or straight leaves which die back during winter. In spring it bears scented flowers on tall fleshy stems. The large trumpet-shaped flowers are white or pink with rose stripes down the middle of the petals. Certain Bantu tribes use the fibre of the bulb as a dressing on inflamed sores.

C. moorei   CAPE COAST LILY
This is the most decorative crinum for the garden. It has been grown overseas for many years. It flowers in mid-summer more or less at the same time as the belladonna lily with which it is sometimes confused. The belladonna lily flowers without leaves, whereas the crinum when in flower has its leaves. The large, trumpet-shaped flowers appear on stems up to 1.25 m (4 ft) tall from January to March. The flowers are generally

163

◁ Clivia (Clivia miniata) is one of the most beautiful of plants for a shady corner

Orange River Lily
(Crinum bulbispermum)
A handsome plant for
the large garden

white or palest pink. After flowering the plant dies down for a short time before new growth appears once more. The leaves are about 60-90 cm long and 6-10 cm wide. This species grows wild in the forests of the eastern Cape, and should be grown in the garden under trees and in rich soil. It should be watered throughout the summer but may be allowed to dry out in winter.

CROCOSMIA CROCOSMIA, FALLING STARS
DISTRIBUTION: Pretty species are to be found in the eastern Cape, Natal, the Transvaal and parts of East Africa.

DESCRIPTION: In addition to the species which occur in the wild there are now many beautiful hybrids. The plants bear dainty spikes of flowers of luminous shades of flame, coral and orange. They make a fine show in the garden and are charming in arrangements, too.

CULTURE: They grow from corms which should be planted in August or September, fairly near the surface of the soil and about 20 to 30 cm apart. The plants grow best in partial shade and in soil to which some humus has been added. They are hardy to quite severe frost and may be left in the garden for several years until they become over-

Falling Stars *(Crocosmia aurea)* produces its exceptionally pretty flowers in summer

crowded, when they should be lifted and divided. They can be grown from seed but this method takes two to three years to produce flowering plants.

C. aurea   FALLING STARS

This is a charming species which bears a spike of flowers of golden-orange on stems about 60 cm (2 ft) tall. The flowers appear in late summer and early autumn and make a fine show in the garden and when grown in containers. Each flower is about 6 cm across and they bend gracefully on the stem. The long, slender leaves come out like a fan on each side of the stalk. The plants look most effective when massed in the middle of a flower border or grown in colonies in a rock-garden.

C. masonorum
(Tritonia masonorum)

This species occurs in parts of the Transkei and Natal. It has long, pointed, ribbed leaves about 6 cm wide and up to 60 cm in length. The flower stem grows to about the same height and tends to bend over. The individual flowers measure 4 cm across and are brilliant orange. The flowering time is mid-summer and the plant should be watered well from spring, when new growth starts, until the foliage has died down in autumn.

C. pottsii
(Tritonia pottsii)

This is a tall species from Natal with a flowering stem which rises to 90 cm (3 ft) and with leaves almost as long. The flowers of flame appear in mid-summer and the plant is dormant during autumn and winter.

CYBISTETES LONGIFOLIA   MALAGAS
LILY, ST. JOSEPH'S LILY

DISTRIBUTION: This plant is limited in distribution to a few districts of the south-western Cape.

DESCRIPTION: The showy flowers grow in rounded heads of about twenty flowers, each made up of six long petals reflexed at the tips. They are palest pink to rose in colour and appear in late summer and early autumn before the leaves, which grow out after the flowers fade. The leaves are almost prostrate on the ground around the plant. They remain on the plant through the winter and disappear in late spring or early summer.

CULTURE: This plant has a huge bulb which measures up to 20 cm in diameter when fully grown. It should be planted in December or January so that its top is level with, or just beneath the surface of the soil, and left undisturbed for several years as the plant does not flower for a year or two after planting. It can also

The Cape Coast Lily or Sabie Crinum *(Crinum macowanii)* has an elegant and beautiful flower

be grown from seed which should be sown when it is still green. The plants should be watered well during autumn and until spring.

CYRTANTHUS FIRE LILY, INANDA LILY, IFAFA LILY

DISTRIBUTION: *Can be found in many parts of the country. The common name of fire lily was given to some species because they seem to come up more prolifically after a fire has burnt out the veld.*

DESCRIPTION: The flowers are carried at the tops of stems which vary in height according to species, from a few centimentres up to 60 cm. They are tubular in shape and usually rose or red in colour, although there are also cream, white, yellow and orange species. In most species the flowers hang down from the tops of the stems in clusters. They make an effective show when massed in a mixed border or when grown in groups in pots. They are also charming flowers for small arrangements.

CULTURE: They grow well in any ordinary garden soil, but produce finer flowers on longer stems if planted in good soil and fertilized from time to time. Most species are hardy to moderate frost and also stand a good deal of drought. They can be grown from offsets planted when dormant. Plant the winter-flowering species in summer and the spring-flowering ones in early autumn, setting them 10-20 cm apart and 5-8 cm (2-3 in) deep. They can be grown from seed also but this takes longer to produce flowering plants.

C. angustifolius TULBAGH CYRTANTHUS
This species is to be found in the south-western Cape. It grows to 30 cm (1 ft) and bears drooping flowers which flare out at the mouth. Each flower is about 4 cm in length and, massed together, they make a handsome show. The flowering time is summer and early autumn. The leaves appear after the flowers and disappear again in summer.

C. breviflorus MOCK FIRE LILY
(Anoiganthus breviflorus)
Occurs in many parts of South Africa and in Rhodesia. It bears funnel-shaped flowers in little clusters on stems 15 cm (6 in) high. The flowers appear in spring and the leaves emerge either with the flowers or after them. To make an effective show plant this species in masses, close together.

C. contractus FIRE LILY, BRANDLELIE
This is one of the most attractive of the species. It grows wild through the eastern Cape and Natal coastal belt and up into the Transvaal. The rose-red, funnel-shaped flowers appear in spring on stems 30 cm (1 ft) tall. They are tubular in form

166

and tend to droop from the stem. The leaves are long and slender, seldom more than 12 mm wide. They appear after the flowers have faded.

C. galpinii
Grows naturally in the eastern Transvaal and in Zululand, and bears its flowers in winter. The flowers which are scarlet or rose, measure about 5 cm in length and are carried on stems 20 cm (8 in) tall. It is common to find only a single trumpet-shaped flower on a stem. The leaves, which generally appear after the flowers, are long and slender.

C. mackenii   IFAFA LILY
Grows wild in the Eastern Province and the south-coast of Natal. Has fragrant white, cream, yellow or flame tubular flowers which appear in winter or early spring, on stems about 30 cm (1 ft) tall. The leaves which emerge with the flowers are long and narrow. It is at present the species most widely grown in gardens. In its natural habitat it is to be found growing at the sides of streams, but it flowers well in the garden even when watered rather seldom.

C. obliquus   GIANT CYRTANTHUS, SORE-EYE FLOWER, JUSTIFINA
Can be seen in the veld from the eastern Cape to Natal. In gardens where frosts are severe it should be planted in a sheltered position. This is a most attractive species which has been grown in Europe as a pot plant for more than a century. The stems reach a height of about 45 cm ($1\frac{1}{2}$ ft) and bear clusters of drooping tubular flowers of three colours—yellow at the base, shading to orange in the centre and green at the tips of the petals. The leaves are about 30 cm long and 2-4 cm wide. The flowering time is from September to December.

C. o'brienii   RED IFAFA LILY
This native of the eastern Cape and parts of Natal has scarlet flowers in winter on stems about 20 cm (8 in) tall. The plants usually flower when they have leaves, although occasionally the flowering stem rises before the leaves grow out.

C. sanguineus   KEI LILY, NAHOON LILY, INANDA LILY
Is one of the most decorative species but unfortunately it is now rare, though it may still be found in a few places in the eastern Cape and Natal. It bears two or three large salmon-red flowers on stems about 30 cm (1 ft) high. The plants flower in late summer and need to be kept well watered throughout the summer to produce good blooms. At the coast they grow in full sun-

Cyrtanthus tuckii

Giant Cyrtanthus *(Cyrtanthus obliquus).*

Hairbell (Dierama) looks charming hanging over water

DESCRIPTION: The outstanding characteristic of this plant is the fineness of the long hair-like stems which support the flowers. Being so slender the stems never seem to be still, even on a calm day and the continual movement adds animation to the part of the garden where they grow.

The flowers, which hang down like bells are usually mauve but sometimes white, pink or carmine. The buds open in succession so that the flower stem remains decorative for quite a time. In warmer parts of the country some species flower before the end of winter but the main flowering season is spring and early summer. The leaves which grow in clumps are long and slender, rather like those of gladioli, and the thin flower stems rise above them to a height of 1.25 m (4 ft) or more.

In districts which have long periods of strong sunshine without much cloud or rain they should be planted where they have afternoon shade. They do best if planted in soil rich in humus. They tolerate severe frost and some species will stand drought, too, but flower best when watered fairly regularly. They have been grown out-of-doors in England and Ireland, and some beautiful hybrids have been raised in Europe.

CULTURE: The quickest way to produce flowers is by planting corms, but plants can be grown from seed sown in spring or autumn. Set out the spring-flowering species in late summer, and the summer-flowering one in late winter. For an effective display set the corms in groups of four to twelve or more, 30-45 cm (12-18 in) apart, and leave them in one place for a few years until they become overcrowded. Some species grow naturally in vleis which dry up at certain times of the year, whilst others are to be found on hillslopes.

shine or in part shade, but in the hot inland districts they should be planted where they are shaded from the afternoon sun.

C. tuckii   BRANDLELIE
Is to be found from the eastern Cape through Natal into the Transvaal. It grows wild in districts which have severe winters. The flower stems grow to about 30 cm (1 ft) and bear a cluster of drooping tubular scarlet flowers in late spring. It makes a good pot plant, and is effective in the garden when massed.

DIERAMA   HAREBELL, HAIRBELL, WAND-
FLOWER, FAIRYBELL, GRASKLOKKIE
DISTRIBUTION: The name comes from the Greek *dierama* which means "like a bell". These plants grow in many parts of Southern Africa on hill-sides and mountain slopes.

D. grandiflorum   LARGE HAIRBELL
Can be found near Somerset East. It has flowers 6-8 cm long of pinky-mauve, attractively marked with a darker shade. They appear in late spring and summer. This species tolerates drought well.

D. igneum   SMALL HAIRBELL, FAIRYBELL
Grows in many parts of the eastern Cape, Natal, Lesotho and Transvaal. Long slender leaves, scarcely 6 mm in width, rise from the ground, and above them, in mid to late spring, the dainty deep mauve buds or the pinky-mauve open flowers sway gracefully on their long thread-like stems.

D. medium SMALL HAIRBELL, FAIRYBELL
Is very similar to *D. igneum*. It flowers from spring into summer and makes an attractive clump for a rock-garden or mixed border. The flowers of *D. medium* var. *mossii* are a more distinct shade of rose.

D. pendulum HAIRBELL
One of the most charming of the hairbells which grow abundantly near Grahamstown and East London. The leaves, about 12 mm wide, reach a height of 1 m (3 ft) and the flowering stems arch high above them. The flowers, from palest pink to mauve, appear from late winter to late spring. This species is resistant to fairly long periods of drought.

D. pulcherrimum EAST LONDON HAIRBELL,
WEDDING BELL, GRASKLOKKIES
This attractive species has magenta to carmine flowers in late summer and early autumn, and can be seen growing wild on the upper and lower slopes of the Amatola mountains near East London. It likes damp conditions and has been grown very successfully in England where it was first established some sixty years ago. It reaches a height of 2 m (6 ft), and flowers in summer.

DIETES WILD IRIS, UILTJIE

DISTRIBUTION: Is widely distributed in Southern Africa.

DESCRIPTION: These plants which belong to the "iris" family were once called moraeas but they have now been separated and re-named. They grow from a rhizome whereas the moraea has a corm. They have very lovely flowers which look rather like diminutive Japanese irises in shape. In most of them the flowers last for only a single day but the stems bear so many flowers that the plants remain decorative over a long period. They grow easily and multiply rapidly and are excellent plants to grow where conditions are difficult. They tolerate poor soil and some of them can endure long periods with little water. When left in one place they eventually form large clumps. They do well in full sun or in partial shade.

CULTURE: The plants have rhizomes which increase rapidly. These may be planted at almost any time of the year but late summer planting is probably the best. They also grow readily from seed sown in autumn or spring. Most species do well in poor soil and endure long periods of

Yellow Wild Iris *(Dietes bicolor)* produces its lovely flowers in spring

drought. Plant them 3-5 cm deep, spacing the small species 12 cm, and the tall ones 30 cm apart.

D. bicolor YELLOW WILD IRIS
(Moraea bicolor)
It grows wild in the eastern Cape and up into the Transkei. The leaves 1-2 cm wide, grow erect like sword blades to a height of about 60 cm (2 ft) or more, and the handsome flowers about 5 cm across are carried on stems above the leaves. The flowers of dusty yellow, attractively marked with brown blotches, appear in spring, but some are produced during summer, too. The flowers last only for a day but there are so many buds that the clumps almost always have some open flowers in spring and summer. In hot, inland gardens it does best in partial shade.

D. grandiflora   LARGE WILD IRIS

This lovely dietes is widespread from the eastern Cape up through Natal to East Africa. Its flowers, more long-lasting than other dietes, measure 10 cm across. They are white with decorative markings of yellow and flecks of brown, and have pale mauve central segments. They appear from mid-spring to summer. The deep green leaves are 12-25 mm wide and 90 cm in height. This one makes a fine show edging a drive in a large garden.

D. iridioides   WILD IRIS
(Moraea iridioides)
Is a summer-flowering dietes to be found growing wild from Caledon eastwards to Port Elizabeth. Its flowers are about 5 cm across and are white with flecks of yellow and brown. It likes rather moist growing conditions and does well in partial shade. The flowering time is mid-spring and summer.

DILATRIS PILLANSII   ROOIWORTEL
DISTRIBUTION: Occurs on plains and mountain slopes in the Cape Peninsula and adjoining districts as far as Tulbagh and Bredasdorp.

DESCRIPTION: This is a perennial which grows from a woody rootstock which is coloured rather bright rose at the top, hence the name of rooiwortel—meaning red root. The leaves which are 10-20 cm long and 6 mm broad emerge in tufts from the top of the rootstock. The flower stems grow to 25-30 cm (1 ft). They are hairy and rose-pink in colour and so are the flower stalks. The flowers are carried in round clusters 6-7 cm across. The individual flowers are small and cup-shaped with broadly oval pointed petals. They are of a charming shade of mauve. The flowering time is late spring and early summer. *D. corymbosa* is very similar and equally pretty. Both would look attractive massed in the garden or growing in containers. *D. ixioides* is to be found in drier parts of the country, near Calvinia. They last well as cut flowers.

CULTURE: I have no data on the growth of this plant in gardens, nor is seed or rootstock yet available. One hopes that nurserymen will, however, soon propagate it.

DIPIDAX TRIQUETRA   STAR-OF-THE-MARSH, VLEIBLOMMETJIE, HANEKAM
DISTRIBUTION: Grows in vleis and marshy areas in the western Cape.

DESCRIPTION: This plant makes a charming show in August and September and certainly deserves a place in gardens where there are shallow ponds or marshy areas. It is one of the prettiest of plants for a water-garden.

The plant grows to a height of 45-60 cm ($1\frac{1}{2}$-2 ft) and bears spikes of flowers measuring 7-15 cm (3-6 in) in length. Each little flower is like a star about 12 mm across. They are white, flushed with pink, with dark purple dots at the base of the petals. The slender, rounded leaves rise to a height of about 30 cm (1 ft).

CULTURE: In nature it grows deep beneath the soil in vleis which dry up in summer, when the plant goes into a period of dormancy. Plant dipidax in tins or plastic containers which allow it to have 10 cm (4 in) of soil above and below the bulbs, spacing them 10 cm (4 in) apart, and sink the container in a shallow pool from autumn until the plant has finished flowering and the foliage has died away. Then lift and store the container during the summer months in an out-of-the-way corner of the garden, watering them occasionally. In late summer the plants should be watered well to promote new growth and the containers can later be put back into the pool.

It can be planted elsewhere in the garden if it can be kept moist throughout the winter months and allowed to dry out in summer. It is not hardy to more than moderate frost.

DISA
DISTRIBUTION: Different species are found from the south-western Cape, along the coastal belt into Natal, and in parts of the Transvaal; some in marshy places and some in dry fields.

DESCRIPTION: Disas vary considerably in appearance from the beautiful red disa which has one or more large flowers, to species which bear many small flowers arranged along the upper part of the stem. They are all what are known as ground orchids and can be grown successfully in the garden if their special wants are observed. They can be recommended as pot plants.

CULTURE: Generally their most important need is thorough, regular watering during their growing season and occasional watering during their dormant period. They grow from a tuberous rootstock, but can be grown from seed too. Unfortunately neither tubers nor seeds are at present obtainable from seedsmen or nurseries, but seeds of the red disa are obtainable from the Botanical

171

Rooiwortel
(*Dilatris pillansii*)
makes a lovely show
growing in masses

Society of South Africa, Kirstenbosch, Newlands, C.P.

D. cornuta   GOLDEN ORCHID

This pretty species can be found from Cape Town to East London either on coastal plains or mountain slopes. It grows to about 30 cm (1 ft) and bears its hooded flowers along the top 15 cm of stem. They are flushed with dull maroon or mauve on the outside and tawny-gold or cream inside. The leaves, which clasp the stem at the base are often decorated with reddish purple blotches. The flowering time is spring.

D. crassicornis

Like many of our more showy plants, this species has become rare although it has been recorded in various parts of the eastern Cape, the Transkei and Natal, growing on rocks in forest streams or on grassy hillsides. The flowering stem grows to as much as 30-60 cm (1-2 ft) and bears flowers with a sweet scent, around the top portion of the stem. Each flower is 2-3 cm across and delicately coloured from pale pink to pinkish-mauve, charmingly spotted with magenta. There is also a white form. The flowers appear in December. Seed of most of these ground orchids is not available as yet and those fortunate enough to be able to collect seed should try sowing it soon after it has been collected.

D. nervosa

This species grows in the highlands of Pondoland, through the Natal midlands and in the eastern Transvaal. It is to be found on grassy slopes or in open patches in forests. It is one of the most attractive of our ground orchids and well worth trying to cultivate. The flowering stem reaches a height of 60 cm (2 ft) and bears a spike of graceful flowers with narrow petals of bright rose colour. The flowers last well on the plant and also when picked. The flowering time is from January to March.

D. polygonoides
(*D. chrysostachya*)

This species occurs from the eastern Cape, through Natal into the Transvaal. It is to be found in marshy places which may dry up during the winter. The plant should therefore be grown where it can get its roots down to water in a boggy part of the garden, or in an area where it can be copiously watered during its growing and flower-

172

ing season. The plant reaches a height of 30-45 cm (12-18 in) and bears a cylindrical head of flowers which are very pretty, particularly when massed. They vary in colour from yellow to orange and from pink to vermilion. It flowers in late spring and summer.

D. scullyi   ELF-CAP DISA

Has been found in various districts of the eastern Cape, Natal, the Orange Free State and the Transvaal, usually in marshy patches and at fairly high altitudes. The plant grows to about 30 cm (1 ft) and has charming pink flowers in a cylindrical spike along the upper part of the stem. Each flower is shaped like a pixie hood with a scarf flaring out below it. It flowers in February.

D. uniflora   RED DISA

This disa from the mountains near Cape Town is the best known of our wild disas, and now that seed has become available through the National Botanical Society of South Africa, some gardeners and enterprising plant collectors will no doubt be anxious to try growing it. This colourful mountain plant with its gay, orange-red flowers was grown in Europe many years ago. In her book "Gardens of South Africa", Dorothea Fairbridge describes having seen this disa on the Royal Horticultural Society's show in London: "hundreds of plants, each bearing three great blossoms and standing a sturdy 2 feet high". That was in 1922!

To have success in growing it one should know something of its natural habitat in order to provide it with congenial conditions. It occurs fairly high up on mountains where it is wet throughout the autumn and winter from the high rainfall, and where in summer it is kept moist by the precipitation caused by cloud and wind. In addition to this moisture from above, the red disa is usually to be found growing along streams, washed by the water and very often shaded by rocks or by the grasses around it. This orchid, therefore, does not need hot-house conditions. In winter the plant is subjected to extreme cold as well as wet, and in summer, when it flowers, it may be baked by the sun on clear days and be cold on other days when the south-east winds blow and clouds form on the mountains where it grows.

I have not grown this plant myself and am indebted for much of the information which follows to Mr H. E. Meyer of the Botanical Garden at the University of Stellenbosch, who has grown plants

successfully. He is of the opinion that we have still a good deal to learn about the red disa as they tend to die off for no reason that he could accurately determine.

1. Sow the seed in late summer or early autumn in soil which is not a rich mixture. One-third each of sand, soil and compost should suit them.

   Another grower advises using a mixture of sphagnum moss and coarse sand with a thin layer of peat on the top where the seed is sown. Whatever mixture is tried, it is advisable to see that the drainage is good through the bottom of the pot, and to cover the pot in which seed is sown with glass to keep in moisture. Stand the pot in a shady place.

2. Until the plants are growing, water the pots by standing them in a bowl of water so that water is absorbed into the growing medium, or allow water to seep through from the top. The question of what water to use appears to be of importance. Two growers affirm that the water should be rain or river water and not water which has been subjected to chlorination. Mr Meyer has, however, grown them successfully using water from the municipal supply.

3. When plants are 2-3 cm (1 in) high—which may take a year or more—prick them out into small pots containing a lean mixture of sand and compost or moss and let them grow on for another year, after which they should be transferred to a 10 or 15 cm (4 or 6 in) pot. Mr K. C. Johnson recommends more frequent re-potting. In order to ensure that there is some moisture in the air around the plants, it is advisable to stand the pot in which the plant is growing in a larger pot, and to fill the space between the two pots with sand. Water the sand every day. The evaporation of moisture from the sand will help to add moisture to the air about the developing plant.

4. It must be remembered that these plants in their natural habitat generally grow with water running over them all the time, or for a great part of the year, and that the running water would leach out nutrients in the soil in which they are anchored. Perhaps, therefore, they would live longer if planted in soil which is not rich and where they can be washed by moving water.

For further information on these plants I can recommend an article by Mr G. M. L. Feinauer in the Jubilee Issue (Part XLIX of 1963) of the Journal of the Botanical Society of South Africa, and another by Mr K. C. Johnson in the same journal—Part 53 of 1967. The address of the Society is Kirstenbosch, Newlands, C.P., South Africa.

ENGYSIPHON PICTUS

DISTRIBUTION: Rather rare. Seen occasionally on lower mountain slopes in the south-western Cape.

DESCRIPTION: This is a charming little plant with flowers which open to a starry face of six petals. It is of a soft terra-cotta to salmon shade, beautifully streaked with a darker colour. The flowers are carried on slender, wiry stems about 30 cm (1 ft) high and the leaves are long and very slender. Unfortunately, being rare, it will possibly be several years before seed is available but one hopes that plant collectors will soon introduce this into cultivation as it would make a wonderful addition to the garden. It flowers in spring.

CULTURE: Plant bulbs in late summer 3-6 cm deep and about 10 cm apart, or sow seed in late summer. The plant seems to like sandy or gravelly soil.

EUCOMIS

PINEAPPLE FLOWER
WILDEPYNAPPEL

DISTRIBUTION: They occur naturally in many parts of the country but particularly from the eastern Cape, north through Natal, Lesotho, the Orange Free State, the Transvaal and Rhodesia.

DESCRIPTION: The word *eucomis* means beautiful hair and refers to the decorative tuft of leaves at the top of these unusual and handsome plants. The common name of pineapple flower is very descriptive, too, because the top of the flower spike is rather like the top of a pineapple. It is recorded that in 1760 plants were raised from seed, in the Chelsea Gardens in England. And yet today, 200 years later, few South Africans know or grow this decorative plant. The flowering period is summer and because the flowers remain fresh-looking for weeks both in the garden and in vases, they can be considered first-class plants for the garden and to provide flowers for arrangements. They should be more widely grown in large pots or tubs as well as in the garden.

CULTURE: Although they will tolerate poor soil, they perform so much better in soil to which some

Pineapple Flowers
(*Eucomis clavata*)
last well in the garden
and in arrangements

The Wine Eucomis is another handsome species

leaf mould or peat has been added, that it is worthwhile taking trouble to prepare the soil properly. The bulbous roots are huge, sometimes measuring 15 cm (6 in) across. Plant them high in the soil so that the top is just below the surface. They grow well in sunshine or in light shade. Eucomis become dormant in winter and can stand severe frost. In spring when they emerge into new growth again they should be kept well watered until the foliage dies down again. The best time to plant them or to divide the plants is in late autumn or winter.

They also grow readily from seed which should be sown in autumn or spring but this takes much longer to produce flowering plants.

E. clavata   PINEAPPLE FLOWER
(E. undulata)
The large strap-like leaves bend down towards the ground and the sturdy flower stem grows to 45 cm (1½ ft) in height with a cylinder of flowers on the top section of the stem. The flowers are usually green and make a fine show in vases and the garden.

E. pole-evansii   GIANT PINEAPPLE FLOWER
Has a tall flower stem up to 2 m (6-7 ft) high, the top 60 cm (2 ft) of the stem being crowded with green flowers in summer. The plant should be staked to keep the flower erect. The shiny leaves are 60 cm long and 15 cm wide.

E. punctata   WINE EUCOMIS
This handsome plant has large leaves measuring about 45 cm in length with undulated edges. The base of the leaf is spotted with purple blotches. The flowerheads of established plants rise to 60 cm (2 ft) in height and bear numerous flowers tightly clustered in a long cylindrical spike at the top 30 cm (1 ft) of the stem, with the characteristic pineapple tuft above the flowers. The stem is spotted with purple and the flowers are usually green with purple ovaries but may vary in colour, sometimes tinged with pink or deep mauve. It makes a splendid cut flower as it lasts for 3 weeks in water. An arrangement of the green seed heads of agapanthus, with green hydrangeas and eucomis is very striking. The Xhosa people stew the

175

Engysiphon
(*Engysiphon pictus*)
should be planted at
the front of the border

Freesias make a pretty
show in the rock-
garden, in arrange-
ments and in pots

bulb to make medicine for the relief of rheumatism.

FREESIA Freesia, Kammetjie, Flissie

DISTRIBUTION: Most of the wild freesias are from the south-western and eastern Cape.

DESCRIPTION: The freesia has for many years been one of the best-known of our small winter and spring-flowering plants. It was being cultivated in Europe more than a hundred years ago and many beautiful hybrids have been created from the original species taken across. Unfortunately, these colourful hybrids do not have the characteristic perfume of the wild ones, although they make a more decorative show in the garden because of their size and colour. They are also popular plants for pot culture. Their flowering time is late winter and early spring.

CULTURE: Freesias grow very readily in all parts of the country although they need some protection from very severe frosts.

Plant the little corms in February, setting them 4-6 cm (2 in) below soil-level. To make a show they should be planted in colonies of about fifty or more, set out 5 cm (2 in) apart. They can be left in the same position for 3-4 years until they show signs of becoming overcrowded. If, however, the ground is required for other plants they may be lifted as soon as the foliage has turned yellow, and stored in sand in a box until the following planting season.

In regions which suffer from severe frost they should be planted where they are shaded from the first morning sun to obviate frost damage, and, in areas which have excessive sunshine all day, they flower best if they have light shade.

Freesias have an annoying habit of canting over when they are flowering and close planting helps to keep them fairly upright.

Although it is usual to plant corms, they are also easily grown from seeds which may be sown from February to April. Very often these will produce flowering stems by spring and they will certainly produce good spikes by the following spring. In New Zealand freesias are grown as florists' flowers for autumn and winter by sowing the seed in October.

Although most garden freesias are hybrids, mention is made here of some of the species worth finding and growing.

F. armstrongii

This species which grows wild between Humansdorp and Port Elizabeth has pink flowers. It was crossed with another wild species to give rise to many of our colourful hybrids.

F. corymbosa

Grows wild between Grahamstown and Port Elizabeth. Its flowers are not arresting but they are sweetly scented, particularly in the evening.

F. flava

Has creamy to yellow flowers with a yellow blotch on one of the petals. Its flowers are distinctly fragrant.

F. refracta

Bears flowers more than 3 cm in length on stems about 30 cm (1 ft) tall. The flowers are lime-yellow tinted with dull mauve on the outside of the petals. It is native to the area from Worcester to Swellendam. There is also a white variety of this one.

GALTONIA CANDICANS Cape Hyacinth, Summer Hyacinth, Berg Lily

DISTRIBUTION: Galtonia grows wild on the slopes of the Drakensberg mountains in Natal, the north-eastern Cape and Orange Free State.

DESCRIPTION: It is at its best during the summer when it bears its drooping, white, bell-like flowers. It grows to a height of 1.25 m (4 ft) and is therefore more suited to the large garden than the small. It can be planted in a border of perennials, or shrubs and perennials combined.

CULTURE: Plant the bulbs which are very large (5-10 cm across) in late winter so that the top of the bulb is just beneath the surface of the soil. See that the soil is friable, as heavy clay, because of bad drainage, may cause the bulb to rot. It should be watered regularly until after its flowering period, when it can be left dry until it shoots again in spring. It need not be lifted and, in fact, does best if left in the same place for some years. It grows readily from seed too. This, sown in early autumn or in August, will produce flowering stems eighteen months later.

GEISSORRHIZA Sequins, Wine cups, Sysie, Syblom

DISTRIBUTION: Geissorrhiza grows naturally in the western Cape near Cape Town and eastwards

towards Humansdorp, but most species are in or near the Cape Peninsula.

DESCRIPTION: The name is pronounced G-ice-o-riza. Some of the species are not more than 10 cm (4 in) high whilst others grow to as much as 30 cm (1 ft). The flowers are either cup-shaped or bowl-shaped and vary in colour from the palest cream and white to vivid shades of burgundy and purple. Their flowering period is early spring. Massed along the front of a border they make a striking show. They are also splendid pot plants.

CULTURE: They like plenty of water in winter and a dry summer, but they grow extraordinarily well in the summer-rainfall area, too, provided they are watered sufficiently in winter.

Very often they can be found growing in ground which is marshy in winter and dries out in summer. Plant the corms in February, 5 cm (2 in) deep and 10 cm (4 in) apart, grouped in colonies

of fifty or more to make an effective show. They grow in full sunshine but also do well in light shade for part of the day. In areas where severe frost may damage them it is advisable to plant them where they are shaded from the first rays of the morning sun. Seed sown in February will often produce flowering plants by the following spring.

G. erosa RED SEQUINS, ROOISYSIE
This brilliantly coloured species grows to about 30 cm (1 ft) in height and has carmine, cup-shaped flowers in September. The slender leaves are prominently veined.

G. rochensis WINE CUPS, WYNKELKIE
This charming plant is well-named for the cup-shaped flowers look as though they are half-full of wine. The bottom half of each flower is coloured burgundy-red and the top half is deep blue; the

178

two colours are distinctly separated by a white line running right round the flower. Several flowers are carried on stems about 20 cm (8 in) high. It has slender, sword-like leaves. This is a fine plant for pot-culture as well as the garden.

G. secunda   BLUE SEQUINS, BLOUSYSIE
(New name is *G. aspera*)
This dainty plant bears tiny, starry flowers of a rich shade of mauve, on stems up to 30 cm (1 ft) in height. The stems are wiry and the plants should be set close together to make a show.

GLADIOLUS   VARIOUS

DISTRIBUTION: Many of the 150-200 known species of gladioli grow wild in Africa but some of them are to be found in the Middle East and Europe. They occur in all provinces of South Africa and in Rhodesia, but the most decorative of the small species are to be found in a fairly small area of the south-western and eastern Cape.

DESCRIPTION: Very few flowers have met with the acclaim accorded to the hybrid gladioli in horticulture. Grown extensively all over the world as one of the most decorative of garden flowers it is, at the same time, one of the easiest to grow. It has been used for many years in floristry, not only because of its beauty but also because of its long-lasting quality.

These majestic and beautiful hybrids were bred from wild gladioli which were largely native to Southern Africa, a fact worth remembering when one admires their classic beauty. Recently those engaged in creating new types have turned their attention to producing smaller flowers on shorter stems as these are now in greater demand for floristry and gardens than the large types. The result is that some of the newest hybrids are very like their original parents.

Some of our native species have been cultivated in Europe for more than 250 years yet one rarely sees them in our South African gardens. They are, however, charming little plants well worth trying, some for their beauty, some for their scent and some for both.

CULTURE: When planting corms of the wild gladioli, one should divide them into two broad groups—those which grow naturally in the summer-rainfall region and those which are native to the winter-rainfall region. When growing these last-named in regions which have summer rains,

care should be taken to see that they are watered adequately during the winter months. Those which are native to the winter-rainfall region also like to be kept rather dry during summer, and in gardens where they are likely to receive too much water in summer, they should either be planted in porous soil which drains readily or else they should be lifted in summer when the leaves have turned yellow and be replanted in February. They do best in friable soil.

Some of the species from the winter-rainfall region are not able to withstand severe frost and should be protected during winter when grown in parts of the country where frosts are severe. To produce good results grow these gladioli in soil which is fairly porous. If the soil is clay, lighten it by adding plenty of compost. Although most of these gladioli grow in full sunshine, some do much better in partial shade.

Many of our native gladioli grow fairly easily from seed and produce flowering stems in the second season. Seed should be sown in February and March in containers which can be kept moist and shaded until well after germination has taken place.

Plant corms of the spring-flowering species from January to March. Those which flower in late summer and early autumn may be planted in spring. Low-growing species should be planted in colonies, spacing the plants 10 cm apart, whilst tall species may be interplanted with other flowers or grouped together, 20-30 cm from one another.

G. alatus   KALKOENTJIE
This species, native to the south-western Cape, is one of the most unusual gladioli in colouring. The flowers are somewhat hooded and the three upper and broader "petals" are terra-cotta or salmon-pink, whilst the three lower ones, which are narrower, are lime-green to yellow-green with orange tips. The leaves are very narrow and about 15 cm long. The flowers are carried on stems 15-30 cm (6-12 in) high. Planted close together in colonies or drifts they make a charming show. They are also decorative when grown in window-boxes. The flowering time is early spring.

G. blandus   BROAD-LEAFED PAINTED LADY,
(New name is *G. carneus*)   BERGPYPIE
Other gladioli with the common name of painted lady are *G. debilis*, *G. macowanii* and *G. ornatus*, but *G. blandus* is to date the only one of

Kalkoentjie *(Gladiolus alatus)* makes an effective show grown in colonies at the front of a mixed border

which seed is available. The word *blandus* means delightful, and this is indeed a delightful flower. The flower stem grows to 30-45 cm (1-1½ ft) and sometimes more, and the flowers of blush-pink or pale-rose measure about 5 cm across. The three lower petals are marked with crimson spade-shaped blotches. There is a white form of this one, too.

It grows wild on mountain slopes in the south-western Cape and needs plenty of moisture in winter. The flowers appear in spring and the corms should be planted from January to March. In hot, inland districts it is advisable to plant this one where it has some shade for part of the day. It is hardy to frost.

G. bullatus   Caledon Bluebell, Bakpypie
(G. spathaceus)
This is always one of the outstanding flowers on the Caledon Wild Flower Show in early Septem-

ber. It has a very thin stalk about 45 cm (1½ ft) long on which the graceful, drooping, bell-shaped flowers hang. It is of a pastel mauve to jacaranda-blue colour with markings of deeper blue or mauve and yellow or cream.

G. cardinalis   Waterfall Gladiolus, Nuwejaarsblom
This gladiolus is to be found in nature along streams and waterfalls in the south-western Cape, often growing in shady places. Its flowering stem rises to 60 cm (2 ft) and bears bright scarlet flowers with spade-shaped white blotches on the three lower segments. The flowering time is summer. It should be planted in February and kept watered adequately throughout the year. This species does best in partial shade. It is hardy to frost.

181

◁ The Painted Lady *(Gladiolus blandus)* is a most decorative small gladiolus. (New name is *G. carneus*)

The Caledon Bluebell *(Gladiolus bullatus)* bears its elegant flowers on slender stems

G. carinatus   MAUVE AFRIKANDER,
             SANDPYPIE
This is another gladiolus from the south-western Cape where it grows in sandy places to a height of 30-45 cm (1-1½ ft), and flowers from winter to mid-spring. The flowers, in shades of mauve, have yellow markings on the lower segments. Its most outstanding characteristic is its delicate scent and it has, therefore, been used as one of the parents of scented hybrids recently developed.

G. carmineus   CLIFF GLADIOLUS
Grows to about 30 cm (1 ft) in height and has salmon to carmine flowers in late summer. The three lower segments of the flowers have creamy-yellow flashes bordered on either side with red. The leaves grow out in autumn and persist through the winter, dying down again in late spring.

182

G. carophyllaceus   PINK AFRIKANDER,
(G. hirsutus)   SANDVELDLELIE
The flowers carried on stems 45 cm (1½ ft) tall, measure up to 5 cm across and are various shades of pink, rose and cyclamen, often with a deeper shade in the centre. Because of its strong scent and handsome flowers this species has also been used for the development of new hybrids. It is native to the winter-rainfall area and flowers in spring.

G. cruentus   RED GLADIOLUS
This is a handsome species from the highlands of Lesotho and Natal. It has large, scarlet flowers measuring up to 10 cm across, with white markings on the lower segments of the flowers. The flowering stems grow as high as 90 cm (3 ft). This species, which has been used as a parent for some of the large modern hybrids, flowers during the summer months and is dormant during winter. It is quite frost resistant.

G. debilis   PAINTED LADY
Grows to about 30 cm (1 ft) and bears pretty flowers of off-white or palest pink, marked with faint rose stripes and spade-shaped marks on the three lower petals. This charming species flowers in spring.

G. ecklonii
Is native to the eastern Cape, the Transkei and Natal. It grows to 60 cm (2 ft), and bears flowers in summer which are distinctly speckled, dusty-pink and mauve.

G. liliaceus   LARGE BROWN AFRIKANDER,
(G. grandis)   AANDBLOM, RIBBOKBLOM
Grows wild from the Cape Peninsula to Port Elizabeth and is usually found in sandy soil. The flowers, which measure 8 cm across are carried on stems 60 cm (2 ft) tall. The colour of the flowers varies from subtle shades of brown to pale yellow flushed with ice-green in the throat. They are spectacular and unusual in form and colouring. In addition they have a delightful scent which is strong in the evening. The flowering time is spring.

G. macowanianus   PAINTED LADY
Can be found from the western Cape, where it flowers in spring, to the eastern Cape, where it flowers in summer. This dainty species grows to 30 cm (1 ft) and has flowers of pale pink to salmon

The Large Brown
Afrikander
(Gladiolus liliaceus)
is worth growing for its
scent and unusual
colouring

with distinctive red blotches on the three lower
segments.

G. milleri
(New name is *G. floribundus ssp. milleri*)
Can be seen growing wild in grassy areas near
Humansdorp and Port Elizabeth. Its flowering
stem grows to about 30 cm (1 ft) and carries rather
pretty flowers of pale cream in October.

G. oppositiflorus   TRANSKEI GLADIOLUS
The flowering stem of this species, native to the
eastern Cape and the Transkei, grows to about
60 cm (2 ft) in height and bears beautiful flowers
of white or palest pink, the lower segments always
being marked with maroon stripes. It flowers in
November.

G. orchidiflorus   GREEN KALKOENTJIE
Can be found growing in sandy places near Clanwilliam and in the south-western Cape. This little

Pink Afrikander *(Gladiolus carophyllaceus)* is another
pretty, scented species

gladiolus which grows to 30 cm (1 ft), has enchanting flowers of amber, suffused with palest green, with a maroon stripe on the two side petals, and maroon and lime-green on the lower segments. It flowers in August and September.

G. ornatus   PAINTED LADY

This is a most attractive little species which bears its lovely flowers at the end of winter and early in spring. It likes damp places and care should be taken to see that it does not dry out in autumn and winter, when it is grown in regions which are dry at this time of the year. The flowers are carried on stems 30-45 cm (1-1½ ft) tall, and are of a delightful shade of blush-pink. The three lower segments of the flowers are handsomely marked with cream or white flashes edged with crimson.

G. platyphyllus

Grows wild in the Transkei. It reaches a height of 60 cm (2 ft) and has hooded flowers of apricot to salmon in December.

G. psittacinus

(New name is *G. daleni*)   PARROT GLADIOLUS
This robust and handsome gladiolus is to be seen growing wild in parts of the Transvaal, Rhodesia and Portuguese East Africa. It flowers in late summer and early autumn making a sparkling addition to the garden. It is particularly useful where growing conditions are difficult, as it is determined to grow whatever the soil and situation. It reaches a height of 1.25 m (4 ft) and has long spikes of flame-coloured, hooded flowers with yellow markings on the lower segments. This species, too, played an important part as a parent of many hybrids.

The corms should be planted in late winter or early spring. A variety of this known as *G. psittacinus* var. *cooperi,* grows wild in parts of Lesotho and the Transvaal. Its flowers are lemon-yellow and excellent for arrangements but it does not make as striking a show in the garden as the one mentioned above.

G. salmoneus   SALMON GLADIOLUS
(New name is *G. oppositiflorus ssp. salmoneus*)
This charming species grows naturally in the eastern Cape. It has six to eight rigid, linear and strongly ribbed leaves and the flower stems rise to a height of about 60 cm (2 ft) with beautiful salmon-pink flowers. The flowering time is summer.

G. saundersii   SAUNDERS' GLADIOLUS
A summer-flowering species from the north-eastern Cape, Lesotho, Naṭal and the eastern Transvaal. The flowering stems grow to about 60 cm (2 ft) and bear flowers up to 10 cm across. They are of a rich vermilion hue and the lower segments have white patches spotted with red. The slender leaves are long and rigid. It is dormant in winter and stands severe frost.

G. stanfordiae
(New name is *G. ochroleucus* var. *ochroleucus*)
Can be found in the East London district in summer. It grows to about 25 cm (10 in) and has charming little flowers of blush-pink marked with rose.

G. tenellus
This little gladiolus can be found in the area between Piketberg and Bredasdorp. It is, however, rare, and as far as I am aware, it has not been grown in South Africa but has been cultivated in England. It is certainly worth a place in the garden for its funnel-shaped flowers of pale to sulphur yellow are very pretty and they give off a delightful scent. It grows to 20-30 cm in height.

G. tristis   YELLOW MARSH AFRIKANDER,
VLEI-AANDBLOM
Grows in marshy places in the eastern Cape, Natal and south-western Cape. The slender stems reach a height of about 45 cm (1½ ft) and bear flowers measuring about 5 cm long. They are of pale ivory to sulphur-yellow or greeny-cream, tinged on the outside with mauve or grey, and

Gladiolus tenellus with its prettily coloured, scented flowers deserves a place in gardens and window-boxes

have a strong carnation scent which is heaviest in the evenings. The flowering time is September to November. In the garden it will do well if watered regularly throughout its growing period. The variety *concolor* has larger flowers of palest yellow.

G. tysonii
(Now included with *G. daleni*)
This is a robust species from the eastern Cape, which grows to 60-90 cm (2-3 ft) in height and bears handsome, hooded flowers coloured pale tan or salmon with flushes of green on the three lower segments. The flowering time is summer.

G. venustus
(New name is *G. scullyi*)
This little gladiolus has a distinct scent which continues throughout the day. The flowers have pointed petals of dull yellow with purple or mauve tips. They grow to about 30 cm (1 ft) in height. To make an effective show the plants should be set close together in the garden or window-box. It is hardy to frost.

G. virescens
Grows to 25 cm (10 in) and has three slender spoon-shaped petals of pale mustard and lime-green at the bottom. The other petals are of the same shades suffused with dusky maroon.

GLORIOSA   GLORIOSA, FLAME LILY
DISTRIBUTION: A charming plant which can be found growing equally well in the shade of the dense bush along the coast of the eastern Cape and Natal, and in the open or amongst bushes in the Transvaal and Rhodesia.

DESCRIPTION: They are climbing plants which seldom grow more than about 1.25 m (4 ft) in height and which cling to any support they can find to keep themselves erect. The pretty oval, pointed leaves end in a strong tendril which grips the support firmly. The flowers, which appear in summer, are exceptionally decorative and the plant makes a splendid show in a flower border or when grown in pots or tubs on a stoep, patio or balcony. The buds are green, and, as the six petals unfurl, they arch back and out and change in colour to yellow and flame. The plant should be given some kind of support, such as a tripod of sticks, to which it can cling or it should be planted between shrubs so that it can grow up through them. It becomes dormant in winter.

CULTURE: Gloriosa starts into growth only when the spring has become warm, and the plants grow rapidly to 1.25 m (4 ft). It can be grown in gardens with severe frost, as it is dormant until spring is well advanced. Soon after flowering the plant dies down, and during this long period of dormancy it should be kept rather dry. When grown in the winter-rainfall area it should be planted in a loose soil which drains readily, as otherwise the tubers may rot through having too much moisture during the winter. If this is not possible, the tubers should be lifted in autumn and stored in dry peat until late winter. Give the plants plenty of water during the growing season.

The tubers are curiously shaped, somewhat reminiscent of a small sweet potato when they are young, but they grow to quite a large size if they are not disturbed. Plant the tubers 7 cm (3 in) below the top of the soil and see that they are in a light soil with compost added.

If they are to be grown in pots to be brought indoors, plant them in large pots so that there is space for the tuber to grow good roots, and after the foliage has died back store the pot in an out-of-the-way part of the garden or in a shed until growth starts again. The tuber is said to be highly poisonous.

Flame lilies can also be grown from seed. They take a fairly long time to germinate and should therefore be sown in soil to which peat has been added to prevent it drying out quickly. The seed will give rise to small tubers at the end of the growing season and these can be left to grow on in the same place for another year until they are big enough to plant out in their permanent place. It usually takes two or three years to produce flowering plants from seed.

G. superba GLORIOSA, FLAME LILY
Grows naturally in the Transvaal, Rhodesia and further north. The flowers have distinctly wavy, curled and twisted petals which arch up and back, and are shaded from yellow to bright flame colour.

G. virescens FLAME LILY, CLIMBING LILY, GEELBOSLELIE, ROOIBOSLELIE
This species grows wild along the coast from the eastern Cape into Natal and further north. The petals differ from those of *G. superba* inasmuch as they are narrow at the base and broaden half way up before tapering to the tip. They curve inwards at the tip. They are wavy only along the edge in the top half and less curled than those of *G. superba*. The depth of colour seems to depend upon the amount of sunlight the plant gets—those growing in shade being paler than those growing in the open. They are usually yellow at the base and shaded to crimson at the tips of the petals.

HAEMANTHUS
CATHERINE WHEEL, PAINT BRUSH, APRIL FOOL, SNAKE LILY, TORCH LILY, MARCH FLOWER, MAARTBLOM

DISTRIBUTION: Haemanthus grow naturally in many parts of the country and in all the provinces.

DESCRIPTION: These are unusual plants which can be described as handsome rather than beautiful. They make a fine contribution to the garden and they can also be grown as indoor plants in pots, or as stoep or patio plants in tubs. Haemanthus produce large heads of flowers at the end of thick, fleshy stalks. The flowers vary in form and in their arrangement. Some are star-shaped and carried in rounded umbels whilst other species have flowers arranged close together to look like a round brush. The flowers are in shades of cream and pink to red, but a white one is also known. In some species the flowerhead is surrounded by colourful bracts and later, when the flower fades it gives way to large scarlet berries which are also decorative. The leaves vary considerably according to the species. In some they grow more or less upright whilst in others they spread flat on the ground.

They grow from huge bulbs which have a definite period of dormancy when they require little or no water.

CULTURE: Although haemanthus grow fairly freely in the veld, as yet most of them have proved difficult to raise in the garden. Some of them prefer growing in the shade, although near the coast they may often be found growing out in the open. They should therefore be tried in partial shade in inland districts. Species from the summer-rainfall area which are dormant in winter should be tried in districts which have severe frosts. Other species may not be damaged by frost if they have shade over them to keep off the early morning sun in winter.

Natal Paint Brush (*Haemanthus natalensis*). Plant this pretty species in groups in front of a shrub border or singly in pots (New name is *H. puniceus*)

Once planted they should be left undisturbed for many years and it is advisable therefore to prepare the ground before planting. The big bulbs send out large roots, and holes 45 cm (1½ ft) across and of at least this depth should be made, and compost added to the soil at the bottom of the hole. Plant the bulb so that the top is at, or just below, soil-level. Those native to summer-rainfall regions should be planted out in August, and species from the winter-rainfall region in December and January. Although they like plenty of water when growing, they should be kept fairly dry when dormant, and for this reason they should be planted on their own under a tree or in large pots or tubs where they can be watered and kept dry at the appropriate times.

Haemanthus can be raised from seed. This sometimes takes three seasons to reach flowering size. The seedlings, like the parent plants, should be allowed to become fairly dry during their dormant period.

H. albiflos   APRIL FOOL, POEIERKWAS

This species is found in many parts of the eastern Cape and further north into the Transvaal, often in the coastal bush or along shady river banks. It has leathery leaves, edged with white hair, which spread flat along the ground. The flower stem rises to about 45 cm (1½ ft) and when the flower has faded, the red berries are almost as attractive as the flower. The flowerhead, which appears in April, consists of a tightly packed mass of creamy-white flowers surrounded by large bracts which so enclose the many flowers that the bracts themselves appear to form the flower, which probably accounts for the common name of April fool. The name of *poeierkwas* is more apt

as the flowerhead looks rather like a brush for applying powder.

H. amarylloides   PINK HAEMANTHUS

Bears round heads of cream to pale pink starry flowers on thick 30 cm (1 ft) stems. Each flower is about 6 mm across and attached to the top of the stem by its own short stalk. The bracts around the flowerhead are narrow and pink. The flower stem rises from the bare ground when the plant is without leaves in October and November. Immediately after the flower fades the leaves appear and remain green until winter when they die down.

H. coccineus   MARCH FLOWER

In late summer or early autumn this species from the winter-rainfall region sends up from the bare ground a thick stem mottled with brown which bears a head of coral-pink flowers enclosed in wide scarlet bracts. Later two large leaves grow out. They may be up to 18 cm broad and 30-60 cm long and lie almost prostrate on the ground.

H. incarnatus

May be seen growing in the scrub in parts of the eastern Cape near Port Elizabeth. The bulbous rootstock is rather flattened instead of rounded, as is usual in other species. The leaves, which rise after the flowers, are about 22 cm long with a purple margin and spotted with the same colour on the underside. The flower stem is crimson, about 20 cm (8 in) tall, and bears a brush-like head of rose-coloured flowers enclosed in scarlet bracts. It is decorative, although not as large as some other species. Its flowering period is summer.

H. katherinae   CATHERINE WHEEL,
(New name is *H. multiflorus*)   BLOOD FLOWER,
                                 BLOEDBLOM

This species is to be found in the veld in the eastern Province, Natal, Swaziland, the eastern Transvaal and Rhodesia. It is one of the most handsome of the species and the most widely known for it was grown in Europe in the latter part of the last century, usually as a pot plant.

It bears a huge round head of flowers measuring 25 cm across on sturdy 60 cm (2 ft) high stems speckled at the base. The flowerheads are made up of small scarlet flowers each on its own stalk. Its large, deep green, undulated leaves grow to a length of 45 cm and are often 15 cm at their broadest. The scarlet berries are decorative long after the flowers fade. It flowers in late summer or early autumn. The plants should be kept fairly dry in winter when grown in the winter-rainfall region as they are dormant at this time.

H. magnificus   PAINT BRUSH, MIELIEGIFBOL
(New name is *H. puniceus*)

Grows wild usually in coastal bush and under trees or scrub in the eastern Cape, Natal and the Transvaal. This most ornamental species has a flowerhead like a paint brush or a large shaving brush. It consists of brilliant scarlet filaments tipped with golden-yellow anthers and the whole is surrounded by crimson bracts. There is also a variety with pink flowers. The flower stem, liberally speckled with maroon at the base, grows to about 30-45 cm (1-1½ ft) high. It produces its flowers in late spring and early summer before the leaves, which develop while or after flowering. The leaves emerge from a thick stem about 60 cm (2 ft) high and are large, measuring about 40 cm in length. The plant is dormant during winter.

H. multiflorus
(*H. sacculus*)

Can be found in the eastern Transvaal. It has large, round umbels of coral-pink to rose flowers with prominent anthers, and upright-growing leaves.

H. puniceus   NATAL PAINT BRUSH, BLOOD
         FLOWER, BLOOD LILY, SNAKE LILY,
              SEEROOGBLOM, POEIERKWAS

Found in the eastern Cape as well as Natal, this is another haemanthus with a brush-like inflorescence. The filaments in this case are coral to red with golden anthers and the surrounding bracts are of a brownish hue. It is very like the species mentioned above but not as colourful, and

the flower stem is often much taller (30-90 cm) with undulated leaves which develop after the flower. It is dormant in winter and bears its flowers in summer.

HOMERIA   CAPE TULIP, TULP

DISTRIBUTION: Although these plants are to be found growing wild in all the provinces, only a few species from the western Cape are attractive enough for garden show.

DESCRIPTION: The flowers last for only a day but as there are many buds which open in succession, the plants remain decorative for quite a long time. The flowers are made up of six oval or oblong segments. As the plants are fairly small it is advisable to plant them close together.

CULTURE: The species described below flower in late winter or early spring and the corms should therefore be planted in January or February, 2-3 cm (1 in) below the soil and 8-12 cm (3-5 in) apart. They should be watered regularly during the winter, and on the highveld, where severe frost is experienced, they should have some protection or be shaded from the early morning winter sun. They also grow readily from seed sown in late summer. They are not particular as to soil.

H. collina   SALMON HOMERIA, ROOITULP
(*H. breyniana*)

Has flowers which appear along the ends of stems 30-45 cm (1-1½ ft) tall. They are about 3-4 cm across and generally salmon to yellow in colour. The leaves are slender and arching. Massed, it is decorative. This species is poisonous to stock, and can easily become a weed; it is therefore not recommended for farm gardens.

H. comptonii

Has leaves about 25 cm long and 18 mm wide at the base, tapering to the tip. The flower is about 4 cm across and made up of six widely separated petals with rounded tips. It is most attractively coloured lemon-yellow at the centre and salmon-pink along the upper part of the petals.

H. elegans   PAINTED HOMERIA, POUBLOM

This species is a most decorative plant and should be grown in gardens and window-boxes everywhere. The flowers are about 5 cm across and of bright yellow with gay splashes of green or orange on the petals, or with three yellow and three

The Painted Homeria (*Homeria elegans*) produces delightful flowers in early spring

orange petals. It grows to 30-45 cm (1-1½ ft) and flowers in early spring.

HOMOGLOSSUM — FLAMES, RED AFRIKANDER

DISTRIBUTION: Most of the decorative species grow wild in the western Cape.

DESCRIPTION: In late winter and early spring they produce flowers which look somewhat like gladioli in shape. Planted close together in a rock-garden or the front of the flower border, they make a striking show.

CULTURE: Corms should be planted in January or February, about 2-5 cm (1-2 in) beneath the soil. They grow well in partial shade as well as in full sun, and are not particular as to soil.

H. hollandii — FLAMES, RED AFRIKANDER

Can be found growing wild in the area around George and eastwards into the Transkei. It has pretty flame-coloured flowers on slender stems about 45 cm (1½ ft) high. The leaves are long and slender. It flowers in late winter and early spring. Planted in groups it makes a splendid show.

H. merianellum — FLAMES
(*Antholyza merianella*)

A plant from the Cape Peninsula which bears its flowers in winter. The stem grows to 30-60 cm (1-2 ft) in height and bears flowers made up of a thin tube flaring out into a cup—the whole flower being of a vivid flame colour.

H. watsonium
(*Antholyza revoluta*)

Grows in fields and on the slopes of mountains near Cape Town, and produces coral-red flowers on stems 30-45 cm (1-1½ ft) tall, in winter. Each flower consists of a slender tube ending in six widely flared petals. This is a fine plant to produce colour in winter on a rockery or elsewhere in the garden, or to grow in pots or window boxes.

IXIA — IXIA, WAND FLOWER, CORN LILY, KALOSSIE

DISTRIBUTION: The most decorative species grow wild in the south-western Cape.

DESCRIPTION: Although ixias were first grown in Europe 150 years ago, they are as yet very rarely seen in gardens in Southern Africa. This is probably due to the fact that they do not make a good show unless massed, yet individually they have great charm. The plants now grown in Europe are hybrids with more showy flowers than their parents.

These plants vary in height from a few centimetres to 60 cm (2 ft) and the flowers are carried in loose clusters at the ends of slender, straight, wiry stems, which accounts for the common name of wand flower. The flowers vary in shape according to species, sometimes being rather funnel-shaped, sometimes saucer or bowl-shaped, and sometimes with an elongated tube ending in a starry face. They are decorative in the garden and the smaller ones make an enchanting show in pots and window-boxes.

CULTURE: Ixias grow very readily from little corms which should be planted about 2-3 cm (1 in) deep and 7-10 cm (3-4 in) apart to make a mass of colour. They should be grouped in colonies of fifty or more. The best time to set them out is from January to March. Plant them in porous soil and in full sunshine, except in hot, inland gardens where they seem to prefer some shade. They grow readily from seed sown at the same time of the year, to produce flowering plants the following season.

When grown in the summer-rainfall area they should be watered well during winter and, after the bulbs have finished flowering and the leaves have died down, they may be lifted, dried off and stored, allowing the space they occupied to be filled with other plants during summer, or they may be left in the ground, and shallow-rooted annuals set out over them to cover the ground in summer.

I. columellaris PURPLE IXIA
Is one of the most decorative of the species with flowers of a pleasant purple hue on 60 cm (2 ft) stems. It flowers in September.

I. lutea YELLOW IXIA
Has bright yellow flowers on stems 30 cm (1 ft) high in September.

I. maculata YELLOW IXIA, GEELKALOSSIE
This fine species bears bowl-shaped flowers 2-4 cm across on stems up to 45 cm ($1\frac{1}{2}$ ft) high. The flowers are yellow or orange, usually with a coral-red flush on the back of the petals and a purplish-brown centre marking. The flowering time is from August to October.

I. monadelpha
A small plant which grows to 30 cm (1 ft) in height and has charming little flowers of mauve, misty blue, or yellow with a flush of darker blue and tan at the centre. It flowers in late spring.

Flames,
Red Afrikander
(Homoglossum
hollandii) looks
lovely in the
garden and in
arrangements

Ixia
(*Ixia monadelpha*).
This species bears
attractive flowers of
unusual shades

An arrangement of
orange Ixias

192

I. orientalis

This species is found from George eastwards to Port Elizabeth. It bears its fairy-like flowers of pink or pinky-mauve on stems about 45 cm (1½ ft) high. It flowers in spring. *Ixia scillaris* is another pretty species with pink flowers.

I. polystachya   CORN LILY, KORINGBLOMMETJIE

This species grows to 60 cm (2 ft) and has fragile flowers of white, palest pink or misty mauve, often with a central green flush to enhance the colours. It seems to prefer damp places and light shade to full sun. Its flowering time is mid-spring.

I. trifolia   THREE-LEAFED IXIA

A species native to drier areas of the south-western Cape, this one makes a colourful show if massed, and is a fine rockery plant. It has a flower stem 15-25 cm (6-10 in) high. The flowers of carmine to cyclamen appear in winter to early spring.

I. viridiflora   GREEN IXIA, GROENKALOSSIE

Any green flower commands attention because it is a rarity. The sea-green ixia is worth trying because it is attractive, as well as rare. The colour is subtle and enhanced by a circle of deep purple to maroon in the centre of the flower. The flowers are about 2-3 cm across and carried on stems up to 45 cm (1½ ft) in height. It flowers in spring.

KNIPHOFIA   RED-HOT POKER, TORCH LILY

DISTRIBUTION: Widely distributed in all provinces of South Africa and in Rhodesia.

DESCRIPTION: Red-hot pokers make a fine show in any garden and well deserve their popularity. They look handsome at the back of a mixed flower border, in groups in the front of a shrub border, or lining a long drive. They are splendid flowers for planting in bold groups in large gardens and parks.

Some species were already being grown in England in the eighteenth century and records show that one of them, then referred to as an aloe, flowered in Kew Gardens in 1735. Many charming hybrids have been developed since then but as yet both these named hybrids and our native species are not easy to obtain under their correct names. The plants grow from a fleshy rootstock and most of them are tall and handsome with flowers closely attached to the top section of the stem, opening from the lower ones upwards.

South African gardeners generally grow only two of the hybrids, referred to as "summer-flowering" and "winter-flowering" red-hot pokers. Gardeners keen on having more variety should try some of the species mentioned below.

CULTURE: Some species grow in full sunshine and rather dry places but most of them grow in areas which become damp or marshy for part of the year. None of them likes to be disturbed and it is, therefore, advisable, when planting, to prepare the ground so that the roots can be left undisturbed for several years. When poor flowering seems to indicate that they may need dividing, lift the clumps, cut through the fleshy roots with a sharp spade, and re-plant sections of them. They can also be grown from seed but this takes a long time to produce flowering plants. They tolerate frosty winters but will not flower well unless watered fairly regularly, particularly when they are coming into flower.

K. caulescens   BASUTO TORCH LILY

This is a big, bold plant suitable only for large gardens. It grows naturally in the highlands of the north-eastern Cape and Lesotho where there is an abundance of rain in summer and a dry winter. The thick flower stem grows to as high as 1.25 m (4 ft) and bears flowers which are coral-red in the bud and flushed yellow as they open. The leaves are big and arched. It flowers in spring.

K. linearifolia
(K. longiflora)

Is to be found in damp places, particularly near the coast from the eastern Cape up into Natal. The stem grows up to 90 cm (3 ft) and has flowers of sulphur-yellow followed by seeds which look like large beads. The flowering time is summer.

K. multiflora   BULRUSH POKER

Grows wild in the highlands of Natal and the eastern Transvaal and requires to be kept fairly moist throughout its growing season.

Because of its size, this is a plant for the large garden rather than the small. It reaches a height of 2 m (6 ft) and has long, slender flower spikes with small flowers closely packed. The flowers may be cream or yellow with red buds. The plant is dormant in winter and bears its flowers in autumn.

K. praecox

Occurs generally in marshy places and often at

Red-hot Poker
(Kniphofia hybrid.)
Plant them in groups in
front of shrubs, along
the sides of a long drive,
or at the back of a
flower border

high altitudes from the eastern Transvaal south through Natal to the eastern Cape. It is a tall-growing species up to 1.75 m (5 ft), flowering from March to May. The buds of rich crimson open to yellow.

K. rooperi   SPRING TORCH LILY
Grows in marshy places in the eastern Cape and Natal. This is a tall species to 90 cm (3 ft) or more, with leaves almost as long. The flowerhead is unusual in that it is round rather than cylindrical. The flowers are orange-yellow.

K. splendida
This is another Transvaal species which produces its flowers in autumn. The stems grow to about 1.25 m (4 ft) in height and the long spikes of flowers are orange in the bud and turn yellow as they open. It is dormant during winter.

K. triangularis subsp. **triangularis**   DWARF
(*K. macowanii*)   RED-HOT POKER
A charming small species with spikes of salmon to coral flowers which droop down from the top of the stem. It grows to about 45 cm (1½ ft) and flowers in summer. In its natural habitat, in the

eastern Cape, it favours marshy places, and, in gardens it should be watered well, specially in spring and summer. It is more suitable than the large types for gardens of average size. It is interesting to note that amongst certain African tribes it is believed that if a pregnant woman wears the root threaded on a sinew, she and her child will never be struck by lightning.

K. uvaria   RED-HOT POKER
(*K. aloides*)
A handsome species which occurs in the western Cape. It is to be found growing in moist places and grows to a height of 90 cm (3 ft) with big flower spikes. The buds are bright red and open to equally bright yellow flowers. A clump of these in full flower is very striking. The flowers appear during summer.

LACHENALIA   CAPE COWSLIP, LACHENALIA,
                   NAËLTJIE, VIOOLTJIE
There are many species of this decorative plant which grows naturally in the south-western Cape.

DESCRIPTION: Lachenalias have been grown in Europe for more than a hundred years and some remarkably attractive hybrids have been raised there from our wild ones. Many of the species are very, very lovely and deserve a prominent place in gardens and window-boxes. They are widely grown in Australia and New Zealand as well as in Europe. It is a pity that these lovely flowers, so well known around the globe, are seldom planted by gardeners in their homeland.

They are small plants usually growing to only between 15-30 cm (6-12 in) in height but they nevertheless make a fine show when massed and are excellent for the front of a border, as the flowers are colourful and last for a long time on the plant. For this reason they are also admirable plants to grow indoors in containers. The fact that they start flowering in autumn and continue through winter is an additional attribute.

The flowers are generally tubular in form, composed of six segments of unequal size forming one tube inside another. Some are of a single colour, whilst others are of two or three colours. The flowers are waxy, carried in spikes, and very, very attractive in the garden and in arrangements.

CULTURE: Plant the bulbs about 3-5 cm (1-2 in) deep and 10 cm (4 in) apart to make a massed show. One needs at least fifty of them in a group in the garden to look effective. As the different species flower at different times, I think that each group should be composed of a single species. The best time to plant them is from January to March. The flowering period is from April to October. After flowering, the bulbs may be left in the ground, but as one usually needs the ground for other plants, and because the bulbs are apt to rot if over-watered during their period of dormancy in summer, it is advisable to lift them *after* the leaves have faded in late spring and to clean them off and store them until the following January or February. Store the bulbs in vermiculite or soil in a shady place, and water them occasionally during their period of dormancy.

When lifting the bulbs, be careful to lift them so as not to lose the tiny offsets which form around the parent bulb. Separate these from the parent bulb, and plant them in pots or boxes or special raising beds for a season, before planting them out into the garden. Lachenalias may also be raised from seed sown in March. This should produce flowering plants in the following year, although some species take a further season to grow to flowering size.

Like many other South African bulbs lachenalias prefer a friable soil which drains readily. In gardens where the soil is a heavy clay, compost should be added to the top 25 to 30 cm (10 to 12 in) of soil. When grown outside in areas where winters are very cold they should be protected from frost. Although they do well in full sunshine near the coast they should be planted where they are shaded for part of the day when grown inland. They grow and flower quite well under the shade of tall trees and they flower very well when brought indoors as pot plants.

L. aloides var. quadricolor   KLIPKALOSSIE
(L. tricolor)

This is one of the most attractive of this charming group of plants. It grows to 15-25 cm (6-10 in) and bears pendulous flowers beautifully formed and coloured. The inner segments are of green tipped with burgundy and the outer segments are deep rose or crimson at the base changing to yellow at the top. The leaves are blotched with mauve markings. The variety, *aurea* has flowers of a deep golden colour.

L. bulbifera   RED LACHENALIA, ROOINAELS,
(L. pendula)   VIOOLTJIE

This species is widely grown in gardens in New Zealand to produce flowers for florists there. It makes the garden or house gay in mid-winter when it bears its beautiful flowers of coral-red. It grows to about 15-45 cm (6-18 in). This is one of the most decorative species for gardens and for growing in pots, bowls or window-boxes for colour in winter.

Golden Lachenalia *(Lachenalia aloides* var. *aurea)*
A pot-plant of delicate beauty

Red Lachenalia (*Lachenalia bulbifera*). One of the best species for garden show, for arrangements and for pots.

L. contaminata   WILD HYACINTH
A small species which grows to only 15-20 cm (6-8 in) in height and has attractive creamy flowers with an open face instead of the characteristic tubular form. The buds and ends of the flower segments are tipped with terra-cotta markings. The leaves are like grass. Its flowering period is mid- to late spring.

L. glaucina   OPAL LACHENALIA
This charming species grows to about 30 cm (1 ft) in height and bears a stem of enchanting little flowers. The inside segments are usually lighter in colour than the outer ones. The tones of misty blues and iridescent mauves of the flowers are reminiscent of the luminous colours of an opal. *L. glaucina* var. *pallida* is a close relation with flowers of a yellow or pale green hue. The leaves are spotted with purple. The flowering period is early to mid-spring. This is an enchanting pot or border plant.

L. mutabilis   FAIRY LACHENALIA
Reaches a height of about 15-20 cm (6-8 in) and has sterile flowers at the tips of the stalks, of fascinating shades of blue, from a fluorescent electric-blue to lavender, whilst those lower down on the stem are from tawny-copper to lime-green.

L. ovatifolia   OVAL-LEAFED LACHENALIA
This species is characterized by its unusual leaves which are rather fleshy and broad. It reaches a height of about 15-20 cm (6-8 in) and has a thick stem bearing a spike of flowers which are white at the base with tips of mauve to purple. It flowers in late winter and early spring.

L. rosea
Grows to only about 15 cm (6 in) and has dainty flowers of beige to pink shaded to cyclamen, or ones that are ice-blue at the base shading to pale rose at the tips.

L. rubida   SANDKALOSSIE, ROOIVIOOLTJIE
Although it seldom grows more than 15 cm (6 in) in height this little lachenalia with its coral-red flowers and large spotted leaves is most decorative. It flowers in autumn and early winter.

L. unicolor
Grows to 30 cm (12 in) and has showy spikes of flowers of lilac to violet in colour, with stamens jutting out beyond the petals.

L. unifolia
Has a slender arching leaf or leaves about 20 cm long and 12 mm wide at the base, grooved along their length and widening to a banded base. The flower stems are about 15 cm (6 in) long and are usually of ice-blue tipped with palest green and maroon, with a tube of alabaster.

L. violacea
Is about 30 cm (1 ft) tall with many stalked flowers on the top part of the stem. They are beautifully shaded from greenish blue to violet.

LANARIA LANATA   COTTONWOOL FLOWER, (*L. plumosa*)   KAPOKBLOM
DISTRIBUTION: Grows in a few places near the coast from the Cape to Port Elizabeth.

DESCRIPTION: This is a useful plant to have in a mixed border of annuals and perennials, for it offers an interesting contrast in form and colour to other flowers. It grows to a height of about 60 cm (2 ft) and bears heads of flowers, the buds of which look as though they have been fashioned from ivory-coloured wool. These open to reveal starry little pinky mauve flowers which are not as decorative as the flowerhead when in bud. The flowering time is spring to mid-summer.

196

Opal Lachenalia
(*Lachenalia glaucina*)
has flowers of en-
chanting tones of
colour

Cottonwool Flower,
Kapokblom
(*Lanaria lanata*)
is an unusual plant
which stands harsh
growing conditions

Springbok Painted
Petals
(*Lapeirousia speciosa*)
does well in dry places

CULTURE: It grows from seed but can also be grown from sections of the root which may be divided up. Lanaria needs to be watered during winter and spring and does best in regions which do not experience severe frost.

LAPEIROUSIA   PAINTED PETALS

DISTRIBUTION: These dainty plants are to be found growing wild in parts of the eastern and south-western Cape, Natal and the Transvaal.

DESCRIPTION: The flowers are composed of very slender tubes which flare out into an open face made up of six segments, the whole flower measuring up to 5 cm in length. The foliage differs according to the species. They look effective massed at the front of a border or when grown in pots.

CULTURE: It grows from a corm which can be left in the ground when the flowering season is over, or they can be lifted and stored. They can also be grown from seed. Species native to the winter-rainfall area must be kept watered well in winter when they are grown in the summer-rainfall area. The species indigenous to the summer-rainfall area are hardy to frost. Spring-flowering species should be planted in late summer, and the summer-flowering ones in late winter.

L. corymbosa   KLIPBLOMMETJIE
A dainty little plant found in gravelly or sandy soil in the Cape Peninsula. It grows to 10-15 cm (4-6 in) and bears charming little clusters of flowers of royal blue to violet-blue marked with a white line circling the inside of the petals half-way down. It flowers in spring.

L. laxa   SMALL RED IRIS
(New name is *Anomatheca laxa*)
This species grows naturally in many parts of the country, from the eastern Cape up into the Transvaal. It is to be found growing in shady places under scrub or trees. It grows to 20-30 cm (8-12 in) and bears dainty little flowers of coral-red. Each of the three lower petals have a darker marking at the centre whilst the other three lack this. The

leaves are 12 mm broad and the same length as the flowering stalk. It flowers in mid- to late spring.

L. speciosa   Springbok Painted Petals
(New name is *L. silenoides*)
A charming little plant which makes a fine show in the dry countryside near Springbok in the north-western Cape, which is its natural home. It is to be found growing in clusters, sometimes in the shade of scrub and sometimes with its roots imbedded in the cracks of rocks which give some shade. The flowers are carried on stems only 10 cm (4 in) high and are of carmine to magenta, with contrasting shading on the three lower petals.

Plant it in clumps in sandy soil where it gets some shade from the hot afternoon sun.

LITTONIA MODESTA   Butterlily, Climbing Lily, Geelklokkie
DISTRIBUTION: An unusual little plant which occurs in parts of the Eastern Province, and up through the Transkei and Natal to the northern Transvaal.

DESCRIPTION: This little plant, which belongs to the lily family, is a climbing or scrambling plant which is like its near relation gloriosa in that it has the same kind of tendrils at the tips of the upper leaves. The flowers of deep golden-yellow are bell-shaped with six pointed segments, measuring about 4 cm in length. When the flowers fade the seed pods continue to make the plant decorative. The flowering time is summer. The plants grow to 60-90 cm (2-3 ft) and in their natural habitat they cling to any support offered by the scrub or bushes about them. Use it as a patio or indoor or balcony plant.

CULTURE: The plants grow from a tuber which should be planted 5 cm (2 in) deep in well-composted soil in late winter or very early spring, in a position which gets shade for the hottest part of the day. When grown in the garden in the winter-rainfall area it might be advisable to lift the tuber at the beginning of autumn, as too much water during its dormant season could cause it to rot. Store the tubers in vermiculite in a cool place until the following July to September when they should be planted again. They do best, however, if left in the ground. They can also be grown from seed sown in spring. The seeds should be kept moist and shaded. Germination sometimes takes several weeks. When the leaves die down

the plants should be watered only occasionally.

Whether the plants are grown in the garden or in pots or tubs they should be provided with some kind of support. Three bamboo canes measuring 60 cm (2 ft) high inserted into the ground to form a tripod, is the neatest kind of support to give them.

MELASPHAERULA RAMOSA   Fairybells, Bruidjies, Baardmannetjie
DISTRIBUTION: This attractive plant grows in the south-western Cape, extending eastwards to Humansdorp.

DESCRIPTION: Although the flowers are small, the whole habit of growth of the plant is such that it would be a charming addition to the garden and useful, too, for providing cut flowers. It grows to about 60 cm (2 ft) in height and bears masses of little flowers about 12 mm across, all along the top part of the stem. The flowers are very dainty with ivory or white pointed petals, some of which have carmine streaks on them. The sword-like leaves measure about 30 cm in length. The flowering period is late winter and early spring.

CULTURE: Plant the small corms 5-10 cm (2-4 in) apart and 2-3 cm (1 in) deep in soil to which compost has been added, and see that they receive water regularly from autumn until flowering is over. In hot inland districts they should be planted where they are shaded for part of the day.

MORAEA   Morea, Tulp
DISTRIBUTION: These plants are to be found growing in many parts of the country from the coast up to the highveld and Rhodesia.

DESCRIPTION: They are members of the iris family and many species have lovely flowers. Furthermore, exceptionally beautiful hybrids have been evolved in Europe from some of them. Certain species which were originally known as moraeas are known now as dietes. The latter have a rhizome or fibrous root whereas the true moraea grows from a corm. They are very like miniature Dutch irises in shape with flowers of charming colours. The flowers of some species have petals as fragile as a butterfly's wings and as beautifully marked as a peacock's tail. Although in many species the flower lasts only for a day, new ones keep opening and a clump of them therefore remains colourful for a long time.

CULTURE: Most species grow well in any kind of

A scene in Kirsten-
bosch Gardens, Cape.
yellow Tulip
(*Moraea spathulata*)
and the grey leaves of
Helichrysum paniculatum

soil. The space apart to plant will depend upon the size of the species grown. Small ones are better planted on their own in clumps whilst larger ones may be planted in a mixed flower border or in groups in front of shrubs. Species native to the winter-rainfall area should be watered during winter, when grown in summer-rainfall regions. They have a period of dormancy for a couple of months after the leaves die down and during this period less water should be given, or they can be left completely dry. If there is danger of their being overwatered during the period of dormancy, because of their being in a bed with other plants which require liberal watering, lift them, when the leaves have died down, and store the corms in a box of vermiculite until the next planting time. When lifting, do this carefully so that you do not lose the tiny offsets which form about the mother corm. Remove these and plant them in a nursery bed, pot or box to grow on for a couple of years until they are large enough to go into the garden.

Moraeas can be easily propagated from seed too. The correct time to plant or sow depends upon the season when the plants flower. Summer-flowering species should be planted or sown in late winter and early spring, and the winter-flowering species in February. They grow well in poor soil and most of them stand long periods of drought and a good deal of frost.

M. fugax UINTJIE
(*M. edulis*)

This delicate little plant occurs in the Cape Peninsula, on mountain slopes and plains. It grows from 15-45 cm (6-18 in) in height and bears small flowers of a delicate shade of mauve, with attractive "peacock" markings of white and yellow. *M. edulis* var. *longifolia* has one very long reed-like leaf measuring up to 40 cm, and flowers of canary-yellow.

M. juncea
(New name is *M. vegeta*)
Grows near Cape Town, usually in shady places, and produces charming little flowers of a buff hue

200

with yellow markings, edged with maroon at the centre. Their height is 15-30 cm (6-12 in). The flowering time is spring.

M. papilionacea   Butterfly Morea
A dainty plant from the western Cape which grows to 20 cm (8 in) or more. It has ethereal little flowers beautifully marked with contrasting shades. The main colours are yellow with salmon-pink markings, or salmon with yellow. To be effective it should be grown in pots or window-boxes or very closely planted at the front of a bed of small plants.

M. ramosissima   Branching Morea
(M. ramosa)
Grows naturally in rather damp places, often in semi-shade, in the south-western Cape. It reaches a height of 60 cm (2 ft) and in spring it produces charming flowers of clear yellow with golden markings in the middle. The flowers are carried like a candelabra which gives the plant a certain elegance, but as the flowers are open for such a short time it should not be used in an important position in the garden.

M. spathulata   Yellow Tulip,
(M. spathacea)   Groot Geeltulp
Grows from Port Elizabeth eastwards and up into the Transvaal. There appear to be differences in growth according to situation. It produces one or two long leaves and has beautiful yellow flowers on stems 90 cm (3 ft) tall. It flowers in winter or spring. As it is said to be poisonous to stock it should not be planted in farm gardens.

M. tripetala   Dwarf Morea
A fragile-looking flower which grows wild in the Cape Peninsula. It has three broad petals and three pointed ones which stand up rigidly at a distinct angle, making it somewhat different in form from the others. The broad petals of misty blue have a central blotch of yellow surrounded by deep blue at the centre. The plant grows to about 30 cm (1 ft) in height and has long, slender leaves. The flowering period is late winter and early spring.

M. villosa   Peacock Morea,
(M. pavonia)   Uintjie
This is one of the most enchanting of our spring-flowering plants and deserves to be more widely grown in pots and other containers as well as in the garden. Many hybrids of different shades have been bred from it. The flowers have three broad, rounded petals which open out flat, and the central ones are reduced to narrow, upstanding segments. At the centre of each of the three broad

Peacock Morea
(Moraea villosa) has flowers as fragile as a butterfly's wings and as beautiful

petals are rounded splashes of glowing peacock-blue or green which resemble those on a peacock's tail, both in their form and iridescence. The colours obtainable are misty blue, yellow, orange, beige, cream, pink and mauve. They look as though they have been fashioned from delicate porcelain and are so beautiful that everyone should grow them, regardless of whether they have a garden or not. They do well in pots or window-boxes. When planted in the garden at least sixty corms should be set out in a group, spacing them about 8 cm (4 in) apart. Several corms can be planted together in a small flower pot.

NERINE   NERINA, GUERNSEY LILY

DISTRIBUTION: Species of nerine are to be found growing wild in different parts of Southern Africa from the coast to the highveld.

DESCRIPTION: This plant was an early traveller for it is recorded that in 1634 one species flowered in a garden in Paris, and it was cultivated in England by 1659. The story of how a species from the Cape came to be called the Guernsey lily is an interesting one. In 1659, a Dutch ship proceeding from the Far East via the Cape to Holland, was wrecked on the Channel Islands, and boxes of Cape bulbs consigned to Holland were washed ashore on the island of Guernsey. There they grew and produced their lovely scarlet flowers. The plants multiplied and flourished on the island and in due course became one of the finest flowers grown on the islands for export to florists in Europe. Because it grew so well, and had grown there for so many years, it was named *Nerine sarniensis*, the word *sarnia* being the old name for the island. At one time it was thought to be a native of Japan, since the vessel which was wrecked was on its way from the Orient. It was only a century later, when specimens were found growing on the slopes of Table Mountain that its real origin became known. This species, and hybrids developed from it, are widely grown in England, the United States, Australia and New Zealand as pot plants, as well as in the garden, and to provide cut flowers in autumn.

Nerinas bear round heads of flowers, each one attached by its own stalk to the top of the flower stem—rather like a miniature agapanthus. Each flower has six narrow petals which are reflexed at the ends to show off the stamens. The colours of the flowers vary from palest pink to deep rose and crimson. A hybrid which is white has recently been produced in England. The long, slender leaves appear with, or just after, the flowers.

CULTURE: Nerinas grow from a bulb which should be planted so that the neck of the bulb is level with the top of the soil. The best time to plant them or to divide them (when necessary) is after the foliage has died down and before they flower, usually December to January. *N. bowdenii*, which is dormant in winter, can however be planted in spring. They should be kept fairly moist during their growing season, which for most species is autumn to spring, and may be allowed to dry off somewhat during their dormant season when the leaves have died down.

When grown in pots these should be stored, after the flowers have faded, sunk into the ground in an out-of-the-way corner of the garden to prevent them from drying out too much. The bulbs should not be disturbed for three or four years as they do not always flower the first year after being transplanted. They should be planted in soil to which some compost and peat have been added. Nerinas increase from baby bulbs which arise from the parent one. These can be removed when the bulbs are lifted after four or more years and planted in nursery beds, boxes or pots to grow on for a couple of years until they are large enough to go into the garden. Nerinas are hardy to moderate frost and will grow in full sunshine or light shade. In hot, inland gardens most species do best in light shade.

They can also be grown from seed which should be sown when it falls from the parent plant and whilst it is still green. Plants from seed seldom flower until the third season. Although handsome hybrids have been raised in Europe, Australia and New Zealand, no South Africans appear to have taken an interest in hybridizing these handsome native plants.

N. alta   TALL NERINA
Grows in damp districts of the eastern Cape and produces a head of beautiful pink flowers with crimped petals. The flowers appear in late summer and are carried on stems up to 90 cm (3 ft) high.

N. angulata   TALL NERINA
This species, which grows wild in the mountains near King Williams Town in the Eastern Cape and in the Transvaal, reaches a height of about 60 cm (2 ft) and bears flowers of pale pink to rose. It is usually to be found growing at the edge of

The Grass-leafed Nerine *(Nerine filifolia)* has dainty flowers which make an elegant show when grown in masses

rivers and where there is a good rainfall. The flowering time is late summer.

N. angustifolia RIBBON-LEAFED NERINA
It grows wild from the eastern Cape, north through Natal and Lesotho into the Transvaal. It reaches a height of 45 cm (1½ ft) and bears flowerheads of rose colour. The leaves are less than 6 mm wide and about 25 cm long. It flowers in late summer, together with the leaves, and goes dormant in winter.

N. bowdenii LARGE PINK NERINA
Is a striking plant when in flower. The individual flowers are more than 5 cm long and of a vivid carmine-pink. The flowerheads are carried on stems 45 cm (1½ ft) tall. It flowers in autumn and the leaves, very like those of an agapanthus, appear in September. New bulbs should be planted in August. Plant it where it will be shaded from the hot afternoon sun. It is grown out-of-doors in England and should be quite hardy to severe frost in South Africa as it is dormant in winter.

N. filifolia GRASS-LEAFED NERINA
Its natural habitat is the eastern Cape near Grahamstown and the eastern Transvaal. This is

a small species with pretty pink flowers on stems 25-40 cm (10-15 in) high. To make a show in the garden it should be planted in bold groups rather than singly. The bulbs can be set out 6-10 cm (3-4 in) apart. It has slender, grass-like leaves and rounded heads of pink flowers with slender, undulating petals. The flowering time is late summer.

N. krigei CURLY-LEAFED NERINA
This species grows in the veld in the colder parts of the Transvaal and is sometimes referred to as the "red agapanthus". It bears striking heads of flowers on stems 45 cm (1½ ft) high during midsummer. The leaves, which are about 12 mm wide, are twisted. They grow out in September and die down in autumn. The bulbs should be planted in winter or early spring. It is hardy to severe frost.

N. masonorum
A dwarf species from the Transkei with pale pink flowers with frilled petals. The leaves are slender, like grass. It flowers in summer and is dormant in winter when it can be transplanted.

N. sarniensis RED NERINA, GUERNSEY LILY
This lovely species from the south-western Cape

Red Nerine, Guernsey Lily (*Nerine sarniensis*), lovely in colour and form, has been grown in gardens in England for many years

is the one which was first exported and which has been used extensively as a parent in hybridization. It has a strong stem to 45 cm (1½ ft) and bears scarlet flowers which look as though they have been dusted with gold. The colourful stamens are prominent and add to the beauty of the flower. The flowers appear in February and March, before the leaves, which grow up as the flowers fade and persist through the winter, turning yellow in spring. The bulbs should be planted from November to January. They should be watered well in autumn and winter. In hot, inland areas it is advisable to grow this species where it is shaded during the hottest part of the day.

NYMPHAEA CAPENSIS   BLUE WATER LILY, BLOUWATERBLOM

DISTRIBUTION: This decorative water plant has been noted growing wild in all provinces, except the Orange Free State, and in Rhodesia.

DESCRIPTION: The flowers are different from exotic water lilies in that they do not float on the water but stand 5-8 cm (2-4 in) above it. The flowers vary in colour, generally being from pale to deep blue, but there is a pink one also. They open only in sunshine, closing each night. The large leaves float on the surface of the water. The plants are dormant in winter.

CULTURE: Our native water lily is hardy to frost and grows anywhere provided it has a pool in which to develop and some soil in which the rhizomes can be planted. The soil may be on the bottom of the pool but it is better to plant them in soil in containers sunk into the pool. Good garden soil with some fertilizer added to nourish the plants should be provided. If the pool is deeper than 60 cm (2 ft) it is advisable to stand the container on some bricks to give the stems a chance to grow out to the surface of the water, and then the container can be lowered to a greater depth. To allow for root-spread the container of soil should be at least 30 cm (12 in) deep and as much, or more, across. Plastic basins make excellent containers. After two or three years it is ad-

The Blue Waterlily
(*Nymphaea capensis*)
holds its sculptured
flowers proudly aloft.

visable to lift and divide the plants and give them new soil. This is best done in winter when the plants are dormant. When dividing, cut through the roots with a spade discarding the old central portion and planting the outer sections which have growing points. After re-planting, spread a layer of gravel 3-4 cm (1 in) thick over the soil to keep it from washing out and dirtying the pool.

These lilies can also be grown from seed sown in tins placed where the water will only just cover the top. As the little plants develop, the tins can be put lower in the water. It takes a long time, however, to produce flowering plants from seed, whereas those grown from root-sections will flower in a couple of months after planting. The flowering time is summer.

NYMPHOIDES INDICA   YELLOW POND LILY
(*Limnanthemum thunbergianum*)

DISTRIBUTION: Can be found in ponds in all the provinces and Rhodesia.

DESCRIPTION: This is a dainty, decorative plant

Yellow Pond Lily (*Nymphoides indica*) is another pretty pond-plant

205

for the ornamental pond. It has leaves which are similar in shape to those of a water lily, but much smaller. They float on the surface of the water and the delightful little flowers of bright yellow rise on stems 5 cm (2 in) above the surface of the water. The flowers are 2-4 cm across and have five slender petals with feathery margins.

CULTURE: Plants form below the leaves and send long roots down to the bottom of the pond; once established it multiplies very rapidly and may have to be kept in check. They require no more than 30-45 cm of water in the pond but will flourish also in deeper pools.

ORNITHOGALUM CHINCHERINCHEE, STAR OF BETHLEHEM, TJIENKERETJIE

DISTRIBUTION: Are found in all the provinces.

DESCRIPTION: There are about eighty species of this genus in South Africa and a number of them also in southern Europe and the Middle East. The plants grow readily and it is surprising that more gardeners do not make use of them. Apparently the name comes from the Greek *ornithogalon* which means "birds' milk"—a proverbial expression for something precious or dainty. Ornithogalums bear flowers in small or large clusters at the tops of the stems. The six petals are generally arranged in the form of a bowl and are usually white, ivory, or yellow in colour.

CULTURE: The species which flower in late winter and spring should be planted in February or March. As they are mostly native to the winter-rainfall region these should be watered liberally in winter and spring, when grown in the summer-rainfall region. They will stand the frost of the highveld and full sunshine, but in hot, inland districts it seems that they produce better blooms if planted where they are shaded during the afternoon, Set the bulbs 3-5 cm (1-2 in) below the surface of the soil, and for effect, plant them close together in groups of twenty or more. They thrive in a variety of soils but perform better if the soil is friable and has some humus in it. The bulbs multiply readily, and if they appear to be overcrowded after they have been in the ground three or four years, it is advisable to lift them and separate the new bulbs from the parents before re-planting. The small bulbs can be grown on in a nursery bed for a year before planting them in the garden.

They can also be grown from seed but this is a much slower way of producing flowering plants.

O. flavissimum ORANGE CHINK
This species grows wild in many of the drier areas of the south-western Cape and along the coastal strip as far as Port Elizabeth. It is a pity that bulbs of these are not more widely grown, as it is a colourful little plant with clusters of yellow to orange flowers with a dull green centre. The flowering stem reaches a height of about 30 cm (1 ft) and the leaves are short and arranged about the base of the stem. The plant is dormant for a time and the first leaves usually emerge in mid-winter, the flowers appearing later, in September to October.

O. lacteum STAR OF BETHLEHEM
It grows wild in the south-western Cape where it flowers from October to December. This is a fine species with large white flowers on stems about 45 cm ($1\frac{1}{2}$ ft) tall.

O. miniatum YELLOW CHINCHERINCHEE
This is a most decorative species with flowers of deep, golden-yellow on stems 20-30 cm (8-12 in) high. The backs of the petals are suffused with a tinge of rose. The flowers appear from September to December. The leaves die down for a short period during winter. The Xhosas use the roots of this plant to make an enema for the treatment of worms in children.

O. saundersiae GIANT CHINCHERINCHEE
A tall-growing species to be found growing naturally in Natal, Swaziland and the eastern Transvaal. It has flower stems up to 1.25 m (4 ft), and sword-shaped leaves which grow to about 60 cm in length. The flowers are ivory with a pronounced black centre piece. The flowering time is January. The bulbs should, therefore, be planted four or five months earlier, in August or September.

O. thyrsoides CHINCHERINCHEE
This is the species which has been exported to grace the drawing-rooms of London for nearly a hundred years. The same Hildagonda Duckitt of Darling near Cape Town, who wrote a book on cookery and sent seeds of our nemesias to a big English seed firm, also pioneered the export of flowers from South Africa. Knowing the long-lasting qualities of these flowers she sent a package of them to friends in England—the daughters

This golden Chincherinchee *(Ornithogalum miniatum)* is a gay plant for the garden or for growing in pots ▷

Chincherinchee *(Ornithogalum thyrsoides)* has flowers which last well in the garden and in arrangements

of the Governor, Sir Bartle Frere. As the flowers lasted for several weeks after their arrival in England, Hildagonda was asked to supply more of them the following year. This small beginning has led to an export trade which now numbers millions of flowers annually.

The flowers are carried on stems which vary from 30-60 cm (1-2 ft) or more in height, in well formed pyramidal spikes. The flowers are white with a central marking of light brown. The leaves are slender and tapered and 15-25 cm in length. It is a good garden species as well as being fine for cutting. The plant is said to be poisonous to stock.

OXALIS SORREL, SURING

DISTRIBUTION: Most of the many species native to the country grow wild in the south-western Cape.

DESCRIPTION: Although this plant grows with such vigour that it can be regarded as a weed, some species are very decorative and make a splendid show when massed. It makes an enchanting picture when grown at the front of a low border, between cracks in brick or stone paving, in a wall or in a rock-garden.

Sorrel (Oxalis) of different colours looks effective as a ground-cover or planted in the crevices between paving stones

They have glistening little flowers with five petals opening up from a tube which may be long, or short and squat. The colours of the flowers vary through all shades of yellow, pink, mauve and white. The leaves, generally arranged in threes, are mostly broad and heart-shaped or rounded, but sometimes they are slender or oval. They are low-growing plants ideal for pots and window-boxes in a sunny position. The flowers open only when the sun is bright.

CULTURE: They grow with such reckless abandon that they may become a weed. Plant the little bulbs 5-7 cm (2-3 in) apart and 2-3 cm (1 in) beneath the soil in summer and water them in winter. They also grow from seed which should be sown in spring to summer. They do well in poor soil and sand. The following are the names of a few of the many ornamental species: *O. bifurca* (rosy-mauve); *O. eckloniana* (pink-mauve); *O. flava* (yellow); *O. lanata* var. *rosea* (pink); *O. namaquana* (yellow); *O. pes-caprae* (yellow); *O. purpurea* (rosy-mauve); *O. semiloba* (cerise; flowers in summer).

PTERYGODIUM ACUTIFOLIUM   MOEDER-KAPPIE

DISTRIBUTION: Grows on lower mountain slopes and coastal plains from the Cape to Port Elizabeth.

DESCRIPTION: This is a diminutive member of the orchid family which grows to only about 30 cm (1 ft) and bears little flowers with a pungent odour. Each flower is shaped like the olden-day bonnet or "kappie" worn by women a century or two ago. The flowers are yellow and attached close to the stem along its upper half. The oval, pointed leaves partially sheathe the stem at the bottom and are of a soft green. It flowers in mid-spring and, when planted in drifts or colonies, makes a charming foreground in the border or rock-garden. It is also decorative as a pot plant. Two other very charming species are *P. caffrum* (yellow) and *P. catholicum* (lime-green).

CULTURE: This plant is often found in marshy places but it also occurs in dry, sandy ground, where it is usually rather stunted. Plant them in February, 5-8 cm (2 in or more) beneath the surface of the soil, spacing them 10-15 cm (4-6 in) apart, and see that the part of the garden where they are growing is watered from autumn to when they flower. They do better in soil to which compost has been added than in poor ground, and

Moederkappie *(Pterygodium catholicum)* bears its flowers of subtle colour in spring.

prefer some shade to full sunlight.

ROMULEA   ROMULEA, SATIN FLOWER, FRUTANG

DISTRIBUTION: The species mentioned occur in the south-western Cape, where they are to be found growing wild in fields and on hillsides.

DESCRIPTION: These delightful little flowers with their petals of satiny texture and many colours make a charming show despite the fact that they grow so near the ground. They are excellent plants for the edging of window-boxes, or for mass-planting in a rock-garden or in a bed of low-growing plants. There are few flowers more beautiful than the romulea. Although they open only when the sun is bright and close in the afternoon, they nevertheless make a most wonderful show for a short period in spring.

CULTURE: The little corms should be planted in January or February in well-composted soil 5-7 cm (2-3 in) below the surface of the soil and about 7-10 cm (3-4 in) apart. To make a show they must be massed in a bed where they can be watered liberally during the growing period, which is winter and early spring. When grown in pots, the

Pink Romulea
(*Romulea rosea*)
Close-up of flower

whole pot could be stood in water occasionally to keep them growing well. Soon after the flowers fade they become dormant and the plants may then be allowed to remain rather dry until the following autumn. They need not be lifted each year.

They can also be grown from seed, and it must be remembered, whether growing them from seeds or from corms, that the leaves are very grass-like, as otherwise they may be pulled up as an undesirable type of grass.

R. citrina   YELLOW ROMULEA
Bears canary-yellow flowers about 2-3 cm across from winter to early spring. It grows wild in Namaqualand in vleis which become completely dry by the end of spring.

R. rosea   PINK ROMULEA
The flowers are often more than 2-3 cm across, of a glistening texture and of dazzling shades of pink, rose and mauve. *R. rosea* var. *speciosa* is the showiest of them all as it is beautifully marked. The top half of the flower is cyclamen-pink and the lower half is deep maroon and lemon-yellow. It flowers in early spring.

210

R. sabulosa   RUBY ROMULEA
Has slender leaves 15 cm long and 2 mm wide. The flowers which measure about 4 cm across appear on stems only 5 cm high (2 in). The upper half of their glistening petals is terra-cotta and the lower half is pale cream with lemon and maroon markings. This is a most beautiful little flower.

SANDERSONIA AURANTIACA   CHRISTMAS
                    BELLS, CHINESE LANTERN
DISTRIBUTION: It grows wild in the highlands of Pondoland where winters are very cold, as well as in the warmer parts of Natal.

DESCRIPTION: This delightful little scrambling plant was named after a plant collector, Sanderson, who first introduced the flower. He certainly has a fine memorial in this charming plant. It is a great pity that it is now so seldom seen in nature and not yet easily obtainable from nurseries.

Although it can be considered a good garden plant it is so unusual that I feel that it should stand alone as a pot or tub plant on a patio. The growth of the plant is rather like that of the gloriosa but the flowers are quite different. It grows to 50 cm (20 in) in height and the leaves are oval and tapering like those of gloriosa but they do not end in strong tendrils, so the plant should be tied to a short stake to keep it erect. The flowers, which are of a lovely shade of tawny-orange, have a smooth, shining texture and are shaped like little bells. Each one is attached to the main stem by a slender stalk which droops with the flower giving the whole plant an elegant appearance. The flowering time is November and December.

CULTURE: It grows from fleshy tuberous roots which should be planted in winter when the plant is dormant. In areas which have heavy rain in winter, it is advisable to grow the plant in large pots which can be sunk in the ground for garden show when they are in active growth; the pots can then be moved to dry off in autumn until the end of winter. It is best not to disturb the tubers for a few years. Set the tubers about 5 cm (2 in) beneath the soil which should be improved to a depth of about 45 cm (1½ ft) by the addition of compost or leaf mould. In hot inland districts it is a good idea to plant it where it will be shaded for the hottest part of the day. In areas of heavy rainfall it should be planted in friable soil which drains readily.

SATYRIUM   EWWA-TREWWA

DISTRIBUTION: These unusual and often decorative plants of the orchid family grow mainly in the south-western and eastern Cape, but species are to be found in all the provinces.

DESCRIPTION: They vary in height from 10-45 cm (4-18 in) and bear their attractive hooded flowers at different seasons, according to natural habitat. The leaves vary considerably. They make decorative pot plants, and look effective grown in colonies towards the front of a border. Interplant them with winter-flowering lachenalias as they start flowering when the lachenalias are over.

CULTURE: The plants grow from a tuberous rootstock which should be planted 5-10 cm (2-4 in) deep in soil to which compost and leaf mould has been added. Spring-flowering species should be planted in summer and watered during autumn and winter, and those which flower in summer should be planted early in spring and watered from then until autumn.

S. carneum   ROOIKAPPIE

A spring-flowering species from the south-western Cape with charming cylindrical heads of pink flowers on robust stems 30 cm (12 in) high.

Massed in the veld near Darling the Pink Romulea *(Romulea rosea)* is a ravishing sight

Rooikappie *(Satyrium carneum)* has decorative flowers of unusual form

S. coriifolium EWWA-TREWWA

Its natural habitat extends from the Cape Peninsula somewhat north and eastwards to Port Elizabeth. The plant grows to 30-45 cm (1-1½ ft) high with a sturdy, erect stem which carries a cylindrical spike of tawny orange flowers sometimes flushed with russet-red. The leaves are broad in the middle and partially sheathe the flower stem. In hot inland areas it should be grown where it is shaded for the hottest part of the day, and in regions which have severe frost it should be tried where it is protected and shaded from the first rays of the morning sun which, striking frosted leaves, often do damage which would not occur if the plants are allowed to warm up slowly. The flowering time is spring.

S. longicauda

Is to be found from the eastern Cape up through the Transkei to Natal, at low and high altitudes.

The flowers, which give off a sweet scent, are white, often with a rose-coloured edging to the petals. They are carried on sturdy stems 45 cm (18 in) high. The flowering time varies from mid-spring to mid-summer.

S. maculatum

This species grows in acid soil between George and Humansdorp. It has two leaves, rather thick, fleshy and rounded, which grow flat on the ground. The pale pink flowers, flushed with deep rose, form a spike along the top of the stem which is 45 cm (1½ ft) high. It flowers from October to November.

S. membranaceum

This pretty species grows naturally between George and the Transkei. It has two large, fleshy leaves which lie flat against the ground. The flowers of a charming shade of pink are waxy and carried on stems 30-45 cm (1½ ft) high. The flowering time is from September to November.

S. ocellatum

Its natural habitat extends from the eastern Cape up into Natal, the Orange Free State and Transvaal. It is dormant in winter and best kept fairly dry at this time. New growth begins in spring and the attractive pink flowers appear on stems 45 cm (1½ ft) high in late summer. Closely planted, it makes a striking show.

SCHIZOSTYLIS COCCINEA RIVER LILY, KAFFIR LILY

DISTRIBUTION: This plant, which grows naturally in forest and high country in the eastern Cape, Natal and parts of the Transvaal, is in serious need of protection as it is now seldom found in the wild.

DESCRIPTION: Fortunately, however, it was one of our native plants which became popular with gardeners in England many years ago, and it has been cultivated there far more extensively than in its home country. Probably the best collection of this lovely native plant, and hybrids developed from it, is to be seen in the Inverewe gardens on the north-western side of Scotland. In addition to growing the species, try some of the attractive hybrids developed in England and elsewhere.

It sends up a stem to about 45 cm (1½ ft) at the top of which appear beautiful, scarlet flowers measuring 5-7 cm across. Each flower has six broad satiny petals with pointed ends. The leaves are slender, about 6 mm wide and 20 cm in length. The flowering time is summer.

CULTURE: It grows naturally along the sides of streams, very often where its rootstock is washed by the water. In the garden it should be planted at the edge of a pool where its roots can reach down to the water, or else it should be watered regularly, specially during its period of greatest growth—from winter to flowering time. As it should be left in the same place for several years it is advisable to make deep and wide holes and to put in plenty of compost and old manure or peat. Plant two roots in each hole and in a couple of years these will form nice clumps. In inland districts it should be grown in shade.

Plant the roots in late winter 5-7 cm (2-3 in) deep. They may not flower in the first year as the plant resents being moved.

SCILLA NATALENSIS
WILD SQUILL, BLOUSLANGKOP

DISTRIBUTION: This species can be found in Natal, the eastern Cape, parts of the Orange Free State, and the Transvaal.

DESCRIPTION: Its flower stem reaches a height of about 90 cm (3 ft) with numbers of small, lavender-blue flowers closely carried in a pyramidal spike. Each flower is composed of a very slender tube opening up into a starry face. The leaves are broad and long, sometimes being flushed with purple on the underside. This is a decorative plant in the garden and, because of its long-lasting properties, a good one, too, for arrangements. The flowering time is late winter and early spring.

CULTURE: It has a large bulb, sometimes as much as 12 cm across, covered with dark, brownish-purple, papery scales. Plant the bulbs in autumn so that only the bottom half is below the ground. Prepare the ground well before planting, as they may not flower for a year or two after being moved and should therefore be left in one place for several years. Make a hole 45 cm ($1\frac{1}{2}$ ft) wide and deep, and fill it with good soil and compost. The plant will grow in full sunshine, but in hot districts it seems to do better if shaded for part of the day.

Ewwa-trewwa
(Satyrium coriifolium)
Grow this species in groups in the rock-garden or at the front of a flower border

SPARAXIS
Sparaxis, Harlequin Flower, Velvet Flower, Fluweeltjie

DISTRIBUTION: Is one of the most beautiful of the small flowers of the Cape Peninsula and the south-western Cape.

DESCRIPTION: Sparaxis species and hybrids have been grown as garden plants not only in Europe but also in Australia and New Zealand, where they have become very popular. They have, in fact, naturalized themselves along the roadsides in some parts of Australia. Many very lovely hybrids of our wild sparaxis have been bred in other countries, but in its homeland few gardeners grow this exceptionally pretty flower, which is surprising, as it grows very readily from seeds or corms. Sparaxis have stems from 15-45 cm (6-18 in) tall with flowers at the top. The flowers generally have a velvety texture and the colours vary from cream to the most luminous shades of red, often with contrasting bands of colour. The hybrids have scintillating flowers of the most alluring range of colours—pale rose flushed with cerise; pink with cyclamen; terracotta with maroon; fawn with burgundy and coral with deep crimson. The leaves are sword-shaped and arranged in a fan at the base of the plant. These plants make a lovely show when massed in the garden or in pots or window-boxes. The flowering time is late winter and early spring.

CULTURE: Plant the corms in February or March in friable soil. Although they grow happily in any kind of soil, they produce longer flowering stems if they have good soil which is not too hard. The corms should be planted in groups of fifty or more, setting them 2-5 cm (1-2 in) below the ground and 10-12 cm (4-5 in) apart. They will not tolerate very severe frost, and in gardens which experience very low temperatures, they should be planted in a sheltered position, or shaded from the early morning winter sun. They flourish in full sunshine but seem to perform better where they have high shade for part of the day. The plants should be watered regularly and well throughout the autumn and winter and allowed to become dry in the summer when they are dormant. Left in the ground, they multiply more rapidly than if they are lifted each year, but if the ground is required for other plants in summer, plant the corms in pots or plastic containers which can be buried in the garden whilst they are in flower, then lifted, after the flowers have faded and stored beneath the soil in and out-of-the-way part of the garden until the following flowering period.

They are easily raised from seed, too, which should be sown in March to April. Very often seed produces flowers in the first year but good flowers are generally produced only the following season.

Harlequin Flower
(Sparaxis hybrids)
Few plants bear more
beautiful flowers for a
spring display

The Botterblom
(*Sparaxis grandiflora*)
does well in places
which become marshy
from autumn to spring

S. bulbifera   Dwarf Sparaxis
This charming little plant reaches a height of
about 30 cm (1 ft) and has flowers of white or ivory.
It grows naturally in parts of the Cape and near
Clanwilliam in ground which becomes marshy in
winter and it should, therefore, be kept well
watered at this time of the year when grown in the
summer-rainfall region.

S. elegans
(*Streptanthera cuprea*)
This, together with its gaily coloured hybrids, is
one of the loveliest of flowers and also one of the
easiest to grow. It has slender sword-shaped
leaves, and flower stems 20-30 cm (8-12 in) tall.
The flowers have a velvet-like texture and are
beautifully marked with bands of yellow and
black. They bloom in early spring. Mass them
along the front of a border or plant a dozen or
two in a pot for a window display.

S. grandiflora   Botterblom, Wit Kalossie
Grows to 30-45 cm (1-1½ ft) and bears large white

or ivory flowers tinged with purple on the back
of the petals. A near relation, *S. grandiflora* var.
violacea, has purple flowers which make a sparkling show.

S. tricolor   Harlequin Flower,
                              Fluweeltjies
This is the most outstanding of the sparaxis
species. It has flower stems from 20-45 cm (½-1½ ft)
tall with glistening flowers 5 cm wide in gay
orange and pink shades with a luminous yellow
centre edged with a broad band of purple-black.
The species and its hybrids make a spectacular
show when massed.

SPILOXENE CAPENSIS   Stars,
(*Hypoxis stellata*)   Sterretjie
Distirbution: This little plant with its eye-catching flowers is to be found growing wild in many
districts of the south-western Cape and to the
north of Cape Town.

Stars *(Spiloxene capensis)* are sparkling flowers for the front of a border

DESCRIPTION: It grows to 15-45 cm (6-18 in) in height and bears a flower made up of six widely separated and pointed petals which give it the appearance of a star. Very often the petals are magnificently marked at the centre. They may be white, cyclamen-pink or yellow with iridescent peacock-blue or green splashes edged with deep, velvety maroon. The backs of the petals are often beautifully coloured, too, with bands of claret or green, or both. The flowers open fairly late in the morning and close up again in the afternoon, but they are so beautiful that they are nevertheless worth growing massed in the garden, or in pots or window-boxes. They flower in late winter and early spring.

CULTURE: Plant the corms 4-6 cm (2 in) beneath the soil in February or March and keep the plants watered well throughout autumn and winter. In nature they sometimes grow where the ground is marshy in winter and dry in summer and they will not perform well if they lack water during their growing season. They grow in any kind of soil.

STRELITZIA   CRANE FLOWER, BIRD-OF-PARADISE FLOWER

DISTRIBUTION: Although the most decorative of these handsome plants are to be found growing wild in the eastern Cape and the Transkei, there are species which occur naturally in parts of the Transvaal and Natal.

DESCRIPTION: In appearance the flower looks very like the head of a crane. The spathe, from which the flower emerges, projects at a right angle to the stem and resembles the beak of a bird; the sepals, which stand erect, are like the crest on top of a crane's head. The petals project forward enclosing the stamens and ovary. This unusual shape is no doubt nature's way of attracting birds for the purposes of cross-pollination which is done mostly by sunbirds and sugarbirds. Some species make fine garden or patio plants.

CULTURE: Strelitzias grow readily in the warmer parts of the country. In areas which experience severe frost they should be grown in a sheltered corner because even although the plant may survive frost, the flowers are damaged by it. Strelitzia do not like being moved and often do not flower for a couple of years after being planted. For this reason it is advisable to prepare the ground thoroughly before they are planted. Makes holes 60 cm (2 ft) wide and deep, and put in good soil and plenty of humus. In hot dry in-

216

Crane Flower. Bird of Paradise Flower, Strelitzia *(Strelitzia reginae)* ▷
Plant one as an accent plant in the small garden or set out groups of them in the large garden

land districts they perform better if grown where they are shaded during the hottest part of the day. They may be planted at any time of the year. Generally it is easier to get them established if they are planted at the beginning of the rainy season.

S. alba
Grows in the south-eastern Cape where it reaches a height of 10 m (30 ft). The spathe is of a purplish colour and measures about 30 cm (1 ft) in length. The sepals are white and the petals are not as showy as in some of the other species. It flowers in late spring and early summer, but does not do well in dry areas.

S. caudata
Has flowers which are similar to the above. It grows to 5 m (15 ft) and occurs naturally in Swaziland and the northern and eastern Transvaal. This is a good accent plant for warm gardens. It has a rather palm-like appearance.

S. nicolai   WILD BANANA
Grows luxuriantly in Natal, the Transkei and in warm areas of the Eastern Province. It was named after the Emperor Nicholas in whose garden at Petersburg it grew under glass. Under sub-tropical conditions it can be considered a decorative plant if grown where wind does not make the leaves look tattered, and if such straggly pieces are removed regularly. It reaches a height of 6 m (20 ft) very quickly and has large leaves at the ends of the stems. The flowers are made up of a huge spathe, sometimes 30 cm (1 ft) or more in length. It is coloured purple suffused with rose, and from it emerge smaller spathes. The first spathe may be 45 cm (1½ ft) long. The sepals are ivory and the petals pale blue. The nature of growth of the plant and the fact that it grows quickly, makes it a useful "stop-gap" plant for the new garden. It will grow in highveld gardens which are not subjected to severe frost, provided it is watered abundantly and regularly. It flowers on and off throughout the year.

S. parvifolia   SMALL-LEAFED STRELITZIA
Its native habitat is the eastern Cape. The flowers are very like those of *S. reginae* but the leaves are different. They are much smaller and more slender, rather like a spearhead. *S. parvifolia* var. *juncea* has similar flowers, and leaves like spikes growing to about 60 cm (2 ft).

S. reginae   CRANE FLOWER, BIRD-OF-PARADISE FLOWER, KRAANVOËLBLOM
This species grows wild in the eastern Cape and up into the Transkei and Pondoland. The plant was grown in England for the first time two hundred years ago and it is now in great demand in Europe for large floral displays. In the Northern Hemisphere it has to be grown in glass-houses as it is unable to stand severe frost, but it is widely grown outdoors in California and has been adopted by the city of Los Angeles as its civic emblem.

It bears the most handsome flowers of all and is, in general appearance, the most decorative of the strelitzias for garden show or patio planting. This species grows to 1.25 m (4 ft) in height. The leaves make a fine show even when the plant is not in flower. They are large, markedly veined and consist of a large blade on a strong stem. When they become ragged they should be cut out of the plant to keep it looking neat. The flower spathe which juts out horizontally from the main stem is up to 20 cm (8 in) in length and flushed with mauve and rose. The crests or sepals are of brilliant orange and the petals enclosing the reproductive parts are of bright blue. Each flower lasts for a long time. The flowering period varies according to district, on and off through the year, but mostly in winter and spring. It develops very long roots and, once established, it will stand long periods without water. It does not like being transplanted and may take two years to flower after being moved.

SYNNOTIA VARIEGATA   SYNNOTIA
DISTRIBUTION: A charming little plant native to certain areas of the western and south-western Cape.

DESCRIPTION: It bears its flowers, which measure about 5 cm across, on stems up to 30 cm (1 ft) in height. The flower has petals which are differently marked. The top petal is deep mauve. It is flanked by two white petals with purple blotches near the base; and the three lower petals are narrow and white with yellow and purple bands. The leaves are sword-like and carried in a fan formation.

CULTURE: Plant corms in February or March, 2-4 cm (1 in) beneath the soil and about 10 cm (4 in) apart. Because the plants are small they should be closely crowded in a group of fifty or more to make a lively show. They grow well in pots as well as in the garden. This plant can be grown readily from seed, too. The seeds should be sown in March

◁ Crane Flower, Bird of Paradise Flower, Yellow Strelitzia *(Strelitzia reginae)* This yellow form is rare

or April. Water plants well from planting time and until the foliage dies down. In gardens which have a high summer-rainfall, it is advisable to plant them in pots which can be buried beneath the ground whilst the corms are growing, and then removed from the ground in late spring when the plants are dormant. The containers can then be stored in an outhouse or buried in soil again in an out-of-the-way part of the garden. This will obviate their getting too much water during their resting period.

TRITONIA   TRITONIA, MONTBRETIA, BLAZING STAR

DISTRIBUTION: Tritonias belong to the iris family and are to be found growing wild in different parts of the country.

DESCRIPTION: Species native to the south-western Cape are generally of small stature, whilst those which grow naturally in the summer-rainfall area are often rather tall—up to 90 cm (3 ft). The flower formerly classed separately as montbretia is now included under tritonia.

Tritonias were introduced into European gar-

dens nearly two hundred years ago and many very lovely hybrids have been developed from them and from the crossing of tritonias with crocosmias. These named hybrids are more decorative plants for the garden than their wild parents.

The montbretia, which grows to a height of 60-90 cm (2-3 ft), with its charming arching spikes of coral flowers, has been a popular plant for many years. It flowers in summer and grows so easily that it can be recommended as a summer-flowering plant for the flower border in gardens where growing conditions are difficult. It is a hybrid which resulted from the crossing of a tritonia with *Crocosmia aurea*.

Tritonias are very easy to grow and make ideal plants where growing conditions are not particularly good. The flowers consist of a short tube opening into a six-petalled face. They are carried in spikes which usually arch over to one side. The slender sword-like leaves are often arranged in a fan.

CULTURE: This varies according to the natural habitat of the species. Those native to the winter-rainfall regions have a dormant period in summer

Synnotia
(Synnotia variegata)
A low-growing plant
suitable for pot-culture
or for growing between
cracks in a stone wall

when they need not be watered. Plant their corms in February or March. Those which grow naturally in the summer-rainfall area are dormant in winter and require water from spring to autumn. The corms of these should be planted in spring. They put up with a good deal of aridity and poor soil, but for superior flowers, plant them in good soil and see that they are watered regularly during their growing season.

After flowering, the corms can be left in the ground as they are not likely to rot if watered during their dormant period, unless they are planted in a heavy clay which does not allow moisture to drain away.

T. crocata   ORANGE TRITONIA, KALKOENTJIE
Is indigenous to the south-western Cape and flowers in September and October. This plant has slender, pointed leaves about 10 cm in length arranged like a fan, and a flowering stem 30 cm (1 ft) high. It carries several, brightly coloured orange to coral-red flowers measuring 2-3 cm or more across. There are now many gaily-coloured hybrids of shades of pink, rose, salmon, gold and cyclamen.

T. hyalina   SALMON TRITONIA, SALMON KALKOENTJIE
This species is from the same area as the above and very like it in form. The flowers of salmon to coral-pink appear in September and October. It always has a pale translucent area in the middle which accounts for the name *hyalina* which means "almost transparent".

T. lineata
Has narrow leaves of about 15 cm in length and a stem rising to about 45 cm (1½ ft) on which are carried cream flowers. The cup-shaped flowers open to a six-petalled face which measures 2-3 cm across. Each flower has delicate faint stripes of dark brown. It is not a very showy species but delicately coloured and would show up better as a pot or tub plant than in the garden unless massed at the front of a border.

T. squalida   PINK TRITONIA
This species is native to parts of the south-western Cape. The flowering stem is about 45 cm (1½ ft) high with pale pink flowers. Each flower is flushed with claret-colour markings in the centre. They appear during mid-spring.

Tritonia hybrids are easy-to-grow and colourful plants for the garden or window-box

Sweet Garlic (*Tulbaghia fragrans*) produces its pretty, scented flowers in winter

TULBAGHIA
TULBAGHIA, WILD GARLIC, WILDE KNOFFEL

DISTRIBUTION: Grows wild in many areas of the country, but most species are not particularly showy and they, moreover, have a strong "onion" scent which makes them unsuitable for cutting.

DESCRIPTION: In the species suitable for the garden, the flowers are carried in rounded heads on the tops of rather fleshy stems, each one on its own stalk coming out from the top of the main stem. The flower consists of a squat tube opening to a face with six petals. The leaves are long, slender and fleshy. Some people affirm that planting species with a strong onion or garlic scent deters moles, but I have not noticed this effect. The flowers of the best species for the garden vary in colour from pale to deep mauve. They appear in late winter to late spring.

CULTURE: These flowers, members of the lily family, are very easy to grow. Plant the fleshy rootstock 5-7 cm (2-3 in) below the surface of the soil. Most species grow well in full sun or partial shade. As it is better to leave the plants in the ground for several years to help them to multiply, it is advisable to prepare the ground before planting. Dig holes or trench the ground to a depth of 30 cm (1 ft) and put in compost or old manure. They are not really particular as to soil, however, and will give quite a good show for a couple of years if planted in any kind of soil. They stand both drought and frost. The best time to divide and plant them is in summer.

T. fragrans — SWEET GARLIC

This species from the eastern Transvaal is the finest tulbaghia for the garden. Not only are the flowers very attractive but they also have a sweet scent. It is a rewarding flower for pots and for arrangements, as the flowers last for a long time when picked. The umbels of flowers are carried on fleshy stems 45 cm (1½ ft) tall. They measure about 7 cm in diameter and the flowers are usually of a charming shade of deep mauve, but there is a white one, too. The flowering time is mid-winter and early spring. The fleshy leaves are long and slender, about 2-4 cm wide and about 40 cm long. These usually die back during winter and emerge again in spring. It grows in full sunshine but seems to produce longer stems when grown where it is shaded for part of the day.

T. natalensis — SWEET WHITE GARLIC

This species grows wild in the uplands of Natal and is therefore quite hardy to frost. It is to be found in rather marshy ground and vleis and should be kept watered well, particularly in summer, when grown in the garden. The umbels of white flowers measure about 5 cm across.

T. violacea — WILD GARLIC

Is to be found in the veld, often along streams from the eastern Cape up through the Transkei to Natal and parts of the Transvaal. It makes a charming show in the garden when massed, but the flowers have a strong garlic scent and are, therefore, unsuitable for picking. The leaves are short and slender and the umbels of lilac flowers are held well above the leaves on stems 25-30 cm (10-12 in) high. The flowering time is late spring to summer. It thrives in sun or partial shade.

VALLOTA SPECIOSA
(*V. purpurea*) — GEORGE LILY, KNYSNA LILY, SCARBOROUGH LILY, BERG LILY

DISTRIBUTION: Occurs from Knysna to Humansdorp.

DESCRIPTION: The first two common names given above indicate where this delightful plant grows naturally, and the third one is the name by which it is commonly known in other lands because it appeared to grow naturally near the town of Scarborough in England. It is another plant which, on its journey from the Cape to Holland at the beginning of the nineteenth century, is said to have been shipwrecked and washed ashore on the coast of England, where it took root and flourished. It continues to be popular there as a garden plant and for pot culture, and it is a great favourite also in Australia and in parts of the United States.

The flowers are carried in groups on the end of a thick stem up to 45 cm ($1\frac{1}{2}$ ft) high. They are brilliantly coloured orange-red. Each flower is funnel-shaped, opening to a starry face measuring 5-7 cm across. The leaves are strap-shaped, 2-3 cm wide and 30 cm long. Its flowering period is spring. It makes a fine show when massed, or when grown in a pot.

CULTURE: The plants do not flower well soon after being moved and for this reason they should be planted where they are to remain for several years. Prepare beds incorporating plenty of old manure and/or compost to a depth of 45 cm ($1\frac{1}{2}$ ft) and plant the bulbs 5-7 cm (3 in) below the surface of the soil, in late winter. This pretty plant is often found in nature in somewhat marshy places, and it should therefore be watered regularly throughout its growing period. Plant where it is shaded during the hottest part of the day.

VELTHEIMIA VIRIDIFOLIA   FOREST LILY
(New name is *V. bracteata*)

DISTRIBUTION: This charming flower can be found in the forests of the eastern Cape up through the Transkei and into Natal.

The Forest Lily *(Veltheimia viridifolia)* will enhance a shady corner (New name is *V. bracteata*)

The George Lily *(Vallota speciosa)* is another delightful plant for a shady part of the garden

DESCRIPTION: It bears flowers somewhat like those of an aloe, both in their shape and in their arrangement at the top of the stem. The slender tubular flowers are of a delightful shade of dusty-pink flushed at the tips with lime-green. They are carried on strong fleshy stems of pale green spotted with purple, at a height of 30-60 cm (1-2 ft). The strap-shaped leaves are about 4 cm wide and 45 cm in length, with undulating margins. It is delightful in the garden and a splendid pot plant and cut flower. It flowers in late winter and early spring. Another charming species suitable for the rock garden or for growing in containers is the one known as *V. capensis*—previously *V. glauca*. It grows in dry areas of the Karoo and Namaqualand, and seems to flourish in sandy soil as well as in gravel. The charming little flowers grow to about 30 cm in height and are at their best in midwinter.

Karoo Veltheimia *(Veltheimia capensis)*

CULTURE: The plant should not be moved each year as this inhibits flowering. It is therefore advisable to prepare the ground thoroughly to a depth of 45 cm (1½ ft) by digging in humus. Set the plants out in a shady place and provide them with plenty of water during the winter months when they are flowering. They will endure severe frost if protected from the early morning winter sun which may scorch the plants. The dormant period is in midsummer. In the summer-rainfall area where rainfall is heavy they should be planted in soil which drains readily.

The large bulbs, which measure 7 cm and more across when mature, should be planted from January to March so that they are only 2-3 cm (1 in) beneath the soil. They can also be grown from seed, but this takes two to three years to produce flowering plants.

WATSONIA WATSONIA

DISTRIBUTION: There are fifty or more species of this lovely plant in Southern Africa. Many of them grow wild in the south-western Cape, but they are to be found also in the eastern Cape and parts of Natal and the Transvaal. In addition, there are numerous hybrids of great merit.

DESCRIPTION: Watsonias vary in size considerably, from little plants scarcely 30 cm (1 ft) high to statuesque plants up to 1.5 m (5 ft) and more. The flowers are of many shades of pink and rose, red, mauve, orange and white. They bear their flowers at different times of the year according to the species. Most of them, however, flower in spring. In most species, each flowering stem ends in a spike of funnel-shaped flowers opening to a six-petalled starry face. They have sword-like leaves. Some species are very like gladioli.

CULTURE: Their flowering time depends largely upon whether they come from the winter-rainfall or the summer-rainfall region, and this naturally governs the time when the corms should be planted. The rule generally is to plant the corms when the plants are dormant, which is roughly four to six months before their flowering time. If they flower in spring the correct planting time is late summer, whereas if they flower in summer the corms should be planted out in spring. Some species which flower in spring may suffer frost

Watsonia species and hybrids grow readily in any soil or situation

damage if grown in regions with very cold winters, unless they have protection of some kind. Most watsonias however, are not damaged by frost.

Plant the corms 5-7 cm (2-3 in) deep. There are deciduous and evergreen species. If the space they occupy in the garden is needed for other flowers, it is possible to remove the deciduous species after their leaves have faded, and to store them until the next planting season. The evergreen ones can be moved too, but in their case it is advisable to plant them in an out-of-the-way corner of the garden rather than try to store them in boxes. The evergreen ones do better, however, if they are left to form clumps over a period of at least four or five years. These look effective when grown between shrubs of moderate height which will not obscure them from view.

The spring-flowering species should be watered well in winter and allowed to dry out in summer; and the summer-flowering ones should be watered regularly during the summer. Evergreen species require water regularly throughout the year, whatever their flowering season. They grow very well even in poor soil, but better results will be had if the soil is fairly good and friable.

The mature corms give rise to several new ones each year and these can be detached and planted in nursery beds for a year or two to grow to flowering size. Plants can also be raised from seed sown in spring or summer. Plants grown from seed will flower in the third season. Not all watsonias can be regarded as good garden subjects and a limited number of species is mentioned here.

W. aletroides Tubular Watsonia
This species grows wild from Caledon to George.

225

It has flowering stems about 60 cm (2 ft) high with drooping tubular flowers of luminous tomato-red to rose. The flowering time is September. It is grown in New Zealand for cut flowers.

W. angustifolia

A handsome species with curved coral-red tubular flowers and deep maroon anthers.

W. ardernei   WHITE WATSONIA, WITKNOL

Mr Arderne, whose father established the remarkably fine garden which later became known as Claremont Park in Cape Town, is said to have been the first to cultivate this beautiful plant originally found in the Tulbagh district in the Cape. The plants bear lovely, snow-white flowers on stems 1.25 m (4 ft) high during September and October.

W. beatricis   BEATRICE WATSONIA

This fine species from George has given rise to numerous lovely hybrids, but the species itself is well worth a place in the garden. It is evergreen, grows to about 1.25 m (4 ft) and bears its apricot-coloured flowers in mid-summer. It is hardy to frost and soon forms big clumps if not disturbed and if watered regularly.

W. coccinea   DWARF RED WATSONIA

Grows wild in the drier areas of the Cape near Malmesbury, Bredasdorp and Tulbagh. It is a spring-flowering species, about 30 cm (1 ft) in height with crimson flowers.

W. comptonii   COMPTON'S WATSONIA

This one reaches a height of 1 m (3 ft) and has coral to crimson flowers.

226

W. densiflora NATAL WATSONIA
This is one of the most decorative of the watsonias because of the long flowering stem and the number of flowers which open at the same time. It grows wild in the lower plains of Natal and in the Transvaal, and bears its flowers on stems 60 cm (2 ft) high in mid-summer. The flowers are usually of a glowing cyclamen shade, although varieties with white and carmine flowers are also known. Plant it in good soil and see that it is watered regularly throughout the year. It is better to leave this one in the ground for several years, as lifting may inhibit its flowering for a year or two.

W. fourcadei
Can be seen on mountain slopes and plains in the vicinity of Knysna and eastwards towards Port Elizabeth.

The flowering stem grows to as much as 1.5 m (5 ft) and bears flowers of salmon to coral. It is an evergreen species which should be allowed to grow in the same position for several years.

W. galpinii
This is another species from the George area where it grows wild in wet places. The flowering stem rises to 60 cm (2 ft) and bears pink or coral flowers in late summer.

W. humilis WASPYPIE
A dwarf species from the Cape Peninsula with flowers of a delicate shade of mauve on stems 30-45 cm (1-1½ ft) high. The flowering time is spring to early summer.

W. knysnana
An evergreen species from the Knysna—George area with flowering stems rising to more than 90 cm (3 ft) and flowers of a mauve-pink to cyclamen hue. It needs regular watering.

W. longifolia
A tall species which grows wild in damp places from George to Humansdorp. The sword-shaped leaves are very long and the flowering stem grows to 1.25 m (4 ft) and more, and has flowers from ivory, through palest pink to rose, salmon and terra-cotta. The flowering time is late spring and early summer.

W. marginata
This plant is very tall, the flower stem sometimes reaching a height of 1.75 m (6 ft). The mauve to magenta flowers appear in spring. It is tender to frost and should be protected when planted in cold areas. Being tall it is a good one to plant between shrubs of lower growth which will protect it from frost damage.

W. meriana LAKPYPIE
Grows wild from the south-western Cape into Natal. It reaches a height of about 60-90 cm (2-3 ft) and bears flowers of white, pink, rose or mauve in October. It has been recorded that this species flowered in England as long ago as 1759.

W. pillansii
An evergreen species from the eastern Cape with flower stems growing to over 1.25 m (4 ft) and clear orange flowers. The flowering time is autumn. This is a good species to use in clumps at the front of a shrub border.

W. pyramidata PINK WATSONIA, SUURKNOL
(W. rosea)
This tall species grows abundantly in the Cape Peninsula and eastwards towards George. It bears its flowers on stems up to 1.25 m (4 ft) in height, in spring, from September to November. The flowers are of a clear cyclamen-pink colour which looks particularly effective when planted near plants with blue flowers, such as *Aristea thyrsiflora*, which flowers at the same time. The plant is dormant in summer and the corms should be planted at the end of summer.

W. spectabilis
Grows to 45 cm (1½ ft) and has beautiful flowers of a glowing flame-red. This is a fine species to have massed in the garden or to grow in pots. The flowers are very lovely in arrangements, too. It flowers in spring.

W. stanfordiae
A tall species from near Cape Town with flowers of pinky-purple on stems 1.25 m (4 ft) tall. The flowering time is November and it makes a fine show when massed between shrubs of this size. More handsome still is the watsonia known as Stanford's Scarlet which has bright red flowers in November. It is quite hardy to frost and makes a fine show when massed. It should be interplanted in clumps with *W. ardernei*.

Watsonia spectabilis Should be grown in groups at the front of a flower border

W. vanderspuyae

Grows wild near Piketberg, Tulbagh and Clanwilliam and bears purple flowers on stems 1.25 m (4 ft) high. It is a deciduous species which flowers in spring.

W. versfeldii

Is another species from the Piketberg-Darling area of the Cape. The flower stems rise to 1.25 m (4 ft) and carry large flowers of white, pale or deep pink or mauve, in spring.

ZANTEDESCHIA   Arum Lily, Calla Lily, Pig Lily

DISTRIBUTION: Arums grow wild in different parts of the country from Cape Town eastwards into the eastern Cape and up into Natal, the Orange Free State, the Transvaal, Rhodesia and further north.

DESCRITPION: These lovely flowers are too well known to need description. Their beauty is such that it is not surprising that they have been grown as treasured plants in Europe since the seven-teenth century. The flowers are supremely decorative in the garden and make charming arrangements, either on their own or when mixed with other flowers. They look elegant, too, when grown in pots or tubs.

As long ago as 1697, Simon van der Stel sent specimens to Holland, and early in the nineteenth century they were grown in the United States, where they rapidly became popular. There, they are known by their old name of calla lilies.

What is generally referred to as the flower is really a modified leaf called the spathe. It varies in colour in different species, and may be white, ivory, pink, rose, magenta or pale or deep yellow. The central fingerlike part is known as the spadix. This is really the flower spike closely crowded with masses of minute male flowers near the tip and female ones lower down, near the bottom. Pollination is done by insects walking down the spadix carrying pollen on their legs from the male flowers at the top to the female ones below. The spadix is generally yellow. The attractive flowers are carried on thick, fleshy stems, 60-90 cm (2-3 ft) tall, well above the leaves, which are also decorative. The leaves are sometimes spear-shaped and sometimes shaped like an arrow, and either plain green in colour or speckled. In some districts the Bantu prepare a poultice for inflamed sores from the leaves of these plants.

CULTURE: Most of the arums native to Southern Africa grow in those regions which have rain in summer, but the one first exported and best known throughout the world is the white arum from the south-western part of the Cape, which is known as *Zantedeschia aethiopica*. This species is also to be found in the wild in other parts of Southern Africa. It has a fleshy rootstock whereas the yellow and pink arums have fleshy rhizomes. It likes to be watered very well during its period of growth and tolerates marshy conditions, whereas the other arums, which grow naturally in many parts of the summer-rainfall region, are inclined to rot if over-watered during their dormant period.

Plant the rootstock 5-10 cm (2-4 in) below ground level, in soil to which some compost has been added, and leave the plants in one place for several years to multiply and form clumps. In the south-western-Cape, the species named above should be planted in summer, whilst in other parts of the country it may be planted from summer to spring, to produce flowers in summer. All the other arums mentioned may be planted in autumn or winter as they flower in late spring and early summer. In the Northern Hemisphere all the arums described below may be planted in spring to produce flowers in summer. Although they have been grown as glass-house plants for many years in Europe some species have proved quite hardy in those parts of Europe, such as the south of England and France, where winters are not extreme. In the country of their origin they stand severe frost. During the period when the plants are dormant they should be watered occasionally, but they need not be watered regularly each week. In hot, dry, inland districts they do best when planted in partial shade.

Arum lilies may be raised from seed but this naturally takes longer to produce plants of flowering size than planting the rootstock. Sow the seed, when it is ripe, in spring or summer. Investigations made by Cythna Letty (see Bothalia Vol. II., No. 1 and 2, May 1973) indicate that some of those named here as separate species, namely, *A. angustiloba, Z. melanoleuca, Z. oculata* and *Z. tropicalis* should all fall under *Z. albomaculata.*

Z. aethiopica   WHITE ARUM LILY, CALLA LILY, PIG LILY, VARKBLOM

This species has large ivory-white flowers and has been popular for bridal boquets for many years, particularly in Europe, where it is considered one of the finest flowers for special bouquets and arrangements. It can be grown outside in gardens in the south of England and Europe. In many parts of the south-western Cape this species can be seen during winter and early spring, flowering by the million in fields along the roadside. In summer the fields where they grow become dry and brown, and it is difficult to imagine that anything could be produced from such desiccated earth. As soon as the winter rains come and with no cultivation at all, there is the transformation once more to a sea of lilies. This species occurs also in damp places in the other provinces. In the winter-rainfall area it flowers from mid-winter to early spring, and, in other parts of the country it flowers in late spring and summer. It is said to have been given the common name of "pig lily" because in the south-western

White Arum Lily, Calla Lily (*Zantedeschia aethiopica*) is decorative in the garden and in arrangements

The sculptured form and pretty colour of the Golden Arum *(Zantedeschia jucunda)* make it a desirable plant for the garden or for pot-culture

Cape, where it grows so prolifically, pigs are said to relish the rootstock. In the winter-rainfall area it should be planted in summer; in other parts of the country it may be planted from autumn to late winter, in a position where it has some shade and where it can be watered well.

Z. albomaculata   SPOTTED-LEAFED WHITE
ARUM, KLEIN VARKBLOM
This species, which grows from a fleshy rhizome, can be seen from the eastern Cape up to the Natal midlands. It grows wild in marshy places as well as in dry places. The arrow-shaped leaves are usually spotted with white, and the flowers carried on stems 45 cm (1½ ft) high, are ivory. The leaves come up in October and the flowers a month or two later. After flowering it gradually dies back. Like the other arums it is hardy to frost.

Z. angustiloba   YELLOW ARUM
The natural habitat of this species is restricted areas of the eastern Cape, the Transkei and parts of Natal. It grows from a fleshy rhizome which sends up leaves in October, followed by colourful yellow flowers in November and December.

Z. melanoleuca   SPOTTED-LEAFED YELLOW
ARUM
This is a handsome species which occurs in the Transvaal and Rhodesia, being most abundant in areas which have a heavy rainfall. The fleshy rhizome, which should be planted in late winter or very early spring, sends up handsome, arrow-shaped leaves copiously speckled with white, and when these are fully developed it bears its sulphur-yellow flowers with a deep maroon blotch inside at the base of the spathe. The flowering time is December, or a little earlier.

Z. oculata   CREAM ARUM LILY
This species occurs in Basutoland, the highlands of Natal and in the central and eastern Transvaal. It has a greenish-cream spathe with a large dark patch inside, and the leaves are sparsely speckled with white.

Z. pentlandii   GOLDEN ARUM, MAPOCH LILY,
ARONSKELK
This very handsome arum with golden-yellow flowers grows naturally in the Transvaal and it has been adopted as the flower emblem of that

230

province. The flowers vary in size, sometimes being as much as 15 cm length, often carried on stems 60 cm (2 ft) or more in height. It is interesting to note that during the last century a grower in England is said to have refused ninety guineas for two of his precious plants of this species. It has a definite dormant period in winter and flowers from November to December. Each flower lasts about two weeks in a vase and much longer on the plant. It is therefore a good plant for floral work or as a pot plant. It should be planted from autumn to late winter. *Z. jucunda* is very similar but has leaves which are copiously spotted with white.

Z. rehmannii   PINK ARUM, SWAZILAND ARUM, ROOIVARKBLOM

This is a small arum whose natural home is in the Transvaal, Natal and Swaziland. The flowers vary in colour from ivory to palest pink, rose and deep wine-red. They are seldom more than 7-10 cm long, carried on stems about 30-45 cm (1-1½ ft)

high. The leaves are rather slender, tapering at the tips. This species can be grown successfully where frosts are severe. It flowers in November and is dormant in winter. It should be planted between late autumn and the end of winter, in a position where it has some shade and where it can be watered well.

Z. tropicalis   SPOTTED-LEAFED YELLOW ARUM

Grows naturally in high parts of the Transvaal and Rhodesia. It bears its flowers in early summer on stems 60 cm (2 ft) high. The flower-spathe varies in colour from cream to pale yellow. The spathe is more tubular than that of *Z. pentlandii*, and the arrow-shaped leaves are abundantly marked with white, translucent spots. A coral-pink form has also been found. They have a dark blotch deep inside the spathe. This plant is dormant in winter and need not be watered much until early spring, when old plants may be divided or new ones planted. It does best in partial shade and tolerates quite severe frost.

The Pink Arum
(*Zantedeschia
rehmannii*)
has daintier flowers
than the other species

Part VI
Succulents

Succulents

WHAT ARE SUCCULENTS?

The word "succulent" is derived from a Latin word *succus* meaning full of juice or sap, and it refers to plants with fleshy stems or leaves which store water. Plants of this kind are usually to be found growing naturally in areas with a low rainfall. In Southern Africa the greatest concentrations of succulents are to be found in the semi-arid areas of parts of the Karoo, Namaqualand and further north into South West Africa. The rainfall in some of these areas is 250 mm (10 in) a year and in others it is even less. In the Little Karoo and Namaqualand it falls mainly from autumn to late winter. Many succulents are, however, to be found in the summer-rainfall regions and a few occur at high elevations on the mountains of Lesotho where the rainfall in summer is heavy and where, in winter, they are often covered with snow.

To prevent rapid transpiration and too great a loss of water and to survive intensely hot sun, dry air and parched earth, succulents have become adapted in different ways. Some have leaves and stems with a thickened skin or cuticle; some have stems or leaves, or both, with a covering of hairs or of wax to prevent the rapid loss of water through transpiration; others have a deep root system to keep them alive when the soil is dry;

and in some species the leaf surfaces are very much reduced, which effectively limits transpiration, as is the case with some of the euphorbias and other plants.

The plants described in the section which follows are only those succulents which are of ornamental value in the garden. They do not include any of the many which are "collectors pieces" and which are themselves a fascinating group of plants. Some of the more unusual ones are those which have developed so excellent a camouflage that it is difficult to find them. A walk in the veld of Namaqualand, in parts of the Karoo and in South West Africa will often prove most rewarding for, hidden amongst pebbles and small stones, one finds many small succulents which look, in colour and form, just like the stones amongst which they grow. Between white pieces of quartz are to be found succulents which are grey or silvery-white—the colour of the quartz—whilst in areas where the stones are of a different colour the succulents blend in with the shade of the stones and the earth around them. Obviously the plants have this camouflage in order to ensure survival but for a short period each year when they flower, the veld is brightly illuminated by their flowers, which are often of vivid colours that show up clearly in their drab surroundings.

Succulents can transform a barren hillside into a scintillating picture

WHERE TO PLANT SUCCULENTS:

As the succulents described in this section are only those of ornamental value in the garden, they can be planted anywhere to add to the beauty of the home surroundings. Some of them are prostrate in their habit of growth and make an excellent ground cover. These are admirable plants with which to clothe a dry bank or to have cascading over a wall. They also look decorative when planted in pots or tubs, where they will hang down gracefully over the edges of the containers. The succulents of more shrubby growth can be treated like small shrubs and used either as background plants in the rock-garden or flower border, or grouped with shrubs in a shrub border. The large aloes and euphorbias are plants to use with discretion—where emphasis in the garden is desirable. In gardens where long periods of drought make gardening difficult a single large aloe, such as the kokerboom *(A. dichotoma)*, the tree aloe *(A. arborescens)*, or the tall angular euphorbia *(E. ingens)*, makes a good accent plant.

Succulents should be used to a large extent in gardens where hot dry conditions prevail, but their placing must be carefully planned to ensure an artistic result.

Many of these succulents are also ideal plants to have growing along our national roads. Once rooted they can be planted in any part of the country which does not experience very severe frost and, if this is done at the beginning of the rainy season, which helps them to get established, many of them will flourish with no further attention.

Most succulents are sun-loving plants and they do well in any part of the garden where they have full sunshine, but a few of them do fairly well in partial shade. The Fairy Crassula *(Crassula multicava)*, for example, is tolerant of dense shade and makes a good ground cover under a large tree.

Some succulents stand severe frost but many of them may be cut back by more than 5° of frost. More often than not, however, they come into new growth again when the winter is over, although those which flower in winter may have had their flowers spoiled by the frost. In gardens where low temperatures occur regularly during winter it is advisable to plant them where they benefit from the stored heat that emanates from a wall which helps to keep the air from becoming too cold during the night. In the Southern Hemisphere it is the north wall, and in the Northern Hemisphere it is the south wall, which absorbs

235

and radiates most heat. In gardens where severe frost occurs it is advisable also to plant them where they will be shaded from the early morning sun in winter, as the first rays of the sun striking frosted leaves and flowers tend to cause damage. Once the warm air has melted the frost the plants will not suffer damage from the sun. In fact, most of them must have sun in abundance to promote good growth and flowering. A number of succulents which are tender to frost when young become hardy to frost as they grow older and they therefore need protection only when young.

SOIL FOR SUCCULENTS:

They should be planted in soil which drains readily as otherwise they may be overwatered and rot. In gardens where the soil is a heavy clay, and where succulents are interplanted with other plants which need a good deal of water, one should make the soil where they are to grow more porous, by digging in coarse river sand or by replacing some of the soil with a mixture of light soil, compost and gravel.

Succulents are ideal plants for gardens where the soil is sandy and where water percolates through rapidly, as they can stand long periods with little water. In fact, many of them flower better when grown in sandy soil than when grown in clay. This does not mean, however, that succulents need no nutrients. Many of them, including some of the aloes, do best when planted in soil to which some humus has been added.

CARE OF SUCCULENTS:

Although succulents are adapted to stand long periods of drought, it must not be thought that they will grow and flower with no water at all. In areas where rains fall in summer and where the autumn to spring period is dry, most of the plants mentioned in this section of the book should be watered occaisionally during these months, as this is their period of greatest growth, and the time when they flower. In cold parts of the Northern Hemisphere these succulents should be grown in containers which can be kept in a glass-house in winter, and they should receive little water during the northern winter. In spring the containers can be brought out-of-doors and sunk into the soil in the garden or stood on a sunny terrace or patio until autumn, as, in cold parts of the Northern Hemisphere most of them produce their flowers at the end of summer, whereas in the Southern Hemisphere and in warm parts of the Northern Hemisphere they flower mostly in spring.

Plants grown in pots or tubs dry out more quickly than those planted in the soil, and it is therefore necessary to guard against their becoming too dry during their growing and flowering season. It is true that succulents generally do not die because of a lack of moisture, but it is also true that they may look parched and produce few flowers if they are kept dry during their growing period. They are never quite dormant, but after they have flowered and set seed they should be allowed to remain rather dry for a period of three to six months, as this is the time when they are not actively growing and when they are most likely to die through being over-watered.

PROPAGATION OF SUCCULENTS:

(a) By cuttings

The quickest and easiest way of adding to your collection of succulents is by taking cuttings, as many types root readily from pieces of the stem or leaves. The cutting should be a piece of stem, preferably from near the growing tip, measuring between 5 and 15 cm (2-6 in) in length and it should be made just below a joint or pair of leaves. Remove the bottom leaves (if any) and push the cutting into friable, porous soil to a depth of about 3-6 cm and water it to settle the soil around it. Thereafter water again only when the soil appears to be dry. Succulents are apt to rot instead of rooting if they are over-watered before they have made roots.

Some succulents, such as the crassulas, root very readily also from leaves. If new plants are to be made from leaves, place the leaf flat on the soil or else push the bottom of the leaf, where it was joined to the stem, down into the soil for about 12 mm ($\frac{1}{2}$ in). If many cuttings are to be made from leaves or stems it is advisable to procure some horticultural vermiculite and to fill a seed-tray or shallow box with this. It is pleasant material with which to work and has the advantage of retaining moisture, which obviates a good deal of watering. It also enables one to pull cuttings out to see whether they are rooting, without damaging the roots, if they have. Once the cuttings have rooted they should be put into soil to grow on.

Cuttings will root in sunshine, but generally it is easier to raise them in partial shade as there is less danger of the soil drying out in the shade. In some cases cuttings of succulents seem to root better if they are allowed to dry out a little before being put into the soil. This is particularly true of the euphorbias. When making cuttings of these, let the cutting remain exposed to the air for a few days before putting it into the soil. When making cuttings of other succulents, experiment by putting some of them into the soil soon after making the cutting and leaving others to dry out for three or four days or even longer before planting them. The time it takes for a cutting to root varies with different plants and at different times of the year. Some of them root in three or four weeks, whilst others may take some months. The best time of the year to take cuttings is between spring and autumn.

(b) From seed

This method is not as quick in producing new flowering plants as rooting cuttings, but in cases where it is difficult to obtain cuttings or plants it is worth trying. Seed should be sown in a mixture which is not rich. Such a mixture can be made by combining:

2 parts of soil or horticultural vermiculite with
2 parts of coarse river sand, and
1 part of leaf-mould, compost or shredded peat.

The best time of the year to sow seed depends upon the flowering time of the plants, and whether they are annuals or perennials. Perennials which flower in winter and spring are usually sown in spring, whilst annuals which flower in late winter and early spring should be sown in late summer or early autumn.

The depth at which seed is sown is governed by the size of the seed. The general rule is to bury the seed two or three times its own diameter, but seed which is as fine as powder is usually left with no soil covering at all.

It is difficult to sow this fine seed thinly and it is advisable therefore to mix it with an equal quantity of fine sand and to sprinkle this over the surface of the soil as thinly as possible. It is also difficult to water fine seed with a watering-can or spray, as the finest of sprays tends to dislodge the seed. When sowing fine seed, do so in pots which can absorb water from below. Place a few small sharp stones in the bottom of the pot to ensure that soil does not block the drainage hole and fill it with the recommended soil mixture to within an inch of the top. Press the soil down and, before sowing the fine seeds, stand the pot in a basin of water until the soil and the pot are thoroughly soaked. If terra-cotta pots are used it is important that they should be soaked, as otherwise, if only the soil is watered, the pot tends to absorb moisture from the soil thereby causing it to dry out rapidly. Sow the seed on top of the soil, cover the pot with a piece of clear glass and stand it in a shady place. As water from the soil tends to condense on the glass, it is advisable to lift and wipe it clean from time to time. When the surface of the soil appears to be drying out, stand the pot in a basin of water again so that the water will be absorbed through the pot. Do not water from the top with a spray or watering-can until the seedlings are up.

The above applies only to very fine seed. Seed which is of ordinary size can be sown in beds or boxes, covered with a thin (3-6 mm) layer of soil and watered with a fine spray from the top. Whatever the size of the seeds, it is important that once they are sown they should be kept moist until they have formed roots which are able to draw moisture from the soil.

Pots or boxes which have been covered with glass to keep in moisture should have this cover removed altogether once the seedlings appear and the plants should be gradually accustomed to full sunshine. When the little plants are 12-24 mm ($\frac{1}{2}$-1 in) high they should be pricked out. If, perchance, the seeds have been sown too thickly and the plants are crowded, this pricking out should be done even before the plants are 12 mm high, as otherwise they tend to become weak and leggy and seldom develop properly. Those plants which are annuals may be planted out at this stage direct into the garden where they are to grow to maturity, whereas perennial plants should be transplanted to other pots, boxes or nursery beds where they can be more easily looked after until they have grown a little larger.

The time that seeds take to germinate varies considerably not only between different plants, but also at different times of the year. The seeds of some plants germinate in a matter of days, whilst others may lie dormant for several weeks and even months. Seed sown in cool weather takes longer to germinate than seed sown when the weather is warm. One should not, therefore, be over-hasty in discarding pots or boxes of seeds if they have not produced plants within a couple of weeks.

**Adeniums are
fascinating plants
for hot,
dry gardens**

Adenium obesum var. *multiflorum* (Impala Lily Sabie Star)

ADENIUM OBESUM var.   IMPALA LILY,
MULTIFLORUM   SABIE STAR

DISTRIBUTION: Found in warmer parts of the eastern Transvaal, Natal, Zululand and Rhodesia.

DESCRIPTION: This is an unusual plant which grows to about 1.5-3 m (5-10 ft) and looks somewhat like a miniature baobab in form. The stumpy, succulent stem and branches are unique in character and certainly not without charm. For most of the year they have no leaves or flowers but when in flower they are most attractive. The flower has a tube of pink which opens up to a starry face made up of five white petals with crinkled pink to rose margins. The leaves, which are broadly oval, appear about a month after the flowers. The flowering time is July to September. Another species, *A. swazicum*, which occurs also in the warm districts of the eastern Transvaal and the lowveld of Swaziland, is smaller and has its flowers in summer. It has leaves 7-10 cm long and about 2 cm wide, broader at the apex than at the base. The stem narrows sharply as it comes up from the ground. The clusters of flowers are very showy. Each one is a tube 3-4 cm in length with an open face of five rounded petals. They are a

Adenium boehmianum (Impala Lily) ▷

charming shade of rose. *A. boehmianum* has similar flowers but much larger leaves. All three species make good accent plants for a rock-garden.

CULTURE: They are slow-growing but long-lived plants which thrive in sandy soils and in hot conditions. The thick tuberous underground stems which develop help the plants to survive long periods without water. These are not plants for cold or damp gardens.

ALOE   ALOE, AALWYN

DISTRIBUTION: The name aloe is an old Greek one related to the Hebrew *allal* meaning bitter. They all have a bitter sap. There are 139 species of aloe recorded in Southern Africa distributed over the whole country. They grow naturally from the coastal grasslands where there is fairly high humidity and no frost, to the dry plateaux of the interior where severe frost is not uncommon. They grow from the semi-desert parts of Namaqualand and South West Africa to the snow-clad mountains of Lesotho. Over eighty species occur in the Transvaal, mainly in the eastern and north-eastern parts.

DESCRIPTION: The aloe, with its unique foliage and form and its showy flowers caught the eye of plant collectors centuries ago. In 1674 it is recorded that some were collected in the Caledon district of the Cape and that offshoots of these were planted in the Company's Garden at Cape Town to see whether they would thrive there. Descriptions and drawings of four aloes made by a member of Simon van der Stel's party which made an historic journey to Namaqualand in 1685, still survive.

The sap of some aloes is used to-day in pharmaceutical practice but Bantu tribes have used aloes through generations both in medicine and in magic. In magic it is thought to avert danger, and in medicine the fleshy leaves are cut up and applied to festering sores.

Aloes grow in areas where the rainfall varies considerably from about 150 mm (6 in) a year, falling mainly in winter, to 1500 mm (60 in) in summer, as in the mountains of Lesotho.

Aloes certainly deserve a more prominent place in our gardens than they have been given up to now. They can stand difficult growing conditions and many of them make a splendid show in winter when gardens and the countryside generally look rather bare. Plant the small ones singly or in groups in a rock-garden, patio or along a drive, and set the tall ones out as accent plants. They could be used far more extensively, too, in public parks and they should certainly be planted more along our national roads to brighten the many miles of road leading through desolate stretches of country.

Aloes are succulent plants which belong to the lily family. They show tremendous variation in size from species such as *A. aristata* which is hardly 7 cm (3 in) high to *A. bainesii* which grows to 9 m (30 ft) and more. They generally have fleshy tapering leaves arranged in a whorl or rosette at ground level or carried on a stout trunk or stem, which may be simple or branching. The flowers are tubular and narrow as a rule, and carried close together usually in cylindrical or conical spikes. The colours of the flowers vary from the typical aloe-red to coral and yellow. Very often they are attractively shaded in two or more colours. Their chief flowering season is winter, but the time of flowering varies with the different species, and by planting species which flower at different seasons, one can have aloes in flower almost throughout the year.

It is not always easy to recognise a species of aloe because they may show quite marked differences in character when grown elsewhere than their natural habitat, and, even in nature they differ when found in different places. Furthermore they hybridize freely in nature and it is sometimes difficult to identify plants with certainty. Many hybrids are exceptionally fine and well worth a place in gardens in all parts of the country. The late Mr G. W. Reynolds in his book *The Aloes of South Africa*, remarks that "There is almost as much individuality and variation among some species of Aloe as there is among human beings".

As it is not easy to make a selection from the many names in books and catalogues, I am listing here a dozen which could make the nucleus of a collection. The names include small aloes, those of medium size and large ones. *A. africana, A. arborescens, A. chabaudii, A. comptonii, A. cryptopoda, A. ferox, A. melanacantha, A. petricola, A. reitzii, A. saponaria, A. striata* and *A. wickensii.*

CULTURE: Aloes are succulent plants adapted by nature to stand rigorous conditions, but this does not necessarily imply that you should plant them in the garden and neglect them entirely. It is true that most of them will survive this harsh treatment but it is advisable to give them the same kind of conditions as they have in their natural habitat. If the species is native to an area which has a fairly high rainfall then see that it is watered regularly in the garden during the period when it would have been watered well in nature; if it comes from an area which has warm, damp conditions do not be surprised if it succumbs to frost; and if it is a species from an area of little rain there is the possibility that too much water may cause it to die off. On the whole, however, aloes adapt themselves, as they grow, to conditions which are very different from their native haunts. Some of them thrive in brak soil where few other plants grow well, and some prefer acid soil.

Although in nature they appear to thrive in poor soil, this soil often contains the nutrients they need, and in the garden it is advisable to add some compost or manure to the soil where they are planted. They can be grown from offsets from the parent plant or from sections cut off with a piece of stem or a rosette of leaves. The dividing of plants is best done in spring. Aloes can also be grown from seed but this takes a long time to produce flowering plants. The resulting plant may be unlike the parent, but this does not always matter, as often the hybrids are as pretty or even prettier than their parents. Fortunately there are now nurseries which specialize in growing aloes for sale and the gardener can therefore purchase most of the species described here. The seed of aloes should be sown in spring and the seedlings transplanted to a nursery bed to stand a few centimetres apart when they are 2-3 cm (1 in) high. It is inadvisable to plant them out into the garden until they are a year or more old.

A. aculeata

This is a handsome species common in the northern and eastern parts of the Transvaal and Rhodesia. It grows from 1-1.25 m (3-4 ft) and has greyish-green leaves in a big rosette, the leaves curving upwards at the ends. They are about 10 cm broad at the base, 60 cm long and tapered to the tip. The lower surface of the leaf is convex and the margins have sharp reddish-brown teeth or spines. There are thorns of this colour on the upper sides of the leaves, too. The flower stem grows up and branches like a candelabra to bear two to four long cylindrical spikes of flowers 1 m (3 ft) high. The flowers are densely packed on the spike and shaded from yellow to orange. It flowers in late autumn and early winter. This species stands fairly severe frost.

A. africana UITENHAGE ALOE

This species is found growing in the bush between Swellendam and Grahamstown. It reaches a height of 2-2.5 m (6-8 ft) and has leaves which are long and a dull green or yellowish-green colour. They curve out and down and their margins have reddish-brown teeth. The inflorescence is branched to form a simple candelabra, each section being elegantly shaped like a slender pagoda. The flowers are coral-orange changing to yellow. The ends of the flowers always turn up, which makes this one easy to identify. The old leaves cling to the bottom part of the stem giving it a rather untidy appearance and it is therefore a good idea to use this species as a background plant so that its base is hidden by shrubs of lower growth. It is unlikely to stand severe frost. The flowering period is long, from winter to mid-spring.

A. arborescens TREE ALOE, KRANSAALWYN

This decorative shrubby aloe occurs in many parts of Southern Africa, generally where the rainfall is 500 mm (20 in) or more a year, from sea-level to the top of the escarpment in the eastern Transvaal, at an altitude of 1800 m. It grows to a height of from 2-3 m (6-10 ft) and has a spread of as much. The plant sends out numerous branches, each of which has a rosette of leaves at the end. The leaves are 45-60 cm long and 7-10 cm broad at the base, tapering to a point. Each rosette of leaves gives rise to one or more flower stems which carry short spikes of coral-red flowers that make a wonderful picture against the blue of the winter sky. This is a fine species to use on its own as an accent plant in the garden or at the back of a shrub border. In gardens which have very cold winters it should be given some protection when young. Some fine hybrids have been produced from this one crossed with other species. The flowering time varies according to locality from April to July.

A. aristata GUINEA-FOWL ALOE

The guinea-fowl aloe grows wild from the mid-Karoo to the Orange Free State into Lesotho and the highlands of Natal. It is a small aloe with a flower stem growing to about 45 cm (1½ ft). The plant measures only about 12 cm (5 in) across and 5-7 cm (2-3 in) high. It is a good species for planting in pots or at the front of a rock-garden. It has

241

Aloe ciliaris is a scrambling species with vivid flowers

numerous little leaves which are arranged in whorls within whorls. They are 8-10 cm long and very slender. The under side of the leaf is convex and there is a scattering of white spots on both upper and lower surfaces. The margins of the leaves have small white teeth. The flower stem divides into two to six branches with loose clusters of terra-cotta flowers. It flowers in late spring and early summer. This little plant stands severe frost but seems to do best in partial shade.

A. bainesii   TREE ALOE
This aloe is to be found in the eastern Cape, the Transkei, Zululand, Swaziland, Natal and the south-eastern part of the Transvaal, mostly where the rainfall is good. It was named after Thomas Baines who described and sketched specimens he saw at Greytown in Natal in 1873. It is the tallest of the aloes and a dramatic plant. It is like a tree in size and branching and can be used as an effective backdrop in the garden. Under optimum conditions it will reach a height of 9-18 m (30-55 ft). The trunk of mature specimens measure 1-2 m in diameter at ground level, narrowing as it rises. Generally, however, this species seldom grows to more than 7 m in the garden. The branches start about half-way up the stem, each one ending in a rosette of leaves. In winter it bears small cylindrical spikes of apricot to rose-coloured flowers at the ends of the branches. It tolerates mild frost and grows easily from cuttings.

242

A. brevifolia   MINIATURE ALOE, KLEINAALWYN
This small aloe which occurs in the Bredasdorp and adjoining districts of the south-western Cape is a charming one for the front of a small rock-garden or to use as a pot or tub plant. It bears thirty to forty curved leaves in a tight rosette. Each leaf is only about 7 cm long and less than 3 cm wide at the base, and the whole plant measures only about 10 cm (4 in) across and 7 cm in height. There are, however, forms of this species which grow to larger size, measuring about 30 cm across. The margins of the leaves are edged with little white thorns. The tomato-red flowers appear in spring on a stem which grows to 45 cm in height. The plant is hardy to frost but needs well drained soil, particularly when grown in regions of high rainfall.

A. candelabrum   CANDELABRA ALOE
The candelabra aloe can be seen in large numbers on the hillslopes in the valley of the Umkomaas River between Ixopo and Richmond, and in other parts of Natal and the Transkei. It is a striking plant when young, but as it ages its lengthening stem sometimes looks untidy, for as it grows taller the old leaves persist and tend to look straggly. In the garden it should be used as a background plant so that other plants will hide this lower part of the stem. This species grows to 2-3 m (6-10 ft). The leaves, arranged in whorls, curve up and then out and sometimes down. They are of a blue-green colour with hard margins and small reddish-brown teeth along the margins. The inflorescence is like a giant candelabra. The flower stalk is branched into six to twelve erect stems with one taller than the others. The orange-red flowers are carried in long cylindrical spikes 50-80 cm long. In winter, when in flower, it is a very handsome plant. The Zulus burn the remains of the old, dry leaves which cling to the stems and mix the ash with tobacco to make snuff. This species stands moderate frost.

A. chabaudii
Occurs in Zululand, the lowveld of the Transvaal and in Rhodesia. The leaves of this species are arranged in a loose whorl near the ground. They are about 45 cm in length and 10 cm broad at the base, of a dull green often flushed with rose and with a tough edge or margin armed with sharp little teeth. The flower stems rise to 60-90 cm (2-3 ft) and branch freely near the top. The coral-red flowers appear in short loose clusters at the ends

of the stems. This is a very decorative species which flowers in winter. It is sensitive to frost and in cold gardens should be tried only in a sheltered corner.

A. ciliaris

Grows in the bush near the coast in the eastern Cape and Transkei. It has a stem which branches rather freely and may grow to 3-4 m (10-13 ft) in length, scrambling up through the bush and appearing over the tops of scrub to bear its bright flowers in the sunshine. The lower part of the stem generally has few or no leaves. These appear towards the ends of the stems and are long and tapering with a regular saw edge. The tomato-red flowers are tipped with green. This is a fine plant to have growing amongst shrubs or cascading over a bank. It also makes a decorative hedge if trained along a fence. It bears most of its flowers in spring but has some during other months of the year, too. It grows easily from cuttings. This species stands only moderate frost.

A. comptonii

Can be found near Uniondale and Willowmore and towards Laingsburg in the Karoo. This is a showy species. It has leaves forming a compact rosette on the ground. They are grey-green, sometimes tinged with rose. Their margins have small, fawn teeth. The flower stalk rises to 60-90 cm (2-3 ft) in height and branches from about the middle into several stems which bear heads of coral-red luminous flowers in a rounded or slightly conical cluster. It flowers in spring or summer according to locality. As it stands frost and drought, it is a useful one to have planted along our national roads.

A. cooperi

This species which occurs at sea-level in Natal and up into the mountains of the eastern Transvaal and Swaziland has long, slender, upright leaves arranged in a fan-like fashion. The margins of the leaves have a white edging with small even teeth. The flower stem is about 1 m (3 ft) tall and carries a single cone-shaped inflorescence of salmon-pink to coral-red flowers prettily tipped with dull lime-green. In gardens which have severe frost it may lose its leaves during winter but the plant is seldom killed by frost. This is a charming aloe with a long flowering period in summer. It does well under wet, even bog, conditions. Some native tribes cook the shoots and flowers and use them as a vegetable.

Aloe africana (Uitenhage Aloe) has a flowerhead of unusual form

A. cryptopoda   Spire Aloe

Can be found in many parts of the Transvaal, Swaziland, Botswana, Rhodesia and further north. The leaves, which are deep green to blue-green in colour, rise from the ground in a crowded whorl. They grow erect and have small reddish-brown teeth along the margins. The flower stem grows to 1-2 m (3-6 ft) and is much branched with numerous tapering flowerheads measuring about 25 cm in length and coloured scarlet and sometimes yellow. This species makes a fine show in late summer and autumn. It is a very good garden variety which holds its flowers for a long period.

A. dichotoma   Kokerboom, Tree Aloe

This sculptured plant grows in the driest parts of the country, from Upington south to Calvinia and west to Springbok, and into the dry parts of South West Africa. It is of such unusual form that it could well be used as an accent plant standing alone, or with low-growing plants around it, and it is an ideal plant for gardens where there is a scarcity of water and where the air is hot and dry for most months of the year. It stands quite considerable frost, but it is likely to rot in areas of high rainfall.

It was first recorded when Simon van der Stel made his expedition to look for copper near Springbok in the northern Cape. The note made then reads as follows: "*Aloe arborescens:* its trunk is sometimes 12 feet high, and it has beautiful clear and copious sap from which excellent *gumma aloes* could probably be made in large quantities. Its bark is rather hard but the pith within is soft, light and spongy. The branches of this tree are used by the natives as quivers for their arrows. They hollow them out and cover one end with a piece of leather". The Dutch word "koker" means a pipe or quiver—hence the common name of kokerboom. The botanical name of this species has since been changed.

They look like trees which belong to ages long past and give one an impression that they should perhaps have died out with the dinosaurs! The plant grows rather like a tree to a height of 3-5 m (10-16 ft). At ground level the trunk of mature plants is about 1 m across, narrowing and branching out half-way from the top. These branches give rise to further branches, and it is only at the top of the plant that the leaves appear in rosettes of about twenty together. It is a dramatic kind of plant at any time and quite spectacular when it flowers in June and July. The flowers are carried in cylindrical spikes. In bud they are yellow tipped with green, and they open to shades of yellow, from sulphur to bright canary-yellow.

A. ferox   BITTER ALOE, KRAALAALWYN
This aloe is common in parts of the eastern Cape from Swellendam east up through the Transkei to Natal. It can also be found in the Karoo and Lesotho. It is the one often noticed along the road, particularly in the Transkei. It is very showy in winter when it flowers, but as the remains of the old leaves tend to make the bottom of the stems look untidy, it should be grown as a background plant behind shrubs which will hide the lower sections of the stems. The plant grows to 2 m (6 ft) high, the leaves crowning the plant being arranged in a whorl, whilst dried remains of the leaves of previous years cling to the bottom section of the stem. The leaves are sharply tapered and of a dull but pretty shade of green, and in dry weather they become flushed with rose. The margins of the leaves have strong teeth tipped with red. The flower stalk which emerges from the centre of the whorl of leaves branches to form a candelabra which bears long spikes of orange-red flowers. There is also a white form but it is rather drab. The flowers have an abundance of nectar which attracts birds from far and wide. This is the species of aloe which provides sap in commercial quantities for pharmacy. The plant stands moderate frost.

A. fosteri
Its natural habitat is the warmer parts of the eastern and north-eastern Transvaal where summer temperatures are high and the rainfall is low. This is a handsome plant which bears a loose whorl of leaves on the ground. They are covered with a bluish-grey bloom which can be rubbed off to reveal the green of the leaves underneath. The leaves are marked with longitudinal lines and pale spots, and in dry seasons they turn a russet shade. The margins of the leaves have small, sharp, light-brown teeth. The flower stem rises to 1-1.5 m (3-5 ft) and branches about half-way up to form a fine arrangement of long and somewhat conical heads of flowers of coral-red or yellow. It flowers in autumn when few other species do. It is hardy to moderate frost.

A. globuligemma   KNOPPIESAALWYN
Occurs in some districts of the eastern and northern Transvaal and in Rhodesia. This is an attractive species which has a creeping stem which gives rise to numerous new plants as it grows along the ground. The leaves grow in a rosette and bend up sharply and are recurved at the tips. They are glaucous green and have pale teeth along the margins. The flower stem rises to 1 m (3 ft) and branches out horizontally or obliquely. The flowers are closely crowded in cylinders along the ends of these stems. The colour varies from brick-red in the bud to ivory in the open flower. The flowering time is winter. One Bantu tribe living in a district where these aloes are abundant declares that the flowers point in a different direction to indicate the nature of the coming season. If pointing towards the east the season will be dry, and if to the west, there will be good rains. The plant stands moderate frost and likes a well-drained soil.

A. hereroensis   HERERO ALOE, SANDAALWYN
Its natural habitat is the dry areas of the north-western Cape eastwards to the Orange Free State and north into South West Africa. It is generally found where temperatures may rise above 38 deg. C (100 deg. F) and where the rainfall is seldom more than 250 mm (10 in) a year. The leaves of this species are of a pallid green and in hot, dry areas they sometimes turn russet-red for a time. They have a tough margin with reddish-brown teeth.

244

Herero Aloe
(*Aloe hereroensis*)
stands intense heat
and aridity

The flower stem rises to 1 m (3 ft) and is much branched with loosely arranged flowers in rounded clusters. They vary in colour from a glowing flame to crimson and yellow or orange. The flowering time is July. More use could be made of this species to brighten our national roads in desolate parts of the country. It stands considerable frost and dryness and is a fine species therefore for hot, dry gardens. It grows well in alkaline soil but is not recommended for regions with a high rainfall.

A. humilis   Dwarf Hedgehog Aloe, Krimpvarkieaalwyn
Can be found in the Little Karoo from north of George across to Grahamstown. This is a splendid little species for small rock-gardens and for pot culture. It has been used as a pot plant in Europe for many years. This was one of the first aloes cultivated in the garden of the Dutch East India Company at the Cape as early as 1695. The leaves are only 7-10 cm (3-4 in) long and the plant does

not measure much more than this across. It multiplies rapidly to form clusters of plants. The flower stem is about 25 cm (10 in) tall and bears coral-red, tubular flowers in late winter. It is hardy to frost and grows well in sandy and in alkaline soil.

A. karasbergensis   Karasberg Aloe
Occurs in the Richtersveld, Namaqualand and parts of South West Africa—all hot, dry regions. The leaves are very broad at the base and carried in a loose whorl. They are bluish-green with pronounced longitudinal stripes of a darker hue running down them. The margins have no teeth but a tough ivory edging. The flower stem rises to 45 cm (1½ ft) and is broadly branched, the lower branches being horizontal to the main stem. The flowers are small and carried in loose clusters. They vary in colour from coral-pink to strawberry-red. The plant stands frost but not much dampness.

245

Miniature Aloe *(Aloe krapohliana)* A dainty species for the small garden

A. khamiesensis   TREE ALOE
This species, which occurs in Namaqualand, is tall with a stem which grows up to 2.5 m (8 ft) in height. Unfortunately the remains of the old leaves persist at the bottom of the stem making the plant rather untidy, but, if it is planted behind shrubs where only the flowering stem can be seen it makes an attractive show. It could also be used extensively for roadside planting in hot dry districts of the country. It has a dense rosette of leaves of greyish-green with ivory spots scattered on the upper and under surfaces. The margins of the leaves are edged with reddish-brown teeth. The flower stem rises to 60 cm (2 ft) above the rosette of leaves and sends out branches from half-way up, each of which bears, proudly erect, a conical head of coral-red flowers. Its flowering time is winter.

A. krapohliana   MINIATURE ALOE
This aloe grows in a few districts of the north-western Cape where the rainfall is less than 250 mm (10 in) a year. It is a charming small species with a compact rosette of curved leaves which are quite decorative. The margins of the leaves have small white teeth. Two to four flower stems rise from the rosette of leaves to about 45 cm (1½ ft) and bear loose, rounded heads of rose to scarlet

flowers tipped with green. The flowering time is winter. This species needs good drainage and dry conditions.

A. longibracteata
Can be found in the north-eastern Transvaal. It has a loose whorl of leaves which are different from the usual aloe leaf, inasmuch as they are almost as broad as they are long. The upper surface is spotted and the margins are toothed. The flower stem grows to about 1 m (3 ft) and branches from low down into three erect stems which bear long, slender cylinders of strawberry-red flowers. The flowering time is winter. It stands frost and alkaline soil.

A. longistyla   KAROO ALOE
The Karoo aloe occurs in parts of the southern Karoo from Laingsburg across to Bedford. It grows to 30 cm (1 ft) and forms rosettes of leaves at ground level. The leaves are grey-green to blue-green and have white spines not only along the margins but also on the upper and under surface of the leaves. The whorls of leaves look extremely effective at the front of a rock-garden or when planted in pots. The flowers are carried on stems just above the leaves in cone formation. They are coral-pink to coral-red. The styles and stamens protrude, giving the flowers an elegant appearance. The flowerhead is large in comparison to the plant and very showy. The flowering time is winter. This little aloe can stand quite considerable frost, but in regions with a high rainfall it should be planted in a well-drained position.

A. marlothii   BERGAALWYN
Grows wild in the warm parts of the Transvaal and Swaziland, in the north of Natal and Zululand, along the eastern border of Botswana and in Rhodesia. This species is suitable for background planting in a large garden where the untidy lower stem of the mature plant is hidden by a foreground of other plants. It grows to 3-4 m (10-13 ft) and has leaves of grey-green to green. In dry seasons they have a dull red tinge. The margins of the leaves have regular reddish-brown spines and there are also spines of the same colour on the upper and under surfaces of the leaves. The cylindrical spikes of flowers are carried horizontally or obliquely and not erect, as in many other species. The flowers of yellow to orange and red appear in late autumn and winter.

Karoo Aloe
(*Aloe longistyla*)
is a charming species
for the rock-garden or
to plant on a bank

Blackthorn Aloe
(*Aloe melanacantha*)
This species was first
grown in a garden
two-hundred years ago

A. melanacantha   BLACKTHORN ALOE
This little aloe which grows wild in the dry areas of the north-western Cape and South West Africa, was one of the first recorded in the history of South Africa. It is mentioned in Simon van der Stel's records as having been found on the 24th October 1685 "in rocky and sandy places and near the ore mountains". The name *melanacantha* refers to the black thorns which are found on the leaves. The plant has small leaves in a dense rosette 20-30 cm across. The flower stem rises to a height of 60-90 cm (2-3 ft) and has a cylindrical spike of flowers which are scarlet in the bud but turn yellow as they age. It is hardy to frost but needs dry growing conditions in well-drained soil.

A. microstigma
Occurs from the Worcester region of the Cape eastwards through the Little Karoo to Grahamstown. This is a handsome species which flowers for a long period. It has a rosette of leaves which measure about 30 cm in length. The leaves are green, often with a russet-red suffusion and usually with light coloured spots on both surfaces of the leaves. The margins of the leaves have sharp reddish-brown teeth. It sends up two to three stems from the middle of the rosette of leaves to a height of about 60 cm (2 ft) on which appear conical spikes of flowers varying in colour from red to yellow. They are red in the bud and yellow in the open flower. It flowers in winter. The plant is hardy to frost and tolerates long periods of drought.

A. mutabilis   KRANSAALWYN
This aloe can be seen growing in mountainous parts of the south-eastern and central Transvaal. It grows to about 1 m (3 ft) with the rosette of leaves usually at an angle to the soil or cliff on which it grows. The glaucous leaves have a narrow pale edge and yellow teeth along the margins. Two or three flower stems come up from each rosette of leaves and bear conical heads of flowers which are scarlet in the bud and lime-yellow to yellow in the open flower. The flowering time is winter. This species is hardy to frost.

A. petricola
Is to be seen on the hills and mountains of the eastern Transvaal. It has a rosette of blue-grey leaves which are sharply tapered and curved inwards at the apex. The margins have dark brown

teeth and there is a scattering of teeth on the surfaces of the leaves too. The flowers are carried on branched stems 1 m (3 ft) tall, with three to six flower spikes coming off the central stem to form a candelabra. They are beautifully coloured crimson and white or orange and yellow. It makes a splendid show in winter when it flowers.

A. plicatilis   FAN ALOE
The natural habitat of the Fan Aloe is the mountainous area of the south-western Cape from Franschhoek to Tulbagh—areas of high rainfall in winter where snow is not uncommon. This is an unusual aloe, for its leaves are quite different from those of other species. Instead of being tapered and arranged in a whorl or rosette, they are strap-shaped and arranged in layers like a fan. They are pale green edged with red. The plant grows to a height of 2-3 m (6-10 ft) and looks like a gnarled tree when it is mature. The lower part of the plant is bare of leaves. Each fan of leaves is carried at the end of a branch and from it emerges the flower stem which stands above it and shows off its loose clusters of tomato-red flowers. The flowering time is late winter. This species stands frost. It prefers acid soil to an alkaline one. When grown in the summer-rainfall area it should be watered in winter.

A. polyphylla   BASUTOLAND ALOE, SPIRAL ALOE
This unusual aloe comes from the high mountains of Lesotho where it is often buried in snow and where the rainfall is heavy. It is made up of a mass of leaves in rosettes arranged in tiers with a twist making a kind of spiral. The leaves are grey-green with an ivory edging and with teeth of the same colour. The flower stem rises from the centre of the plant branching low down to produce three to eight heads of salmon to coral-red flowers on stems 45 cm (1½ ft) high. This species should be planted in well enriched soil, preferably acid in nature. It does best in part shade and when watered liberally. The flowering time is spring.

A. reitzii
This is an attractive species from the eastern Transvaal highveld. The plant is made up of whorls of fleshy leaves which turn up sharply. They are dull green with brown teeth along the margins and occasional spines on the leaf surface. The flower stem rises to 1 m (3 ft) or more

248

Aloe petricola bears gaily coloured flowers in winter ▷

Aloe sessiliflora
A handsome plant for
the dry garden

and branches out near the base to form stems which stand erect like a candelabra to display the long cylindrical heads of flowers. The striking flowers are bright red on the upper side and paler on the underside. The flowering time is late summer.

A. saponaria   SOAP ALOE

Is one of the most widely distributed and also one of the most variable. It is to be found from the Cape Peninsula eastwards through the eastern part of the Cape and the Transkei, in Natal, Lesotho, the Transvaal and Rhodesia. It grows, therefore, naturally, in both the summer and winter rainfall regions from the coast up to an altitude of 2000 m. The common name is derived from the fact that the leaves when cut yield a flow of sap which froths like soap when the two ends are rubbed together. It bears its rosette of leaves either at ground level or else on a short

stem. Each leaf tends to curve up and then down at the ends. The upper surface of the leaves has pale spots and the margins are lined with sharp dark-brown teeth. The flower stem grows to 45 cm (1½ ft) or more and has two to four branches which end in loose clusters of flowers varying in colour from yellow to salmon-pink, orange and red. The flowering time varies according to the locality in which it is grown from late winter to summer. It stands severe frost but may get rust in areas of heavy rainfall.

A. sessiliflora

This species grows naturally in warm parts of the eastern and northern Transvaal, Swaziland and Zululand. The plant reaches a height of 1 m (3 ft) or a little more and tends to sprawl in a rather attractive fashion. The leaves spread out and are often channelled. They are green in summer and turn a bright russet colour during the dry months of winter. The margins of the leaves have closely set red teeth. The flower stem grows to a height of about 90 cm (3 ft) and bears a slender cylinder of closely packed sessile flowers of orange yellow in late winter. Although the plant stands moderate frost, the flowers are often damaged by frost and it is therefore more suited to the warm garden than one where temperatures drop low in winter.

A. speciosa   SPAANSAALWYN
Occurs in dry parts of the country from Swellendam across the Little Karoo to the Kei River. The plant grows to a height of 3-4 m (10 ft). It branches sometimes near the ground and sometimes fairly high up and has rosettes of bluish-green to silver-grey leaves which are obliquely tilted. The margins of the leaves are rose-coloured. The flower stems are densely crowded with flowers in long cylinders which are very showy. The buds are rose to pale tomato-red and the open flowers are white flushed or striped with green. The flowering time is late winter and early spring. This aloe tolerates moderate frost.

A. striata   CORAL ALOE
The coral aloe which can be seen in many districts of the southern Karoo from the Hex River across to the Kei River, is one of the prettiest of the aloes for the garden. It is one of the few aloes which have no teeth or spines along the margin of the leaf. The fleshy leaves are flat and broad at the base and bluish-green or grey-green with red margins. In dry periods the leaves become suffused with rose. They are in themselves decorative and when it flowers it makes a really striking show. The flower stem rises to 1 m (3 ft) and branches about half-way up and then branches again and bears rounded heads of bright coral-red flowers. There is also a pure yellow form which is to be found in the eastern Cape. This species flowers in August and September. It is hardy to frost and does well in alkaline soil.

A. tenuior   FENCE ALOE
This species is found in the eastern Cape near East London, in the Transkei and in Zululand. It has a long, rangy stem which often needs support of some sort to keep the plant erect. The leaves are long and narrow and not very fleshy, with minute teeth along the margins. The flower-head is cylindrical with the flowers fairly far apart. The colour of the flowers varies from coral to yellow and the buds are often lime-green. It

The Coral Aloe *(Aloe striata)* is one of the most decorative for gardens large and small.

flowers for a long time and the flowers last well in vases. It can be planted between shrubs to scramble over them, trained along a fence or pruned hard to form a bush. The flowering time is mainly summer. In the Transkei the root and leaves are used by the Xhosa people in the treatment of tape-worm, and washing in the foam made from the crushed leaves stirred up in water is said to ensure success in an undertaking and to avert danger.

A. thompsoniae   THOMPSON'S ALOE
This little plant grows in the mist belt of the mountains of the north-eastern Transvaal where the rainfall is high. It grows to only about 25 cm (10 in) and is a fine plant for pots or window-boxes and for small gardens. It has bright green leaves in a loose whorl. They taper to a point and tend to curve over at the ends. The upper surface of the leaf has a scattering of pale spots near the base and the lower surface is similarly marked. There are minute teeth along the margins of the leaves. The flower stem is about 20 cm (8 in) tall and has little heads of flowers of orange-red. It flowers in early summer. Plant this species where

it can be kept cool and moist and provide it with soil rich in humus.

A. thraskii — COAST ALOE

Occurs in the coastal strip of Natal near Durban. Very often it is found in the coastal bush along the sand dunes. This is a tall plant growing to 2 m (6 ft). The leaves are a bright green and attractively curved. They arch up for a little way and then turn over backwards in a graceful fashion. The margins have small russet coloured teeth. The flower stem rises to form a candelabra which holds erect the cylindrical spikes of flowers of yellow to orange with green tips. The flowering time is June and July. This is a most useful plant for coastal gardens as it does well on the beach. It is sensitive to frost.

A. vanbalenii

Can be seen growing wild on hills and rocky slopes of mountains and in river valleys in Zululand, Swaziland and the south-eastern Transvaal. This little species grows to about 1 m (3 ft) and sends out its whorl of leaves from ground level. They tend to spread out and down and are green with russet margins and in dry seasons the whole leaf becomes russet in colour. The margins of the leaves are widely toothed and coloured brick-red. The flower stem rises to about 1 m (3 ft) and is often branched with spikes of flowers broader at the base than at the top. The flowers vary in colour from straw-yellow to sulphur-yellow. The flowering time is winter. This species needs good drainage and will stand moderate frost.

A. variegata — PARTRIDGE-BREAST ALOE, KANNIEDOOD

Is of widespread occurrence in parts of the Karoo and the north-western Cape, the eastern Cape, the south-western Orange Free State and the southern portion of South West Africa. It is interesting to note that this attractive little aloe was first found in the Springbok district by Simon van der Stel's expedition exploring for copper in Namaqualand in 1685. It had been planted in the Company's Garden at the Cape by 1695. The plants multiply rapidly from underground stolons. The leaves are arranged in layers and their upper and lower surfaces are dark green or brownish-green marked with pale spots. The flowering stem is rose-coloured, about 30 cm (1 ft) long with pendulous flowers in a loose cluster. The colour of the flowers varies from coral-pink to coral-red. The

flowering time is late winter and early spring. It is hardy to frost and likes a well-drained, alkaline soil.

A. verecunda

The natural habitat of this species is the highveld of the Transvaal, the northern and eastern highlands of the Transvaal and parts of Rhodesia. It is a small plant with long, slender leaves which stand rather stiffly erect. The margins have small white teeth. The flower stems grow to about 30 cm (1 ft) and bear loose, rounded clusters of coral-red flowers. This is a fine plant for the small rock-garden or for growing in pots, as it seldom grows more than 30 cm (1 ft) in height. The flowering time is summer. In cold gardens the leaves may dry out and disappear in winter.

A. wickensii

This species which grows in the northern and eastern Transvaal is a good-looking plant in winter when it is in flower. It is of medium size, suitable for the average garden. It has leaves which grow erect and curve upwards to the top. The margins of the leaves have minute brown teeth. The flower stem rises to 1-1.5 m (3-5 ft) and branches low down to bear the showy flowers at the ends of the stems. They are gaily coloured, coral-red in the bud and bright yellow when open. The flowers remain showy for two to three months in winter. Although the plant stands quite severe frost the flowers may be damaged unless it is in a sheltered position.

CARPOBROTUS — HOTTENTOT FIG, SOUR FIG, GOUNA

DISTRIBUTION: Is limited in distribution to the coastal areas of the Cape Province and parts of Namaqualand.

DESCRIPTION: There are four species of this South African succulent worth cultivating in gardens and along roadsides. One species has in fact been used in all parts of the world to bind the soil on roadside cuttings and railway embankments. It can now be seen growing in California, the south of England and France, Portugal, Spain, Italy, Greece, Israel, Australia and New Zealand.

These plants are not suitable for small gardens unless kept within bounds but they are ideal for large town or coastal gardens, or gardens on farms where space is not limited and where a quick and extensive ground cover is required

which does not need much attention. The leaves are succulent, about 10 cm long and almost as thick as a pencil, often with angled edges. The flowers have thin, silky petals which scintillate in the sunlight and measure 6 cm or more across.

CULTURE: This plant asks for no attention at all. It grows quickly from cuttings and roots itself where it touches the ground, making a dense but rather coarse ground cover. It seems to be able to thrive in any kind of soil, from sand to heavy clay. To encourage flowering, see that it has some water between autumn and spring, but it can be left quite dry for the rest of the year.

C. acinaciformis   GOUNA, HOTTENTOT FIG
This species can be found growing with great vigour in sandy soil. Its large succulent leaves spread across the ground making a coarse carpet of green, and in spring it becomes illuminated by sparkling flowers of a rich shade of magenta. They measure 5 cm across. This is a good species to use for holding coastal sand and for planting on large steep banks to prevent erosion.

C. deliciosus   SOUR FIG, SUURVY, GOUKUM
Has very handsome flowers, measuring 10 cm across, of a glowing magenta colour. The leaves are not as large as some of the other species, seldom more than 7 cm long and about 6 mm across. It is common on coastal sand dunes and is a useful plant for binding the sand. The roots and juice are used medicinally by the Bantu, and the early settlers made great use of the fruit for jam. The fruit is still used for this purpose. In dry areas it is a good plant to grow in tubs on a sunny patio or as a ground cover on large banks. It makes a handsome show in spring when in flower.

253

Carpobrotus acinaciformis (Sour Fig)

Carpobrotus are good plants to use as ground covers in large gardens, to halt the drift of sand at the coast, or to hold the soil on highway embankments

Carpobrotus sauerae (Hottentot Fig)

Gouna *(Carpobrotus edulis)*

Carpobrotus muirii

C. edulis — GOUNA, HOTNOTSVY

Has bright green leaves which are sharply keeled and flowers of a rich straw-yellow shade fading to pink. This plant has been used all over the world, where winters are not excessively cold, to stop erosion, and it has been grown in the south of England for generations under the common name of Sally-my-handsome. The fruits of this species are not palatable.

C. muirii

Is a hardy handsome species from the Riversdale district where it flourishes in sandy places. Its leaves are more slender than those of the other species described and they make a neat carpet on the ground. It is therefore better suited to the small garden than the other species. The leaves carpet the ground and will hold the soil on a bank and help to control the drift of sand along the coast. In September and October it bears flowers 5-6 cm across with very narrow, glistening petals of a beautiful shade of amethyst.

C. quadrifidus — GIANT SOUR FIG

This species from Namaqualand is a rugged plant only too ready to grow, however poor or sandy the soil. In late winter and early spring it produces its huge white flowers which fade to a dusky pink. They are as much as 12 cm across.

C. sauerae

This is a good species for a dry bank, for planting in tubs or for covering a large piece of bare earth along a driveway. It has large leaves very like those of the other species and very large flowers of a rich magenta to cerise colour. The flowers are very showy, and similar to those of *C. acinaciformis.*

255

CEPHALOPHYLLUM   Mesem. Vygie

DISTRIBUTION: Different species are to be found growing in dry areas of South West Africa, Namaqualand, parts of the western Karoo and southwards to the Riversdale district of the Cape.

DESCRIPTION: They are rampant-growing plants with succulent stems and leaves. The leaves are sometimes cylindrical and sometimes angled about their length. The length of the leaf varies from 4-12 cm and the thickness is about 6 mm. The flowers have numerous slender, glistening, silky petals radiating from the centre. A plant in full flower is a ravishing sight. The stems are often prostrate, rooting themselves readily along the ground. The space between the nodes where leaves emerge is usually fairly long. These are ideal plants to cover large dry banks or to have in a border or lining a drive. They are also most decorative when grown in pots or tubs on a sunny patio.

CULTURE: Being plants from the winter-rainfall region they should be watered from autumn to spring, but they do not need much water even at this time of the year. In summer they do best if rather dry and in regions which have heavy summer rains it is advisable to plant them on a slope which drains readily or in soil which is sandy or gravelly. They grow easily from cuttings but can be grown from seed also. This should be sown from spring to autumn. Plant them in full sunshine.

C. alstonii

A charming plant for banks, window-boxes or tubs. It is rather sprawling in growth with flowers of a rich, glistening wine-red colour, measuring about 5 cm across. The flowering time is late winter and early spring.

Other fine species are the following:

C. aureorubrum which is tufted in growth with flowers of different shades from yellow to rose.

C. baylissii a compact species of more restricted growth with lavender flowers.

C. ceresianum is prostrate with slender leaves and yellow flowers.

C. cupreum is low-growing and has large flowers shading from copper to apricot.

C. frutescens is shrubby in habit to a height of 60 cm (2 ft). The flowers are pale yellow.

C. gracile sprawls along the ground forming mats of leaves from which emerge magenta flowers.

C. littlewoodii is a small species with slender leaves and magenta flowers.

C. pillansii is tufted in growth with yellow flowers.

C. spongiosum is a rampant plant with long trailing stems and large terra-cotta flowers.

C. subulatoides is low in growth and rather prostrate with large, magenta flowers.

CONICOSIA PUGIONIFORMIS   Conicosia

DISTRIBUTION: This plant grows in sandy soils north of Cape Town to Namaqualand.

DESCRIPTION: It sprawls along the ground covering the dry, sandy soil with its fleshy pencil-like leaves which are about 10 cm (4 in) long and pointed at the tips. In August and September it becomes covered with large, shining, yellow flowers with slender petals which look as though they are made of strips of satin. It is a good plant to use on a sunny bank or in a rock-garden, or mass-planted to bind the soil on a slope. *Conicosia robusta* is another vigorous succulent with creamy yellow flowers.

CULTURE: Conicosia grows from cuttings and does well in poor sandy soils. It needs some water during the autumn and until spring.

COTYLEDON   Pig's Ear, Plakkies, Hondeoor

DISTRIBUTION: Cotyledons have a wide distribution but the decorative species are mostly from rather dry areas of the eastern and western Cape.

DESCRIPTION: These are succulent plants with fleshy leaves often carried near the ground. The leaves are different in shape according to species. In some species they are almost as broad as they are long and thickly covered with a white bloom. They make good plants for a rock-garden as the leaves blend in with the rocks and the flowers rise above them. The flowers are tubular in form with petals often reflexed at the ends. The leaves of *C. orbiculata* when split and firmly bandaged against planter warts are said to draw them out. Some native tribes heat the leaves and use the warm juice for ear infections.

CULTURE: These drought-resistant plants thrive in poor soil and dry places. They are easily propagated from cuttings of the stem or from the leaves. Very often a leaf falling to the ground will

Conicosia (*Conicosia pugioniformis*) flourishes in sandy soil in dry areas   ▷

Cephalophyllum spongiosum (Vygie) A splendid plant for dry banks or walls, or to plant as a ground cover in hot, dry gardens

root on its own. They may also be raised from seed, but this takes more than a year to produce plants of flowering size. They withstand fairly severe frost.

C. decussata   BERGBESIE
This species, which is widely distributed throughout the country, is a very attractive one with fleshy, blue-green leaves 10-12 cm long shaped like a finger. The flower stem is about 45 cm (1½ ft) long and the flowers are shaded apricot or rose. It flowers in late winter and spring.

C. ladismithiensis   LADISMITH COTYLEDON
This species from the dry area of the Little Karoo is shrubby in habit, growing to about 25 cm (10 in) in height and spreading across twice as much, or more. The leaves are carried in whorls and are thick and succulent with a triangular claw-like tip. The flowers appear on the ends of maroon-red stems a few inches higher than the mass of leaves. They are apricot to rose.

C. macrantha var. **virescens**   PIG'S EAR, HONDEOOR
A species common in the eastern Cape near East London. It is bushy and grows to 60 cm (2 ft) and does well in sandy soil and in coastal gardens. The large, succulent leaves are covered with a waxy bloom and the bright coral-red flowers appear in winter.

C. mucronata   WILLOWMORE COTYLEDON
Has fleshy, flattened leaves clustered about the base of the plant. The leaves are broader at the apex than the base and covered with a white bloom. It grows to only about 30 cm (1 ft) in height and has salmon-pink flowers in spring and summer.

C. orbiculata   PLAKKIES, HONDEOOR
This hardy and decorative succulent is found in dry areas such as South West Africa and Namaqualand. It has a thick stem with large, thick, succulent leaves covered with a silver-white

bloom. Each obovate leaf is 5-7 cm long edged with a narrow red margin. The leaves are in clusters and the flower stems rise to about 60 cm (2 ft) above the ground. The flowers are carried in a cluster and each flower hangs down on a short stem which comes off the flower stalk. The individual flowers are tubular, ending in five re-curved petals. The colour varies from apricot to terra-cotta and crimson. This is one of the most attractive of the species. It flowers in spring and summer.

C. phillipsiae
Is shrubby in habit with leaves almost like a rosette. They are 4-5 cm long and dark green on the upper surface with a square apex which turns rosy-red in strong sunlight. The flowers are orange-red.

C. tomentosa
An attractive succulent with thick obovate leaves, rather square and tinted red at the apex. The whole plant is covered with white bloom. It bears clusters of flowers which are red and furry in the bud, opening to an apricot shade.

CRASSULA
DISTRIBUTION: Can be found growing in many parts of the country, generally in dry places. Only a few of the many species which grow wild are sufficiently decorative to be used in the garden.

DESCRIPTION: These succulent plants vary a good deal in the forms of the leaves, the flowers and the manner of growth. Further descriptions are given below against the names of species. They are good plants for the rock-garden and some of them make pretty pot plants.

CULTURE: Most of them prefer bright sunshine to shade but one species at least makes a fine ground cover in shady places. They can endure drought but are somewhat tender to frost, and, in regions which have very cold winters it is advisable to plant them against a wall or hedge which affords them some protection. They can be grown easily from stem cuttings or from leaves. They can also be grown from seed, but this takes very much longer to produce flowering plants.

C. dregeana
Is an attractive branching species with fleshy leaves obliquely keeled and covered with white spots. The tiny flowers are carmine to white.

C. falcata   RED CRASSULA
This is one of the most decorative of the cras-sulas. The plants have a thick stem growing to about 60 cm (2 ft) and broad, flattened, fleshy leaves of grey-green. They are closely and neatly arranged rather like tiles on a roof. The tiny

Plakkies
(*Cotyledon orbiculata*) is an admirable plant for the rock-garden or for large pots or tubs

Plant Red Crassula
(*Crassula falcata*)
for a bright show in
late summer

Fairy Crassula (*Crassula multicava*) makes a good
ground cover in a shady corner

flowers are carried in fairly large flat heads measuring about 15 cm or more across. They are long-lasting and of a brilliant scarlet colour. It is decorative in the garden and as a pot plant. It was grown in conservatories in Europe in the eighteenth century. The flowering time is summer and early autumn. It is easily propagated from leaves placed flat on the ground in a shady place. Red crassula is a splendid plant for hot dry gardens and those near the sea.

C. marginalis
Is a rather prostrate succulent with weak fleshy stems, ideal for hanging over a bank or planting in a hanging basket. It has tiny, round, sessile leaves, grey-green in colour with red spots along the margins. The flowers are crimson.

C. multicava   FAIRY CRASSULA
This is an excellent plant for covering ground under trees where little else will grow. It does better in light shade than in dense shade and it also grows well in the sun. The leaves carpet the ground throughout the year and in autumn it becomes a frothy mass of minute pinky-white, star-shaped flowers which are decorative in the garden and in arrangements. The leaves are oval and fleshy. The plant spreads itself freely by rooting where it touches the ground. It grows to a height of 20-30 cm (8-12 in).

Pink Joy
(*Crassula portulacea*)
brings colour to the
garden in winter

C. namaquensis

Has thick fleshy rounded leaves on the lower part of the stem which is wine-red in colour. It bears clusters about 5 cm across, of tiny ivory or pink flowers. The plant grows to about 20 cm (8 in) in height.

C. perfoliata   POINTED-LEAF CRASSULA

Grows to about 60 cm (2 ft) and has pointed opposite leaves carried close along the stem. The flowerhead bears flowers of white, pink or red. The flowering period is summer and early autumn.

C. portulacea   PINK JOY, PLAKKIES,
                      BEESTEBUL

This attractive species grows naturally in dry areas of the eastern Cape near Grahamstown and Somerset East. It is a shrub in habit of growth and makes a pretty show in winter when it bears masses of flowers. It grows to 2 m (6 ft) and sometimes more but can easily be kept down to smaller size. The leaves and stems are thick and succulent. The obovate leaves are edged with rose. The neat, round heads of star-shaped flowers of palest pink or white remain decorative for a long time in winter. It is a good plant for seaside gardens as it does not mind sandy soil and salt winds. *C. arborescens* from the south-western Cape is very similar but it has white flowers. In gardens where severe frosts occur they should be planted against a wall which reduces the possibility of the temperature dropping too low at night. Both species grow very quickly from stem cuttings. The roots of these species were eaten by the Hottentots and the leaves boiled in milk were used in the treatment of diarrhoea.

C. rupestris   ROSARY VINE

A shrubby little plant with scandent stems on which the triangular light green leaves are arranged opposite each other. The flowers are pink.

C. vaginata   YELLOW CRASSULA

Grows in many parts of the country from the eastern Cape up through Natal, and in the Transvaal. This showy species has flowers of sulphur-yellow on stems 60 cm high. The fleshy leaves are fairly long and pointed, and partially embrace the flowering stem. It flowers in late summer or early autumn.

DELOSPERMA   MESEM, VYGIE

DISTRIBUTION: Species of delosperma are to be found in all the provinces—from the coast to plateaux of the Free State and Transvaal and on mountain slopes and plains in Natal.

DESCRIPTION: These are succulent perennials

generally of creeping habit or growing as small, tufted bushes. They are closely branched with leaves which are decorative because of their glistening quality. This is due to water-containing cells on the surface which catch and reflect the light. The leaves are round or angled along their length, fairly pointed at the end and often curving towards the tip. The flowers have many slender petals radiating from the centre. They are not as showy as some of the other succulents, but the leaves make a good permanent ground cover, and the plants are therefore excellent for holding the soil on a slope or bank. They flower from late winter to early summer, according to species.

CULTURE: All species grow very easily from cuttings which should be made in late spring or summer. They also grow from seed but this method of propagation takes a long time to produce flowering plants. They are resistant to long periods of drought but to encourage good flowering, water them in late winter and spring. They tolerate a good deal of frost and grow very quickly again even when damaged by frost. Porous soil suits them best.

DIDELTA CARNOSA var. DIDELTA TOMENTOSA

DISTRIBUTION: This plant grows along the coastal sand dunes from the south-western Cape north to South West Africa.

DESCRIPTION: Didelta is a decorative shrubby perennial for coastal gardens. Its attractive leaves are thickly covered with silver-grey felt and they make a coarse mat across the sand. In late winter and early spring the plant becomes a mound of gay, daisy-like flowers of bright yellow. Each flower measures 5-7 cm across and they remain decorative for some time. Set the plants 90 cm (3 ft) apart. This is a good plant to cultivate in order to stop the drift of coastal sand.

CULTURE: It grows best in sandy soil and does well even when subjected to salty spray. It can be grown from seed or root sections.

Didelta
(*Didelta carnosa*
var. *tomentosa*)
flourishes along the
seashore

Didelta
(*Didelta carnosa* var. *tomentosa*)
showing variation in colour of leaves and flowers

DOROTHEANTHUS   BOKBAY VYGIE, MESEM. ICE PLANT, VYGIE

DISTRIBUTION: The species described grow in abundance in sandy soils north of Cape Town near Darling and further north up to Namaqualand.

DESCRIPTION: This genus of annuals includes some extremely showy plants—one at least of which is acclaimed the world over. They are fairly small plants and are ideal for large or small gardens. The leaves grow in tufts on the ground and have raised water cells which make them sparkle in the sun. The small flowers with numerous slender petals radiating from the centre scintillate in the sunlight, too. They are so prolific in their flowering that the area where they grow becomes a glowing carpet of colour. The flowering time is late winter and early spring.

CULTURE: They grow very readily from seed sown in March or April. Set the plants out about 15 cm (6 in) apart when the seedlings are 2-3 cm (1 in) high. They like a sandy type of soil rather than heavy clay but are prepared to grow almost anywhere provided sharp frosts do not burn them and provided that they are watered occasionally between sowing and flowering time. Plant them in full sunshine.

D. bellidiformis   BOK BAY VYGIE, ICE PLANT, BOKBAAI VYGIE

This most colourful annual is now being used extensively not only in gardens but along roadsides in parts of the south-western Cape where tens of thousands of plants are set out close together to make a solid carpet of vibrant colour for many weeks in late winter and very early spring. The leaves are spoon-shaped and sparkle as they reflect the sunlight. The flowers are of the most glorious array of colours from palest pink to cerise, from salmon to magenta and from straw to deep yellow. The flowers measure 2-4 cm across and have contrasting shades of colour at the centre. Sometimes the central part is white and sometimes a paler shade than the outer part of the flower. Certainly there is no prettier bedding flower and it makes a most wonderful show despite its small size. This little flower has been grown in Europe for almost two hundred years but it is only within recent years that it has become popular in its homeland, which is surprising since few plants are more colourful and few are easier to grow.

The following species are worth trying, too, although they are not all as beautiful as the above.

D. flos-solis with sulphur-yellow flowers.

263

D. gramineus with narrow leaves and magenta flowers.

D. muirii which produces flowers of deep rose.

D. oculatus has flowers of bright canary-yellow with a vivid red centre. Massed it makes a striking show.

D. oculatus var. **saldanhensis** which has orange flowers.

D. rourkei. This little annual becomes covered with brightly luminous flowers in late winter and early spring. The flowers are only about 15 cm (6 in) above the ground and measure 3-4 cm across. They have sharply pointed petals of a scintillating, cyclamen-crimson surrounding a tuft of golden-yellow stamens. It is a splendid little plant to have massed as a ground cover on a bank or in broad bands along a drive, at the front of a flower border or in the rock-garden. Because of its strong colour it should be associated with no colours other than green, or soft shades of straw, white, cream or palest pink or mauve. It will also make a brilliant show when grown as a pot plant. It flowers for a longer period than some of the other species. All species prefer a well-drained soil to a heavy clay and they must have full sunshine. In the Northern Hemisphere they should be sown in spring for a show in late summer. Seed is at present still in short supply as the plant was discovered in Namaqualand only three years ago by Dr. J. Rourke, after whom it is named.

D. stayneri is a tiny annual bearing rose-pink flowers with white centres.

DROSANTHEMUM MESEM, VYGIE

DISTRIBUTION: These hardy plants grow in the western and southern Karoo and dry areas of the north-western Cape.

DESCRIPTION: They include some of the most decorative of all the spring-flowering perennials. They may be bushy in habit of growth or prostrate. Very often the young stems and leaves glisten because of the minute water-containing cells which reflect the sunlight and which look like spots on the leaves. The leaves are generally small and cylindrical or angled. The flowers are daisy-like with very slender petals radiating from a central disc. They are fine plants for dry banks, for making a border, specially in dry parts of the country, or for planting to hang over walls or in tubs on a sunny patio. They flower in spring.

CULTURE: Plant them in friable soil in full sun-

Vygie, Mesem or Iceplant *(Dorotheanthus oculatus* carpets the ground in dry areas

light and, in regions where the rainfall is heavy in summer, see that they have adequate drainage as they like to be dry at this season of the year. They should be watered occasionally from autumn until they flower in early spring. The plants stand fairly severe frost but it is advisable to plant them in a sheltered position to prevent damage to the flowers. Plants may be raised from cuttings made during the warmer months or from seed sown in spring or summer, but seed takes much longer to produce flowering plants. Some species tend to become woody with age, and, as they grow so easily from cuttings it is advisable to raise new plants every three or four years. The following are the names of a few of the many decorative species:

D. bellum is a bushy plant to 60 cm (2 ft) with glistening white or pink flowers shaded to pale green at the centre.

D. floribundum is a spreading plant with magenta flowers.

265

◁ Bok Bay Vygie *(Dorotheanthus bellidiformis)* produces an abundance of jewel-like flowers

Drosanthemum
hispidum (close-up)

*Drosanthemum
speciosum* (close-up
of flower)

**Drosanthemums
produce masses of
scintillating flowers
in spring. They do
well in dry areas**

*Drosanthemum
speciosum*
(manner of growth)

267

Medusa's Head
(*Euphorbia
caput-medusae*)
is an unusual plant for
the rock-garden or for
pot-culture

D. hispidum is prostrate in growth and has shimmering lavender flowers carried in such profusion that one can hardly see the leaves.

D. speciosum is bushy in habit with sparkling flowers of glowing orange or crimson.

EUPHORBIA   SPURGE, MELKBOS, NABOOM
DISTRIBUTION: There are about two hundred species of euphorbia to be found growing in different parts of the country—almost always where the rainfall is low and the heat intense for much of the year.

DESCRIPTION: Euphorbias vary considerably in size from small plants which grow flat along the ground to those which have tree-like proportions. Descriptions are therefore given under the species mentioned below.

CULTURE: These are heat-loving plants able to stand long periods of drought and a few of them are also able to tolerate fairly severe frost, but generally they do best where winters are not severe. They do well in poor soil.

E. caput-medusae   MEDUSA'S HEAD
Is a low-growing species of unusual form. It has been aptly named for the snake-like stems which radiate from the central crown grow into new plants very rapidly. It is valued for its unusual form rather than its beauty although in winter when it flowers it is certainly striking. Plant it at the front of a rock-garden where it can clamber over stones or plant it in a pot and keep it on a sunny window-ledge. It can be grown from cuttings or seeds.

E. epicyparissias   MELKBOS
A bushy plant to 1 m (3 ft) which grows wild near East London. It has slender, oval leaves neatly arranged in tiers around the stems and becomes bright with colour in late spring and early summer when it bears its flowers of greenish-yellow and mustard.

E. ingens   NABOOM
This curious and rather dramatic-looking tree grows wild in the northern parts of the Transvaal, Rhodesia, Swaziland and Natal. It has numerous succulent stems coming off the main stem about half-way up to form a candelabra-like top. It is not pretty but it is certainly striking in form and it is a useful tree for hot dry gardens or as an accent plant. It grows to about 9 m (30 ft) in height and has small russet flowers in late autumn. Some African tribes use the milky latex medicinally. It causes blistering of the skin. They also use it to catch fish, as a branch thrown into a pool seems to stupefy the fish. *E. cooperi* is similar in habit of growth.

E. mauritanica   YELLOW MILKBUSH,
JACKAL'S FOOD, GEEL MELKBOS
This little bush can be found in many of the dry districts of the western Cape through to the

268

eastern Cape and further north into Namaqualand and South West Africa. It grows to 1-1.5 m (3-5 ft) with a spread of as much or more and has smooth succulent stems. The old lower stems have no leaves but the young stems which bear the flowers have small oval pointed leaves of a delicate shade of green. The flowers appear at the end of winter and early spring. They are mustard-yellow. The green of the succulent stems and the yellow of the flowers brings colour to large areas of dry countryside in August-September. This is a pleasing shrub and a most useful one for dry, hot gardens where frosts are not extreme. Cut the plant back after it has flowered to keep it compact and to prevent it from becoming leggy. The latex from the stems was used for catching birds and it is said to have been used also by Bushmen in the preparation of poison with which to tip their arrows.

E. tetragona   TREE EUPHORBIA
A tall-growing species from the eastern Cape and Transkei which grows to about 8 m (26 ft). It makes a good accent plant and should be tried in dry gardens as a background to other succulents.

LAMPRANTHUS   MESEM, SANDVYGIE
DISTRIBUTION: These colourful plants are to be found growing in dry areas of the south-western Cape, the Karoo, Namaqualand and other parts of the north-western Cape, and further north into South West Africa.

DESCRIPTION: The name lampranthus is a very apt one for these spectacular plants. It is derived from two Greek words *lampros* (shining) and *anthos* (a flower) and describes the luminous quality of the flowers. These are perennial plants of different habits of growth. Some are bushy and some are prostrate, but all are succulent in nature. The leaves are generally cylindrical, sometimes sharply angled and sometimes gently angled along their length. They vary in length considerably. There is also variation in the size of the flowers of different species, but they all have many slender, glistening petals radiating from the centre like those of a daisy. They make a wonderful show anywhere in the garden. The prostrate-growing ones look splendid hanging over a bank or wall or the edge of a pot or tub, and the bushy ones make a spectacular background in the flower border or as a foreground to a shrub border. They are also useful plants for lining a long drive. The flowering time is early spring. These are decorative plants for coastal gardens as well as for inland ones.

CULTURE: Lampranthus grow readily in any kind of soil and they endure long periods without water but they should be watered occasionally

Yellow Milkbush
(Euphorbia mauritanica)
does well in areas where drought and frost limit the number of plants which can be grown

This Vygie or
Ice Plant
*(Lampranthus
roseus)* bears
masses of
scintillating
flowers of many
lovely shades.
They grow
exceptionally
well under hot,
dry conditions.

during autumn to spring. They tolerate a good deal of frost and even if cut back they rise again quickly. In very cold gardens where late frosts occur, it is advisable to plant them where they are sheltered. They must have full sunshine to produce an abundance of flowers. They grow very quickly from cuttings made in the warm months of the year, and they can be grown from seed sown in spring or summer, but this takes a year or two to produce flowering plants. When plants become straggly they should be cut back.

The following are the names of some species of decorative value:

L. aurantiacus (Gold Lampranthus) This species seems to require more moisture than many other species. It is a very showy plant with flowers of orange-yellow to gold.

L. aureus (Orange Lampranthus) Grows in bushy fashion to 30 cm (1 ft) with a spread across 45 cm and becomes covered with flowers of a rich golden hue. There are also yellow and white varieties of this very pretty plant.

L. blandus (Pale Pink Lampranthus) Is a rounded, spreading little bush with flowers 3-4 cm across of palest pinky-mauve.

L. brachyandrus (Magenta Lampranthus) Grows to about 60 cm (2 ft) in height and bears masses of amethyst flowers.

L. coccineus (Red Lampranthus) Is a spreading plant with wine-red flowers.

L. comptonii (Compton's Lampranthus) Bears pink flowers on sprawling plants.

L. eximeus (Cyclamen Lampranthus) Is bushy with large flowers of cyclamen colour.

L. explanatus has flowers of bright canary yellow.

L. formosus (Rambling Lampranthus) Bears glowing cerise flowers on a spreading prostrate plant.

L. glaucus (Yellow Lampranthus) A little rounded plant about 25 cm (10 in) high and across with large, glistening flowers of sulphur-yellow.

L. littlewoodii This is a bushy plant to 60 cm (2 ft) with magenta flowers.

L. pittenii Is shrubby to 60 cm (2 ft) with large flowers of pink, cerise or white. (New name is *L. vanputtenii*).

L. roseus Is a spectacular low-growing plant with flowers in varying shades of pink and cyclamen.

L. saturatus A bushy plant to 60 cm (2 ft) with bright cerise flowers.

L. spectabilis (Showy Lampranthus) A spreading species common along the coast in the eastern Cape, with flowers carried about 30 cm (1 ft) high.

Plant Orange Lampranthus (*Lampranthus aureus*) as a ground cover on a dry bank or wall, or in a large pot or tub on the patio

It flowers from spring to summer and bears masses of pink or cyclamen flowers.

L. stayneri Grows to 60 cm and bears cerise flowers.

L. watermeyeri (Winter Joy) This species flowers in late winter and early spring producing large glistening flowers of white or pink on bushy plants with a height and spread of 45 cm (18 in).

L. zeyheri Bushy plant to 60 cm (2 ft) with rich magenta flowers.

MALEPHORA CROCEA COPPER VYGIE
(Hymenocyclus croceus)

DISTRIBUTION: Grows wild in dry areas of the western and south-western Karoo and the north-western Cape.

DESCRIPTION: This is a bushy little perennial of sprawling habit growing to about 30 cm (1 ft). The stems and leaves are succulent. The leaves are 5-7 cm long, triangular along their length about 8 mm thick and covered with grey bloom. The flowers, which are made up of numerous very narrow petals coming out from a central disc, measure about 4 cm across and are of a charming tone of bronze or cyclamen with gold at the centre. The flowering time is late winter. Another species bears larger flowers of bright yellow.

CULTURE: Like other succulents native to the above-mentioned area it likes to be kept fairly dry during summer and to be watered fairly regularly during the autumn to spring period. In regions with a heavy summer-rainfall it is advisable to plant it on sloping ground or in sandy soil which drains easily. Plant it in full sunshine. It can easily be propagated from cuttings made in the warmer months of the year.

MESEMBRYANTHEMUM MESEM, VYGIE, ICEPLANT

DISTRIBUTION: Most of those suitable for the garden are native to the north-western Cape and the western and Little Karoo.

DESCRIPTION: The plant group broadly known as mesembryanthemum consists of about 3000 different species nearly all of them South African. Recently these plants have been re-classified and most of the plants which we refer to as "mesems" or "vygies" are now listed under their new names. There are many genera but only eight of these are described in this book. These are the

273

most decorative ones for garden show. Many of the other genera include most fascinating plants but they are plants for collectors of succulents rather than plants to make a bright show in the garden.

The genera described in this book will be found under the following names: CARPOBROTUS, CEPHALOPHYLLUM, DELOSPERMA, DOROTHEANTHUS, DROSANTHEMUM, MALEPHORA, LAMPRANTHUS and RUSCHIA. Of these Lampranthus, Dorotheanthus and Drosanthemum produce the greatest number of showy plants.

At first sight this may appear to be a formidable array of names, but if one starts pronouncing them out aloud it is surprising how quickly they begin to slip off the tongue, and once one has grown the plants, remembering the names becomes easier because these plants are beautiful and useful in the garden.

Some of these different genera are so alike that it is very difficult to describe them to show up the differences. In some cases it is only by examining the fruit capsules that one can be sure of naming the plant in the veld correctly. This problem, however, concerns the botanist rather than the gardener.

Although the different species flower for only a short time (seldom longer than three weeks) most of them put on such a magnificent and colourful show that the garden looks splendid whilst they are in flower. The leaves in most cases are green throughout the year and many of the prostrate-growing species make a fine ground cover.

The main flowering period of most genera is from late winter to mid-spring, and by planting a number of them you can have a colourful show for quite a long time. Mesems are splendid plants for any part of the garden. They make a most colourful show in the rock-garden and in the border, interplanted with other flowers. They camouflage dry banks with their leaves which are green throughout the year and make them bright with colourful flowers from late winter to late spring. Many of them will drape themselves gracefully over a wall. If you have no garden plant some of them in pots or tubs on a sunny patio, balcony or window-ledge. They do well in coastal gardens.

CULTURE: These decorative succulents grow in any kind of soil and in their natural habitat they are often to be found in sandy soil. They like an abundance of sunlight and they grow naturally where the average rainfall may be as little as 100 mm (4 in) a year, and where it is seldom more than 250 mm (10 in) per annum. In the garden they should be given similar conditions. Sandy or gravelly soil suits them best as this allows water to drain away readily. In areas of the summer-rainfall region where heavy rains occur, great care should be taken to see that they are in soil which allows for good drainage. Although nature has adapted these plants to withstand long periods without any water at all they flower well, as a rule, only if watered occasionally during the period when they are forming new growth and flowers, which is, for most of them, from late winter to spring.

Some of them are tender to frost but most of them will endure fairly severe frost. When they are to be planted in gardens where very severe frosts occur it is advisable to plant them where the early morning sun in winter will not strike the plants while they are still frosted, as this may cause damage to both flowers and leaves. They should in such places be planted where they are shaded until about 9-10 a.m. They need to have full sunshine for the rest of the day as the flowers open properly only when they have bright light. Many of our mesembryanthemums are grown in the cold countries of the world. Some of them grow happily out-of-doors in the south of England but they are unable to stand snow, and where snow falls in winter they should be potted and kept indoors until the winter is over. One enterprising collector of succulents in England has more than six hundred species of those native to South Africa.

The easiest way to propagate mesembryanthemums is by cuttings. Take a piece of stem 5-10 cm (2-4 in) long, push it into friable soil or sand to a depth of about 2-3 cm (1 in) and water it occasionally until the plant roots. The best time to do this is between spring and autumn. If the slip has a flower remove this to encourage better rooting as sometimes the flower might develop into a seed capsule and this absorbs some of the energy of the developing plant and retards it. They can also be grown from seed but this generally takes a year or two to produce flowering plants. Sow the seed in March in areas which do not have cold winters and in spring in the Northern Hemisphere where winters are very cold.

PORTULACARIA AFRA   ELEPHANTS' FOOD, JADE PLANT, SPEKBOOM
DISTRIBUTION: This plant is widely distributed in dry areas of the eastern Cape, the Karoo, Natal and the northern Transvaal. The word "spek" means pork, and refers to the succulent (fat) nature of the stems and leaves of this plant.

DESCRIPTION: It is a quick-growing shrub to 3 m (10 ft) or more with fleshy stems and fairly small, rounded fleshy leaves. The flowers appear in summer in dainty little spikes at the ends of the stems. They are very small with five pink petals. This is an excellent shrub to use in dry areas—in the rock-garden, as a hedge or for background planting to frame and shelter other plants. It can be kept pruned to 60 cm (2 ft) to make a decorative low hedge. It has proved invaluable as food for stock in time of drought and should be propagated more widely for this purpose in dry areas. The leaves have a pleasant tart flavour. A form with leaves tinged with yellow, and rose-coloured stems, is grown in Australia. It is a decorative plant for dry gardens and for growing in a pot or tub.

CULTURE: Spekboom stands any amount of aridity but it is tender to very severe frost. Often, however, when it has been cut down by frost it will grow up quickly again. It is a useful plant for gardens where a shortage of water and general aridity makes gardening a problem. It grows very quickly and readily from cuttings of the stem.

ROCHEA COCCINEA   RED CRASSULA, (pronounced row-she-a)   ROCK CRASSULA
DISTRIBUTION: Grows mainly on mountain slopes and plains in the south-western Cape.

DESCRIPTION: This is a perennial plant which grows to about 45 cm (1½ ft) and bears fleshy, oval leaves about 2-3 cm in length all along the red stems which carry the flowers. The flowers are

carried in flat clusters about 7 cm across at the ends of the stems. Each flower is made up of a long slender scarlet tube opening to a five-petalled starry face. The flowering time is summer. This plant should not be confused with *Crassula falcata* which is also known as Red Crassula. Another attractive species is *R. subulata* which grows to about 30 cm (1 ft) and has clusters of tubular ivory flowers in smaller heads in early spring. They give off a strong scent at night. Both are fine plants for the rock-garden and for pot culture.

CULTURE: This plant grows very readily from stem cuttings and can also be grown from seed sown in spring but this takes very much longer to produce flowering plants. They grow out in the open very well but, in hot, inland districts, they seem to do better if planted where they have some shade for the hottest hours of the day. Where frosts are severe plant them so that they are sheltered by a wall or by other plants.

RUSCHIA
CUSHION MESEM, VYGIE
DISTRIBUTION: Can be found growing in dry areas of the south-western Cape and further north.

DESCRIPTION: This group of perennial plants is not as attractive as some of the other mesems, but they are useful plants for covering dry banks. The plants are either flat on the ground or erect and often grow in a series of tufty mats of leaves. The foliage is compactly arranged and generally smaller than in other related genera. The leaves vary from being cylindrical to sharply angular in form. The flowers seldom measure more than 18 mm across and are not carried in such profusion as on lampranthus and drosanthemum. They flower in spring.

CULTURE: They grow readily in any soil and tolerate long periods of drought and fairly severe frost. They should be watered occasionally from autumn to spring to encourage good growth. They can be propagated easily from cuttings and the plants root themselves as they grow along the ground. They can also be raised from seed sown in spring or late summer but this takes a year or two to produce flowering plants.

The following are some species worth trying:

R. diversifolia has a rambling, shrubby manner of growing and bears magenta flowers.

276

R. dualis Is prostrate in habit, forming little mats of leaves as it grows along the ground. The flowers are lilac.

R. karrooica Is bushy with more succulent leaves than some of the other species. It grows to about 30 cm (1 ft) and has magenta flowers.

R. lineolata Is a neat spreading plant. It makes a good ground cover. In spring it becomes studded with daisy-like flowers about 12 mm across. They have slender petals of palest pink with a delicate stripe of glowing magenta running down the centre of each petal.

R. macowanii Is a bushy plant to 45 cm (1½ ft) with sprawling stems carrying pretty flowers about 18 mm across, of a pinkish-mauve colour. It grows wild near the sea at the Cape.

R. rigida Makes compact mats on the ground. The leaves are small and in tightly arranged clusters. The flowers are mauve.

R. stayneri Is of shrubby growth to 60 cm (2 ft) with deep mauve flowers.

SEMNANTHE LACERA

DISTRIBUTION: Occurs in sandy areas of the south-western Cape.

DESCRIPTION: This plant has large fleshy angled leaves very like those of some species of carpobrotus, but they have fine serrations along one or more edges whereas the leaves of carpobrotus are smooth along the margins. Its flowers are similar to those of carpobrotus, too. They are of a very pretty glowing shade of cyclamen-mauve and have a mass of slender, glistening petals. Each flower measures 4-6 cm across. The big difference in appearance between this plant and the carpobrotus species described is in the habit of growth. Whereas carpobrotus sprawl and form a mat along the ground semnanthe grows into a little bushy plant 30-45 cm tall and much more across.

CULTURE: It does well in dry places and in sandy soil and will tolerate moderate frost. It needs full sunshine to promote good flowering, Semnanthe is a useful plant for coastal gardens.

SENECIO HAWORTHII   GREY-LEAFED
(Kleinia tomentosa)   SENECIO

DISTRIBUTION: Is found in dry parts of the Little Karoo.

DESCRIPTION: This is a fascinating bushy little plant growing to about 30 cm (1 ft). It has an unusual appearance due to the shape of the leaves and their heavy coating of grey to silver felt. Each leaf is round, and pointed like a bullet at both ends. They measure 2-3 cm or a little more in length and are about 8 mm in diameter. The flowers are yellow daisies about 2-3 cm across. It is worth growing for its decorative grey leaves which make a pleasant contrast to the green leaves of other plants or to blue flowers.

CULTURE: The plant grows in poor soil and with little water and stands moderate frost. In areas of high humidity it should be planted in well-drained soil.

Rock Crassula
(Rochea coccinea) will brighten the garden in summer

Index to Common Names

Index to Botanical Names